Pacifist
TO PADRE

Pacifist
TO PADRE

The World War II Memoir of Chaplain Roland B. Gittelsohn,
December 1941–January 1946

*Lieutenant Roland B. Gittelsohn (Chaplain Corps),
U.S. Naval Reserve*

EDITED BY DONALD M. BISHOP

MARINE CORPS UNIVERSITY PRESS
Quantico, Virginia
2021

LIBRARY OF CONGRESS CATALOGING-IN-PUBLICATION DATA

Names: Gittelsohn, Roland Bertram, 1910–1995, author. | Bishop, Donald M., 1945- writer of introduction.

Title: Pacifist to padre : the World War II memoir of Chaplain Roland B. Gittelsohn, December 1941–January 1946 / Lieutenant
Roland B. Gittelsohn (Chaplain Corps), U.S. Navy Reserve.

Other titles: World War II memoir of Chaplain Roland B. Gittelsohn,
December 1941–January 1946

Description: Quantico, Virginia : Marine Corps University Press, 2021. |
Includes bibliographical references and index. | Summary: "Pacifist to Padre deftly threads so many elements of the World War II chaplaincy into a compelling and thoughtful narrative. It offers a personal window into a complex institution. It provides insight into the world of an unusual American space that has been naturalized as normal: of government-sponsored and managed religion. And it brings that world into focus from the vantage point of a man who never would have predicted pinning the Jewish chaplain's tablets insignia to his collar, a Jewish pacifist turned military padre"—Provided by publisher.

Identifiers: LCCN 2020055671 | ISBN 9781732003156 (paperback)

Subjects: LCSH: Gittelsohn, Roland Bertram, 1910–1995. | United States.
Marine Corps—Chaplains—Biography. | World War, 1939–1945—Chaplains—United States. | Rabbis—United States—Biography. | Marines—United States—Psychology. | Military morale—United States. | World War, 1939–1945—Participation, Jewish. | United States. Marine Corps. Marine Division, 5th—Biography. | Iwo Jima, Battle of, Japan, 1945—Personal narratives, American. | World War, 1939–1945—Personal narratives, American.

Classification: LCC D769.59 .G58 2021 | DDC 940.54/78092 [B]—dc23

LC record available at https://lccn.loc.gov/2020055671

DISCLAIMER

The Jacob Rader Marcus Center of the American Jewish Archives in Cincinnati, OH, provided the archival documents that formed the basis for this project: Manuscript Collection No. 704, Box 64, Folder 7, "Pacifist to Padre/Pacifist to Uniform/Pacifist No More."

The production of this book and other MCUP products is graciously supported by the Marine Corps University Foundation.

Published by
Marine Corps University Press
2044 Broadway Drive
Quantico, VA 22134
1st Printing, 2021
ISBN 978-1-7320031-5-6

CONTENTS

EDITORIAL NOTE

In 2019, Donald M. Bishop approached Marine Corps University Press (MCUP) about publishing the war memoir of Rabbi Roland B. Gittelsohn. His personal papers were available at the Jacob Rader Marcus Center of the American Jewish Archives, and though Gittelsohn published prolifically during his career as a rabbi, his participation in the Pacific campaigns of World War II was not as widely known.

MCUP had recently published *Investigating Iwo: The Flag Raisings in Myth, Memory, & Esprit de Corps* (2019) and the timing seemed perfect to continue the conversation on the period, though from a quite disparate perspective. Chaplain Gittelsohn's typewritten manuscript shows he had not decided on a title. Three were listed: *Pacifist to Padre—Pacifist in Uniform—Pacifist No More*. We have chosen the first for this volume. The pages that follow chronicle the days, months, and years prior to, during, and following the war, including Rabbi Gittelsohn's training at chaplain's school, his connection with the Marines and sailors he served, and the emotional and spiritual journey he would experience dealing with the American military at war, the young people he was charged with guiding, and the impact of racism and bigotry at a time when America appeared to be standing united as a country.

In 1995, at the ceremony marking the 50th anniversary of the battle, Chaplain Gittelsohn offered the benediction, repeating some of his words from the dedication of the 5th Marine Division cemetery. He fully understood how usages and word choices had changed between 1945 and 1995. In 1945, for instance, Negro was a term used by both African Americans and whites, but in 1995 Chaplain Gittelsohn said "black." In other ways too, reading the 1946 text in the twenty-first century takes readers on an excursion into an earlier American society. In World War II, Americans commonly referred to all men in the armed forces as boys, and adult women could still be called girls. That none of the few women Marines were at Iwo Jima, and the first woman Navy chaplain was not commissioned until 1973, frames his characteristic use of masculine words. As this volume presents his memoir as it was written in 1945 and 1946, it uses the language of its time. Though some of these terms give offense today, their use here, in their historic context, in no way diminishes Rabbi Gittelsohn's lifetime commitment to equality and inclusion.

The pages that follow offer Gittelsohn at his most honest and, at times, conflicted. To honor his memory, MCUP has done everything to keep his work intact by retaining as much as we could of the typewritten manuscript. This printing represents as closely as possible the original work, with minor alterations to the text based on current standards for style, grammar, punctuation, and spelling. In some instances, we have retained the original spelling of specific places and things as they represent the accepted spelling for the historical period. Further, we have included informational footnotes and citations to educate the reader on historical terms and to assist with later historical research. Every effort has been made to verify the names, ranks, locations, and dates in the content that follows. Due to the passage of time, it was not possible in all cases and we must rely on the author's proximity to the subjects and the topic.

Finally, the illustrations throughout the pages that follow were neither part of Rabbi Gittelsohn's archival record, nor did he make notations in the original manuscript about visual aids. Given the maps and photographs now available for the period from Marine Corps History Division, the National Archives and Records Administration, and the Library of Congress, they were inserted to supplement the text, with the intent of enriching the reader's experience and adding context to a complex time.

Angela J. Anderson
Director
Marine Corps University Press

DEDICATION
To Ruth

—whose insight helped me decide,
—whose encouragement is the fountainhead of my own morale,
—whose love sustains me when the night is blackest.

FOREWORD

My first encounter with "The Purest Democracy"—the moral centerpiece of this volume—was in 1995 as a Navy chaplain assigned to a Marine Corps unit. Our headquarters building was a vast converted warehouse, a full block long, with a cavernous central passageway wide enough for several forklifts. As I exited an office, I was startled to see our three-star commanding general and most of his staff headed my way. I was trapped. There was nowhere to hide. I stopped, snapped to attention, and pronounced the salutation, "Good afternoon, Sir!" His response was, "Chaplain, I want to talk to you. Do you have a minute?" My heart sank. I was petrified. What had I done?

"I just came back from [Washington] DC, where we commemorated the 50th anniversary of the Battle of Iwo Jima," the general told me.

"Everyone from the SECDEF [secretary of defense] to the Commandant and on down was at the memorial. They pulled out all the stops. Then, at the very end of the ceremony, they introduced this little guy to give the closing benediction, announcing he would read the same words he had used dedicating the cemetery on Iwo 50 years ago. He was so short, we could hardly see more than sun reflecting off his bald head peeking over the lectern; but wow, what he said was the most powerful and moving part of the whole day. It was like hearing Abraham Lincoln at Gettysburg. I asked the Commandant's office for a copy. I am sending it to all my officers and noncoms [noncommissioned officers]. Here's yours. The gent's name is Rabbi Gittelsohn. You being a rabbi, perhaps you know him?"

DID I KNOW HIM?

Indeed, from age 6 until his passing when I was 48, Roland Gittelsohn was my family's rabbi, a teacher, a model, and a mentor as I, too, decided to become a rabbi and a Navy chaplain.

My first two memories of Rabbi Gittelsohn were at age six. My mother had coaxed me onto the imposing Temple Israel pulpit for consecration, the ceremony marking the beginning of a child's religious school education. There, standing before the ark, flanked by imposing ornamental pillars, was a bald man with robes and the center of attention as he pronounced a blessing over me and my hundred or so assembled classmates. "Awestruck" hardly describes the effect. The next Sunday at religious school, I was alone on my way up the wide and tall institutional staircase common to school buildings of the day. I looked up, and there on the landing high above me stood the rabbi in full pulpit garb. He was silhouetted by the bright sunlight streaming from the window. Only the glare off his bald head hinted it was a person not an apparition. I was frozen in fear—so petrified that I do not recall the words he spoke. Whatever they were, however, I do recall I was fully reassured. He swept by me on the way down; the encounter was over, and all was fine with my world.

Seven years later, I was in the robing room behind the pulpit about to lead my bar mitzvah ceremony. Everyone I knew, and everyone my extended family knew, sat in the congregation. If I failed, it would be epic—fodder for all manner of jeers from schoolmates and a tale to be recounted for generations around the family holiday table. Gittelsohn arrived, reassured me that Mr. Korinow was an excellent tutor, and I would be fine. That was easy for him to say! An hour later, I visibly trembled as I read the scriptural portion from the handwritten Hebrew text that lacked both vowels and punctuation. The locked arms of Rabbi Gittelsohn and Rabbi Robert W. Shapiro, the assistant rabbi, supported my weight for my trembling knees had long since failed to support me.

Confirmation class at age 16 meant a full semester of twice-weekly classes—four hours a week with Rabbi Gittelsohn himself. He was the author of the one book taught in virtually all Reform Jewish religious schools from Alaska to Panama and New Hampshire to San Diego. The high school grapevine warned us, "Do the assigned homework, keep your head down, and your mouth closed in class. Do not challenge the rabbi!" It was remarkably bad advice.

When else would we have the opportunity to engage with a renowned scholar, an acknowledged leader of the American Jewish community? When I asked questions, sophomoric or astute, he responded thoughtfully and engaged me with respect. At times, our discussion required additional time. Despite his being the leader of the largest synagogue in New England, he found that time. He never patronized me, though surely there were occasions when that was justified. Remarkably, he occasionally conceded that other perspectives could be equally valid or even that his initial understanding was incomplete. All our conversations were thought-provoking and informative.

Our time together, moreover, allowed me a glimpse into his extensive learning on both secular and religious matters. He had, for instance, an expansive knowledge of Western culture, including music and the graphic arts. While I had been studying in Israel, back home in Boston, Temple Israel was building a grand sanctuary. When I arrived back home in 1970 with my new wife, Miriam, Gittelsohn took us on a tour of the new facility. As if he were a professor at the Art Institute of Chicago, he described the architecture and the art installations. He pointed out details and nuances we had missed. He described in detail which school of art each element represented, where there was continuity and where there was dissonance, and what the transitions were intended to evoke. At his insistence, the three of us risked life and limb, crossed the busy multilane parkway, and scaled a guard rail so we could view the monumental entrance sculpture from the ideal perspective.

I attended the same seminary as Roland Gittelsohn had a generation earlier, Hebrew Union College in Cincinnati, Ohio. Throughout my studies, he found time to meet with me. He even intervened to ensure that my graduate work at Hebrew University would be accepted for credit at our seminary.

RESPECT AND ANGER

Rabbi Roland B. Gittelsohn was an acknowledged leader of American Judaism, a prolific author, a powerfully influential leader in the metropolitan Boston religious community, and an original thinker. He followed in the tradition of great twentieth century American Jewish orators, among them Stephen S. Wise, Barnett R. Brickner, and Abba Hillel Silver, as well as nationally acclaimed Protestants such as Harry Emerson Fosdick.

He evoked both admiration and anger, often from the selfsame individuals.

He was scholarly, extremely well read, cultured, and caring; and he was willing to take any risk, personal, political, and professional in fulfillment of our faith's admonition "not the study but the practice is the essential thing," or as we might say, "actions speak louder than words." Based on strong relations with a wide array of non-Jewish clergy, Rabbi Gittelsohn was a key figure in Boston's interfaith community, and "to complete the package," he was a widely appreciated, astute, and effective counselor for both individuals and couples. This memoir of his service as a Navy chaplain during the Second World War gives many more examples of his personal and empathetic ministry.

While I was in Israel for graduate school, the Central Conference of American Rabbis (CCAR) convened for the first time ever in Jerusalem, with Roland Gittelsohn as its president. A lifelong lover of Zion, he presided masterfully. It was a dramatic symbolic shift for a movement that a few years earlier had been riven over Zionism. The rabbi's patient and listening "diplomacy," so to speak, placed the organization on a new and constructive path.

I would not be candid, however, without saying that this erudite and patient leader in the Jewish faith sparked many controversies. He vexed many in public life and even in his congregation. Some regarded him with anger. How can we account for this anger?

Here is a homely example. My extended family's holiday table always included a passionate discussion—or more accurately an argument—revolving around the festival sermon delivered by Temple Israel's senior rabbi Roland B. Gittelsohn. Characteristically, he marshaled facts and the opinions of experts, and then he pronounced in declarative sentences what the moment and Jewish tradition "required" of us. His sermons were the product of a voracious reading, spoken with the passion of biblical prophecy. He spoke truth to power, comforted the troubled, and troubled the comfortable. Around our family table, one adult might declare him excessively "idealistic," another "too strident" or "arrogant," yet another "thoughtful"; but everyone had an opinion. In other words, he had forced us to think deeply about an issue. Not every sermon was in response to the affairs of the day or on what we know as social justice. There were sermons on family dynamics, the elements of Jewish faith, our relationship to the still fledgling state of Israel, and the need for serious Jewish study. Around our family table, however, it was the many "political" sermons that evoked the most passion and discussion, even anger. Again, I frequently asked myself, how could the kind and good-natured man of my experience evoke so much passionate antagonism?

Historic context is part of the answer. It is instructive to note that Rabbi Gittelsohn's sermon "The Purest Democracy" preceded both the widespread and expanding civil rights and interfaith movements of the postwar years. Prior to World War II, America had not yet learned to speak of our religious landscape as later described by Will Herberg in his landmark book, *Protestant, Catholic, Jew: An Essay in American Religious Sociology* (1955), a description now eclipsed by an ever more inclusive understanding of America. He wrote, spoke, and preached on many postwar issues in American life—issues that divided even Americans of good will. He advocated with passion and intensity for civil rights, an end to the arms race, support for Israel, women's equality, reproductive rights, and our withdrawal from

Vietnam. Most congregants respected and even appreciated Gittelsohn's views, while others were enraged. However, these were common rabbinic themes of the day and hardly account for the anger.

For me, an early clue came when Rabbi Gittelsohn pronounced the benediction at our Boston wedding reception. Asked if he wanted a microphone, he responded, "If people listen, they will hear me without a microphone, and even if they don't, God will hear." Of course, he was correct, but still . . . it was as if he and God were having a conversation and we were allowed to eavesdrop. Might this haughty air explain the passionate hostility he aroused?

I found a more complete answer in Lee Mandel's book *Unlikely Warrior: A Pacifist Rabbi's Journey from the Pulpit to Iwo Jima* (2015). Mandel reports that in 1934, Roland's required student sermon was entitled "More Human Bondage." From Genesis 23:12, he evoked the binding of Isaac by Father Abraham and God's command: "Lay not thy hand upon the lad, neither do thou anything to him." For Gittelsohn, that command to Abraham in the ancient moment continues as an imperative for every adult in all succeeding generations. Roland continued, "The days of human sacrifice were to be ended." The sacrifice of human lives, dignity, and talent in the name of any deity, doctrine, or "ism" must cease! In 1934, he saw humanity as an automobile careening toward a crash so extreme and urgent that action was required. The required action, the required remedy, was nothing less than the establishment of economic, social, and racial justice.

Another 1934 sermon displayed how even then he marshaled facts and proffered a vision: "Eight southern states average $44 per year for the education of each white child. . . . For each Negro child they average $12.50. And . . . [yet they] dare to speak of the Negro's low level of culture." Economic justice, equality, and Jewish values demanded that "only after every man has what he needs can any man have what he wants! . . . We must protect the man whose skin is black even if our skin is white, and we must feed the hungry and clothe the naked even if it means less luxury for us." Rabbi Gittelsohn was convinced human history would culminate in humanity's perfection. With every fiber of his being, he worked to ensure the societal changes required by the universal imperative to repair both ourselves and creation. He believed we were coworkers with God and "little lower than the angels."[1]

Naturally, this sort of excited idealism was no surprise coming from a 24-year-old rabbinic student. It has been said that youthful radicals mature into middle-age moderates and age into status quo conservatives. I suspect that this man evoked such passion and anger because he failed to follow that model. His last sermon was the same as his first, brought up to date and preached even more effectively.

There is an apocryphal story of a rabbi that gave the same high holiday sermon every year. After the third occasion, the board of the congregation sent a delegation to demand an explanation. The rabbi responded: "Yes, it's true, and when you show you have taken it to heart, I can move on to the next sermon." Like that rabbi, Roland never veered from his vision for humanity, our responsibility to perfect the human condition, and his abiding optimism that human advancement was our common destiny. I suggest to you that his entire life was the living out of that early sermon. In this light, "The Purest Democracy," his famous sermon at Iwo Jima, was a succinct expression of the same

---

[1] Psalms 8:5.

message, now honed by the awful experience of a world at war in general and more intimately the terrible carnage he witnessed on Iwo Jima.

From that 1934 sermon, Roland Gittelsohn went on to become a prolific author, even while he was still in seminary. The National Federation of Temple Sisterhoods (now Women of Reformed Judaism) commissioned him to write a book for use in Jewish religious schools across North America. In 1943, *Modern Jewish Problems: A Textbook for High School Classes and Jewish Youth Groups* was first published, being revised and updated in 1949 and 1955. His *Little Lower than the Angels*, first published in 1955, became the ubiquitous high school-level confirmation text on Jewish thought across North American for two decades. His books intended for a wide audience include: *My Beloved Is Mine: Judaism and Marriage* (1969) and *Consecrated unto Me: A Jewish View of Love and Marriage* (1965) on marriage in modern America; *Wings of the Morning* (1969), *Fire in My Bones: Essays on Judaism in a Time of Crisis* (1969), and *Man's Best Hope* (1961) on Jewish thought; and his memoir, *Here Am I—Harnessed to Hope* (1988). These books and, more importantly, his life evidenced his unwavering commitment to the ideals of our people as he encountered them in his childhood home and his encyclopedic studies.

So, how did such a kind and insightful man evoke such anger from so many? The answer lies in his staying true to his principles in word and deed. Dr. Albert Vorspan, another great leader in the American Jewish community and also a World War II Marine and sailor combat veteran, remarked, "Roland was fearless—he told people what he believed they needed to hear whether they wanted to hear it or not." Indeed, he did, and often deep in their souls they resented knowing he was correct. It did not soften the effect that he preached from a nationally renowned pulpit and that his subjects included the most contro-versial issues of the day: racial equality, reproductive rights, and economic justice. He epitomized the words of Senator Barry M. Goldwater (R-AZ) (with whom I imagine he otherwise never agreed): "I would remind you that extremism in the defense of liberty is no vice. And let me remind you also that moderation in the pursuit of justice is no virtue."[2] Ever the optimist, Rab-bi Roland B. Gittelsohn believed in the inevitability of human progress and in humanity's capacity to build a divinely inspired and more perfect world. He was indeed "harnessed to hope."

Rabbi Harold L. Robinson, DD, DHumLitt
Rear Admiral, Chaplain Corps, U.S. Navy (Ret)
Centerville, Massachusetts

---

[2] Barry M. Goldwater, "Republican Nomination Acceptance" (speech, Nation-al Convention of the Republican Party, Daly City, CA, 16 July 1964).

PREFACE

The Military Chaplaincy's Chaplain
Roland B. Gittelsohn
in World War II

It is a truism of historical research that you have no idea what you will find in the archives. Even with a good finding aid—and the American Jewish Archives (AJA) in Cincinnati, Ohio, has excellent finding aids—it is hard to anticipate what a Hollinger archival storage box contains. When I went to the AJA to conduct research on military chaplains in 2012, I knew some basic information about Rabbi Roland B. Gittelsohn; he was the first Jewish chaplain to serve in the U.S. Marine Corps, his experience on Iwo Jima included both the painful experience of anti-Semitism and the triumphant call to build a more just future, and (most notably to a graduate student) he was a prolific writer and the papers from his long career are extensive.

The last folder in the final box of MS-704 contained a document labeled "Pacifist to Padre/Pacifist in Uniform/Pacifist No More." It could have been anything, and it appeared likely, based on the other folder titles, to be a sermon or short recollection. It was part sermon and part recollection, but it was also anything but short. At more than 165 typewritten pages, with handwritten corrections, "Pacifist to Padre" (to select one of three suggested titles) packaged anecdotes and reflections into a full-fledged memoir of Gittelsohn's wartime service. True, it languished in his files. But what historian could resist an unpublished memoir, especially one that began by modestly asserting "this is a story that could be written by any one of us" and accurately predicting "we shall—most of us—return one day to our civilian congregations considerably changed. We shall be better ministers, Priests, and rabbis because we have been chaplains."

In my notes from the time, I simply wrote "Box 64/Folder 7 [photographed full memoir]." It would not be until I returned home and started writing a chapter on World War II that I would refer back to the photographs I took and start reading. In many ways, Gittelsohn was correct that his story of World War II chaplaincy was a common one. His memoir corroborated letters, diaries, memoranda, oral histories, and albums preserved by other chaplains. A wry wit studs the narrative. Take, for example, his description in chapter 3 of his Chaplain School class: "As a group, each beginning class at the school is just about as unmilitary a conglomeration of homo sapiens as the eye has ever seen. The first time I wore my Navy uniform, I felt like half policeman and half theater usher." Just as often, a deeply pensive and wise voice emerges. Witness the characterization of Chaplain School that follows: "But the interplay of three major religions in a living democracy was not limited to our personal and informal relationships. It was a conscious and deliberate part of our schooling." Gittelsohn intuited and internalized the message that the military sought to imbue in its chaplains.

Pacifist to Padre thus stands out because it deftly threads so many elements of the World War II chaplaincy into a compelling and thoughtful narrative. It offers a personal window into a complex institution. It provides insight into the world of an unusual American space that has been naturalized as normal: of government-sponsored and managed religion. And it brings that world into focus from the vantage point of a man who never would have predicted pinning the Jewish chaplain's tablet insignia to his collar, a Jewish pacifist turned military padre.

By World War II, clergy from three religious traditions comprised the military chaplain corps. There were Protestant ministers, there were Catholic priests, and there were Jewish rabbis. They were all men. They were predominantly, but not wholly, white. They were well educated, with college degrees, graduate degrees, and formal ordination. They chose to enlist (as clergy, they received automatic draft deferments). And most of the more than 11,000 chaplains who served had no prior military experience.

Demographically, then, Gittelsohn fit in well. Temperamentally, he matched the military's interest in clergy who could boost morale, reach officers and enlisted, and embrace the multireligious milieu of the armed forces. Religiously, his Reform movement rabbinical training meshed well with an institution that valued God but tried to avoid sectarian particularities. When he writes, in chapter 8, that "You and I have such reserves of strength in us too. You can call that strength God, as I do. You can give it any other name you like. The important thing is, it's there," he manifested his commitment to transcending rather than maintaining religious boundaries.

Politically, however, he was less of an obvious fit. His discomfort with the machinery of war was longstanding. Even as Adolf Hitler rose to power, Nazi Germany invaded Poland, and much of the American Jewish community urged President

Franklin D. Roosevelt to fight Hitler, Gittelsohn eschewed violence. But Pearl Harbor—as he relays in the opening of his memoir—made him reconsider his views and apply for a commission as a Navy chaplain.

Like other American rabbis, he applied first to the Jewish Welfare Board (JWB), which reviewed candidates and endorsed those they thought fit to represent the Jewish community in the U.S. military. The JWB, which was founded during World War I, operated as the organizational conduit between the U.S. government and Jewish Americans. While this community was varied and complex, its interface with the military did not allow for denominational differences. The armed forces wanted rabbis who would be Jewish chaplains, not Reform, Conservative, or Orthodox rabbis. Here, too, Gittelsohn embraced the charge to simply be a rabbi. Or, as he discusses in chapter 10, the commitment that "we are still one people with one faith" and cannot "permit our minor differences of interpretation to obscure our major agreement on fundamentals." War, he conjectured, offered Jews "the greatest opportunity . . . in centuries . . . [to] forge a new unity in the religious life of the Jew."

In some ways, Gittelsohn epitomized the goals of the military chaplaincy. In chapter 3, he embraced the multireligious milieu—even Chaplain School was a "living thrill" that he characterized as "an honest effort to understand each other based on an equally honest determination to help each other." He carried that thrill into combat, where his fellow chaplains were most often Protestants and Catholics.

But Gittelsohn was far more than a starry-eyed idealist. "I wish that I could write here the kind of easy, pleasant chapter that most of my friends would like to read," he lamented in chapter 12. "It would run something like this: there are no group prejudices or antagonisms in the armed forces. . . . But it would not be true." His aspirations for unity—among Jews, across religions, and between blacks and whites—were marred by raw encounters with prejudice. Uniforms did not erase bias or discrimination. Limiting Black Marines to scut work as attendants and orderlies was, in his view, "unfair . . . unreasonable . . . [and] a frightful waste of manpower. It is all that, and it is, over and above and beyond all that, undemocratic and un-American." He was dismayed to encounter prejudice in the chaplain corps, among those "who presume to be people of God!"

He reserved his most scathing critique for his most personally searing incident: the refusal of some Protestant and Catholic chaplains to participate in a joint memorial service at Iwo Jima in which he—at the request of his senior chaplain—was supposed to give the memorial sermon. "I do not remember anything in my life that has made me so painfully heartsick," he wrote. "We had just come through nearly five weeks of miserable hell. Some of us at least had served people of all faiths and of no faith, without making denomination or affiliation a prerequisite for help." His rage would fuel the writing of the sermon he did give. In "Pacifist to Padre," he mourned the fragility of religious harmony along with the deaths of his Marines. "Protestants, Catholics, and Jews had lived together, fought together, died together, and now lay buried together. But we the living could not unite to pray together." Then, in his sermon, he argued they could and they should. "Among these men there is no discrimination. No prejudice. No hatred. Theirs is the highest and purest democracy," he proclaimed. And then he warned: "Anyone among us the living who fails to understand that, will thereby betray those who lie here. Whoever of us lifts his hand in hate against another, or thinks himself superior to those who happen to be in the minority, makes of this ceremony and of the bloody sacrifice it commemorates, an empty, hollow mockery."

During his time in uniform, as a pacifist turned padre, Gittelsohn most often acted in his pastoral capacity. He counseled, he listened, he prayed. After all, the Marine he wrote of in chapter 12 was "a human being, coming with a human problem, to a human chaplain." Like World War I Jewish chaplain Lee J. Levinger, Gittelsohn believed "religious unity . . . is more than a far-off ideal." But after weeks of "miserable hell" in the Pacific theater, he cried out in the register of a prophet. He called the chaplaincy, the military, and the United States to task. He insisted the ideals could be real—but only with work. "The Purest Democracy," for which he longed was not predestined. Only with human commitment, "if we understand both the issues and the dangers and play our hand wisely," might it develop.

When Gittelsohn urged his battle-weary congregation onward, when he told them there was work left to do—to "dedicate ourselves: to the rights of Protestants, Catholics, and Jews, of all races alike, to enjoy the democracy for which all of them have here paid the price" and to "consecrate ourselves in memory of those who sleep beneath these crosses and stars"—he evoked the language of another significant war eulogy of another great orator. Amidst the dead at Gettysburg, President Abraham Lincoln exhorted Americans to endow death with meaning. "The living," he argued, must "be dedicated here to the unfinished work . . . to the great task remaining before us . . . that this nation, under God, shall have a new birth of freedom, and that government of the people, by the people, for the people, shall not perish from the earth." And similarly, Gittelsohn, a little more than four score years later, reminded Americans that war represented a beginning, not an end, a starting point for "our generation's struggle for democracy." To consecrate and to dedicate could be an act of holy renewal: to "live together in peace," "to build the kind of world for which you died," to create "the right to a living that is decent and secure."

As a chaplain, Roland B. Gittelsohn exemplified the values the military purported—at least rhetorically—to hold: commitments to religious pluralism, to equality, to security. If that made him a radical in the ranks, so be it. Even in uniform, Gittelsohn was a pacifist who could only countenance war if it produced a just society. Invigorated by the opportunity to live with, learn from, and lead servicemembers from a broad spectrum of American experiences, Gittelsohn never let the military off the hook. And this too is part of his legacy. After World War II, he carried his Marine Corps experience home to his pulpit and to politics, where he continued to speak his mind, to ensure the men he buried had not died in vain. He served on President Harry S. Truman's Committee on Civil Rights, and he condemned the Vietnam War. For the pacifist turned padre, conscientious objection to an unjust war remained as important as donning the uniform in a just war.

Like many other chaplains, he wrestled with his role: invested in interfaith service, compelled by the call to serve Americans in uniform, but motivated by religious and political ideals that the military did not always achieve. In this sense, his desire and commitment to constructing "the purest democracy" animated all of Chaplain Gittelsohn's decisions, as part of and resistant to military force. *Pacifist to Padre* helps show how and why.

Ronit Y. Stahl
Assistant Professor of History,
University of California, Berkeley

ACKNOWLEDGMENTS

This is the place to thank a number of individuals who helped complete this book. Chaplain Harold L. Robinson wrote a revealing foreword, and he improved the volume with his knowledge of Judaism and the unique characteristics of the American chaplaincy. Professor Ronit Stahl alerted the editor to the manuscript at the American Jewish Archives, wrote the preface, and provided valuable counsel on usages. Angela Anderson of the Marine Corps University Press took personal charge of this book project, shepherding it from beginning to end with saintly patience. The staff of the American Jewish Archives provided the original document and answered many subsequent inquiries. Others who made contributions, especially to the footnotes, include Bishop F. Richard Spencer of the Archdiocese for Military Services, a retired Army chaplain; retired Army chaplain Dick Stenbakken; Terese Erickson, the Christian Science Endorser for the Armed Forces; and Rabbi Gittelsohn's former assistant rabbis and students.

INTRODUCTION

by Donald M. Bishop

It was economist Julian L. Simon who first drew my attention to Navy chaplain Roland B. Gittelsohn and his sermon at the dedication of the 5th Marine Division's cemetery as the battle of Iwo Jima closed. During a conference at the Ethics and Public Policy Center in Washington, DC, in 1993, I heard Simon describe how a visit to the Iwo Jima memorial (formally the U.S. Marine Corps War Memorial) in Arlington, Virginia, awakened memories of the sermon and led him to break a new path in his studies of population and economic growth.[3]

Simon had sparked my curiosity. I found the sermon, realized its power, and corresponded with the former chaplain, then rabbi emeritus at Temple Israel of Boston in Massachusetts. Rabbi Gittelsohn pointed me to his 1988 memoir, *Here Am I—Harnessed to Hope*. In one chapter, he told how he wrote the sermon.[4]

Corresponding with an old friend, the author Dan Levin,

---

[3] Julian L. Simon, *A Life Against the Grain: The Autobiography of an Unconventional Economist* (Piscataway, NJ: Transaction Publishers, 2003), 242–43.
[4] Roland B. Gittelsohn, *Here Am I—Harnessed to Hope* (New York: Vantage Press, 1988), 130–33.

a Marine Corps combat correspondent at Iwo Jima, I learned that he had listened to the sermon on the island. In 1949, Levin wrote one of the first novels of the war, *Mask of Glory* (1949), and in 1953 he again recalled the battle in his second novel, *The Dream in the Flesh*. At my urging, Levin gave details of hearing the sermon in his 1995 book, *From the Battlefield: Dispatches of a World War II Marine*.

Some years later, I accompanied the Assistant Commandant of the Marine Corps, General Robert Magnus, on a trip to Iraq and Afghanistan. Joining us on the aircraft was Chaplain Rear Admiral Harold L. Robinson, at that time the Navy's senior Reserve chaplain. I was surprised to learn that Chaplain Robinson had been a member of Rabbi Gittelsohn's congregation; indeed, the Iwo Jima chaplain had encouraged young Robinson to become a Navy chaplain after he finished his religious studies. These personal encounters—Simon, Levin, and Robinson—were milestones on the path to this volume.

After his death in 1995, the papers of Rabbi Gittelsohn were given to the American Jewish Archives in Cincinnati. I asked the archives whether the papers included any materials from Gittelsohn's time in the Navy. Unfortunately, I asked at the wrong time—after the accession of the papers but before their organization and the publication of the finding aid.[5] I was told there were none.

Fast forward to 2017. I attended a talk at Marine Corps Base Quantico, Virginia, by Professor Ronit Stahl of the University of Southern California, the author of *Enlisting Faith: How the*

---

[5] "Finding Aid to the Roland Bertram Gittelsohn Papers, 1934-1996," Manuscript Collection No. 704, Jacob Rader Marcus Center of the American Jewish Archives, accessed 3 April 2020.

Military Chaplaincy Shaped Religion and State in Modern America, published by the Harvard University Press in 2017. She told me that the Gittelsohn papers at the American Jewish Archives included the typed draft of a book written by Chaplain Gittelsohn in the months following the battle but never published. Indeed, she had photocopied this draft for her own research, which she then shared with me.

When I read the pages, I realized that while it told the story of chaplains during the battle, the whole book was much larger in its scope. It was a personal account of moving from an idealistic prewar pacifism to active participation in the Second World War.[6] It provided a valuable record of the wartime Navy Chaplain's School at the College of William and Mary in Williamsburg, Virginia.[7] It was a meditation on relations between chaplains from different denominations, and it offered Chaplain Gittelsohn's considered philosophy on a chaplain's role in a command.

I showed the draft manuscript to the director of Marine Corps University Press. Angela Anderson immediately recognized its value. She made the arrangements with the American Jewish Archive for its publication, and she took on the editorial preparation of the text and its design personally.

Navy Chaplains at Quantico—Captain Maurice A. Buford,

---

[6] See also Gittelsohn, *Here Am I: Harnessed to Hope*, 99-100. The topic is thoroughly explored in Lee Mandel, *Unlikely Warrior: A Pacifist Rabbi's Journey from the Pulpit to Iwo Jima* (Gretna, LA: Pelican Publishing, 2015). Mandel conducted extensive research in the Gittelsohn papers at the American Jewish Archives, and he drew on *Here I Am—Harnessed to Hope* and the manuscript now published in this volume.

[7] For the official history of the school, see Capt Clifford M. Drury, *The History of the Chaplain Corps, United States Navy,* vol. 2, *1939-1949* (Washington, DC: Bureau of Naval Personnel, 1948), 56-67.

Captain Daryl White, and Commander Cristiano DeSousa—also encouraged the book's publication. In the second decade of this century, senior Navy chaplains realize that today's Chaplain Corps has no experience with the large casualties that chaplains might confront in future naval combat against major powers. They agreed that Chaplain Gittelsohn's memoir can help prepare the naval Services for these future challenges.

* * *

The first Marines landed at Iwo Jima on 19 February 1945, and Associated Press photographer Joseph Rosenthal captured the raising of the American flag on Mount Suribachi on 23 February in his now iconic image.[8] The battle—eventually pitting 71,000 Marines against 22,000 Japanese on an island only 13 square kilometers in size—lasted until 26 March, far longer than expected. That only 216 Japanese were captured during the battle gives testimony to its unforgiving ferocity and to the power of the Japanese state under ultranationalist and military influence to indoctrinate and propagandize its youth in its schools and in the army.[9] The tally of American casualties was 26,000, among them 6,800 dead.

With the Marines and sailors on the island were Navy chaplains of the three major faiths. In their number was Gittelsohn, the first Jewish chaplain sent by the Navy to the Marine Corps.

---

[8] The Rosenthal image would become the basis for several Marine Corps investigations into the identities of the Marines who raised the flags that day. See Breanne Robertson, ed., *Investigating Iwo: The Flag Raisings in Myth, Memory, & Esprit de Corps* (Quantico, VA: Marine Corps History Division, an imprint of Marine Corps University Press, 2019).

[9] For more on the Japanese who were taken prisoner during and after the battle, see "The Battle for Iwo Jima," National World War II Museum, February 2020; and Ben Brimelow, "73 Years Ago a War Photographer Snapped the Most Iconic Image of World War II," *Business Insider*, 23 February 2018.

He had left Central Synagogue in Rockville Center on Long Island, New York, for the naval Service.

Americans celebrate how the war, bringing together Americans from all regions, backgrounds, walks of life, and faiths, forged a new and more unified America. Chaplain Robinson emphasized that the war also transformed the chaplain corps and its understanding of ministry in a pluralistic society. Many chaplains developed collegial bonds and friendships across denominational lines, unlike their previous experience in civilian pastoral care. Chaplains ministered to servicemembers of different faiths (and no faith) without hesitation.[10] The issuance of the Four Chaplains postage stamp ("Interfaith in Action") in 1948—honoring the four Army chaplains on the SS *Dorchester* in 1943 who had given their own life vests to soldiers abandoning the torpedoed troop transport—showed how the solidarity among chaplains laid ground for the postwar interfaith movement.[11]

Gittelsohn remembered two chaplains in particular. Protestant Chaplain Herbert Van Meter (1915-82) was "one of his dearest friends." In Hawaii when the 5th Marine Division had no Jewish chaplain, Van Meter organized and led Jewish Sabbath services so often that he was called "Rabbi Van Meter." During the battle, Gittelsohn recalled, Van Meter "would crawl

---

[10] To give but one example, the Jewish chaplain assigned to the 6th Marine Division during the invasion of Okinawa, Morton M. Berman (1899-1986), received a rare Navy citation: "Whenever the situation permitted, he sought to be of help to men of other faiths as well, winning the affection of all in the division who knew of his selfless devotion to his duties." Drury, *The History of the Chaplain Corps, United States Navy*, vol. 2, 205.

[11] The story of the four chaplains has been told many times. A recent title is by Dan Kurzman, *No Greater Glory: The Four Immortal Chaplains and the Sinking of the Dorchester in World War II* (New York: Random House, 2004). For the postage stamp (Scott #956), see "Four Chaplains Issue," Smithsonian National Postal Museum, accessed 24 April 2020.

between attacks from one foxhole to another, trying to reassure his weary, frightened Marines. He would grasp the hand of one, squeeze the shoulder of another and hold firmly to the uncontrollably trembling body of a third. He prayed with them, read psalms to them, helped them feel unashamed of their fear by confessing that he was terrified himself."[12]

Soon after the battle, it was Army chaplain Newton Carl Elder, a Presbyterian, who co-opted a plane, flew to Saipan, and returned with "nearly half a ton" of matzos, gefilte fish, Haggadahs, and wine for the three Jewish chaplains on Iwo Jima to celebrate Passover with their Marines.[13] They were surely grateful that the angel of death had passed over their own foxholes.

Even during the fighting, two large cemeteries were staked out, and the thousands of dead were interred in long trenches with chaplains providing the appropriate rituals.[14] For the unknowns, Protestant, Catholic, and Jewish rites were administered. Having worked together consecrating burials all day and into the night, Gittelsohn wrote, "three chaplains—a Baptist, a Methodist, a Jew—wearier than they had ever been before, climbed into the trench, stood there together before the last row of graves, and held the flashlight for each other as they prayed."

---

[12] Roland B. Gittelsohn, "Padre in Hell," *Leatherneck*, December 1985, 44-47. See also Robert T. Mueller, "Sound Off: Padre in Hell," *Leatherneck*, March 1986, 8.
[13] Gittelsohn, *Here Am I—Harnessed to Hope*, 144-45. The Iwo Jima files in the Historical Resources Branch (previously Archives Branch) of Marine Corps University include a 1988 letter from the Army chief of chaplains, MajGen Norris L. Einerston, appreciating Elder's "assistance to three Marine Corps Jewish chaplains on Iwo Jima."
[14] The letters of Chaplain E. Gage Hotaling of the 4th Marine Division well portray the work of Navy chaplains at the cemeteries on the island. See Kerry Hotaling, *Go Forward into the Storm: An Iwo Jima Journal* (Gleneden Beach, OR: Christopher Matthews Publishing, 2016).

The rabbi said "it was impossible to forget the brotherhood and love of men like these."

Chaplain Gittelsohn provided personal testimony to the solidarity and comradeship among chaplains, but he also knew its limits. He encountered the anti-Semitism of the times. A drunk Marine said, "One good thing Hitler has done is kill the Jews."[15] A chaplain refused copies of Jewish Welfare Board and Anti-Defamation League pamphlets, saying "If you want your Jewish boys to read this trash, give it to them yourself. I refuse to put it on the shelf for Christians to read."[16] Other chaplains voiced demeaning stereotypes of Jews.[17]

DEDICATING THE
5TH MARINE DIVISION'S CEMETERY

The 5th Marine Division's cemetery, laid out in the shape of a cross at the base of Mount Suribachi, eventually held more than 2,200 graves, 38 of them unknowns. The final throes of the battle could still be heard in the distance when it came time to dedicate the cemetery on 21 March 1945.[18] According to plan, the division's commander, Major General Keller E. Rockey (1888–1970), would speak a tribute to the dead for the Marine Corps and the nation. His remarks would be followed by the religious dedication.

There were 17 chaplains in the division. Division Chaplain

---

[15] Gittelsohn, *Here Am I—Harnessed to Hope*, 103–4.

[16] Gittelsohn, *Here Am I—Harnessed to Hope*, 126–27.

[17] Gittelsohn, *Here Am I—Harnessed to Hope*, 127–28.

[18] For instance, one of the Marines who raised the flag on Mount Suribachi, PFC Franklin R. Sousley, was killed by a sniper the day the cemetery was dedicated. See Bob Jordan, "The Youngest Flag Raiser," *Leatherneck* 68, no. 2, February 1985, 26–29.

Warren Cuthriell wanted Rabbi Gittelsohn to speak at a joint funeral service, and the Jewish chaplain wrote out a sermon by hand on onionskin paper. The senior chaplain's plan, however, met staunch opposition that showed the limits of interfaith solidarity. Some Protestant chaplains protested that it should not be a Jewish chaplain who prayed over the graves of mostly Christian Marines. Catholic chaplains voiced their church's traditional objection to all-faiths services. Those objecting to Chaplain Cuthriell's proposal urged a different format for the service: following the commanding general's secular tribute, chaplains and Marines of the three major faiths would move to different corners of the cemetery for their own services.

Cuthriell replied that "the right of the Jewish chaplain to preach such a sermon was precisely one of the things for which we were fighting the war." When he learned of the objections by some of his fellow chaplains, Gittelsohn later wrote, "I do not remember anything in my life that made me so painfully sick." The rabbi might have stood his ground on principle, but sensing his superior's distress, he agreed to lead the Jewish burial service, speaking the same words he had written out for the joint service.[19]

Only 40 or 50 servicemembers, joined by three of the Protestant chaplains who were upset by the decision to hold separate services, gathered around Chaplain Gittelsohn, but his words rank among America's finest eulogies.

> This is perhaps the grimmest, and surely the holiest
> task we have faced since D-Day. Here before us lie
> the bodies of comrades and friends. Men who un-
> til yesterday or last week laughed with us, joked

---

[19] Gittelsohn, *Here Am I—Harnessed to Hope*, 130–33.

> with us, trained with us. Men who were on the same
> ships with us, and went over the sides with us, as we
> prepared to hit the beaches of this island. Men who
> fought with us and feared with us.

Gittelsohn's repeated mentions of "we," "our" and "us," along with his images of shared experiences, set up the sermon's major theme. "We" have become a brotherhood on this battlefield, and we must carry that spirit back to our nation, where Americans are still divided by origin, race, class, and faith. Surely his recent experiences with anti-Semitism suggested the theme, as did seeing how African-American Marines in amphibian truck and depot companies were so often given the grisly duty of recovering remains.[20] From his position on the division staff, Gittelsohn knew there were Army Nisei interpreters among the Marines, along with Navajo code talkers.

> Somewhere in this plot of ground there may lie the
> man who could have discovered the cure for cancer.
> Under one of these Christian crosses, or beneath a
> Jewish Star of David, there may rest now a man
> who was destined to be a great prophet to find the
> way, perhaps, for all to live in plenty, with poverty
> and hardship for none. Now they lie here silently
> in this sacred soil, and we gather to consecrate this
> earth in their memory.

This was the passage that so moved Julian Simon—and still moves me today. Gittelsohn only gave two examples of trans-

---

[20] For more on black Marines at Iwo Jima, see Bernard C. Nalty, *The Right to Fight: African-American Marines in World War II* (Washington, DC: Marine Corps Historical Center, 1995), 22–24.

formative genius, but if "a man that was destined to be" might have come from among ordinary Marines implies to me that Gittelsohn understood that every person has a divine spark and an endowment of talent, however humble. Julian Simon spoke of individuals who "might be a Mozart or a Michelangelo or an Einstein," for sure, but he thought too of individuals who were "simply a joy to his or her family and community, and a person who will enjoy life."[21]

> IT IS NOT EASY TO DO SO. Some of us have buried our closest friends here. We saw these men killed before our very eyes. Any one of us might have died in their places. Indeed, some of us are alive and breathing at this very moment only because men who lie here beneath us, had the courage and strength to give their lives for ours. To speak in memory of such men as these is not easy. Of them, too, can it be said with utter truth: "The world will little note nor long remember what we say here. It can never forget what they did here."
>
> No, our poor power of speech can add nothing to what these men and the other dead of our division who are not here have already done. All that we can even hope to do is follow their example. To show the same selfless courage in peace that they did in war. To swear that, by the grace of God and the stubborn strength and power of human will, their sons and ours shall never suffer these pains again. These men have done their job well. They have paid the ghastly price of freedom. If that freedom be once

[21] Simon, A Life Against the Grain, 242–43.

again lost, as it was after the last war, the unfor-
givable blame will be ours, not theirs. So it be the
living who are here to be dedicated and consecrated.

As he wrote out his sermon, away from a library, exhausted by his chaplain's work every day, the young rabbi, it is clear, leaned on Abraham Lincoln and his Gettysburg Address. The generation of young Marines present on the island had all read Lincoln's words in school; indeed, some would have memorized them. Then, as now, the words are evocative.

WE DEDICATE OURSELVES, first, to live to-
gether in peace the way they fought and are buried
in war. Here lie men who loved America because
their ancestors, generations ago helped in her found-
ing, and other men who loved her with equal pas-
sion because they themselves or their own fathers
escaped from oppression to her blessed shores.[22] Here
lie officers and men, Negroes and whites, rich men
and poor . . . together. Here are Protestants, Cath-
olics, and Jews . . . together. Here no man prefers
another because of his faith or despises him because
of his color. Here there are no quotas of how many

---

[22] For Chaplain Gittelsohn, the reference to escaping from oppression to America's "blessed shore" was more than a historical allusion. His father and grandfather had "fled from the oppression of Czarist Russia. America had opened its ams to them." Moreover, from Jewish Telegraph Agency reports, he knew of prewar German persecution and the outlines of the Holocaust. He knew Soviet forces had liberated death camps in Poland, begiming with Maj-danek near Lublin in July 1944. They overran the sites of Belzec, Sobibor, and Treblinka that summer. It was two weeks after he gave his sermon on Iwo Jima that the U.S. Army first liberated a camp at Ohrdruf, Germany. For more, see "Liberation of Nazi Death Camps," Holocaust Encyclopedia, United States Holocaust Memorial Museum, accessed 4 April 2020.

> from each group are admitted or allowed. Among
> these men there is no discrimination. No prejudice.
> No hatred. Theirs is the highest and purest democ-
> racy. [Gittelsohn's ellipses]

"We," who landed and fought together, then, are the "we" who must return home with a new awareness and pass it on to "our sons." Gittelsohn's "we," spoken at a time when the majority of Americans traced their roots to the British Isles and Europe—only a few years after the first African Americans had been reluctantly allowed to enlist in a traditionally all-white Marine Corps—was, for its time, more inclusive. Gittelsohn perhaps shorted the entirely different ways that the ancestors of whites and blacks had come to America, but for 1945, his expression was liberal and far-sighted. Indeed, he continued,

> Any man among us the living who fails to under-
> stand that, will thereby betray those who lie here
> dead. Whoever of us lifts his hand in hate against
> a brother, or thinks himself superior to those who
> happen to be in the minority, makes of this cere-
> mony and of the bloody sacrifice it commemorates,
> an empty, hollow mockery. To this, them, as our
> solemn, sacred duty, do we the living now dedicate
> ourselves: to the right Protestants, Catholics, and
> Jews, of white men and Negroes alike, to enjoy the
> democracy for which all of them have here paid the
> price.
>
> TO ONE THING MORE do we consecrate
> ourselves in memory of those who sleep beneath
> these crosses and stars. We shall not foolishly sup-
> pose, as did the last generation of America's fighting

men, that victory on the battlefield will automati-
cally guarantee the triumph of democracy at home.
This war, with all its frightful heartache and suffer-
ing, is but the beginning of our generation's struggle
for democracy.

Here, the chaplain was prophetic.[23] The debate about civil rights and equality began immediately after the war and continues to this day. It had starts and stalls, tragedies and triumphs; it was indeed a "struggle." President Truman established the President's Committee on Civil Rights on 5 December 1946. Other milestones included the desegregation of the armed forces in 1948, the Supreme Court's 1954 decision in *Brown v. Board of Education*, the Montgomery, Alabama, bus boycott of 1955–56, the Freedom Summer of 1962, and the passage of the Civil Rights Act of 1964.

When the last battle has been won, there will be
those at home, as there were last time, who will
want us to turn our backs in selfish isolation on the
rest of organized humanity, and thus to sabotage
the very peace for which we fight. We promise you
who lie here; we will not do that. We will join hands
with Britain, China, Russia—in peace, even as we

---

[23] So were others. On the final page of MacKinlay Kantor's *Glory for Me* (New York: Coward-McCann, 1945), 268, are these words: "But savage too the weather of a peace—/When glare exposes class and race/With Bludgeon lifted for a blow—/When staring flash reveals a blackened face/As monster to the babies in their beds/And to the blacks reveals a monster pale/When Star of David is a curse, a jeer/A lodestone and a sacrament in one." This is the epic poem that eventually became the Oscars' best film of 1946, *The Best Years of Our Lives*, directed by William Wyler (Los Angeles, CA: Samuel Goldwyn, 1946), 172 min.

have in war, to build the kind of world for which you died.

This was Chaplain Gittelsohn's rebuke of prewar isolationism. Even as the battle raged on Iwo Jima, President Roosevelt was engaged in diplomacy to establish a postwar United Nations organization. Delegations from 49 countries would meet in San Francisco, California, only a month after the 5th Division cemetery was dedicated, and the United Nations Charter was signed on 26 June 1945.

The reality of "we will join hands with Britain, China, Russia" did not unfold, however, as the young chaplain hoped. Even as the fighting on Iwo Jima was underway, President Roosevelt and Prime Minister Winston Churchill were distressed by Joseph Stalin's evident design to place Poland and other countries of Central and Eastern Europe under Soviet control. Seeds of the Cold War were sown by the Soviets even before the fighting wars in Europe and the Pacific had concluded.

> *WHEN THE LAST SHOT has been fired, there will still be those eyes that are turned backward not forward, who will be satisfied with those wide extremes of poverty and wealth in which the seeds of another war can breed. We promise you, our departed comrades: this, too, we will not permit. This war has been fought by the common man; its fruits of peace must be enjoyed by the common man. We promise, by all that is sacred and holy, that your sons, the sons of miners and millers, the sons of farmers and workers—will inherit from your death the right to a living that is decent and secure.*

In the decade that followed, the American economy boomed so that large numbers of America's miners, millers, farmers, and workers indeed found jobs and prosperity. Home loans and educational benefits for veterans allowed many to join the middle class. In retrospect, we realize, the benefits were uneven, and practices such as residential redlining and segregation of schools and institutions of higher learning kept African Americans behind. After the war, Rabbi Gittelsohn kept his own commitment. He was a member of President Truman's Committee on Civil Rights, and he strongly supported the civil rights movement.

> WHEN THE FINAL CROSS has been placed in the last cemetery, once again there will be those to whom profit is more important than peace, who will insist with the voice of sweet reasonableness and appeasement that it is better to trade with the enemies of mankind than, by crushing them, to lose their profit. To you who sleep here silently, we give our promise: we will not listen: We will not forget that some of you were burnt with oil that came from American wells, that many of you were killed by shells fashioned from American steel. We promise that when once again men seek profit at your expense, we shall remember how you looked when we placed you reverently, lovingly, in the ground.

Here, Gittelsohn criticized the American companies that sold scrap iron and oil to Japan even as the prospect of war loomed. The chaplain's words might help us consider American firms that have helped China develop its internet firewall and visual monitoring technology.

> THUS DO WE MEMORIALIZE those who, hav-

ing ceased living with us, now live within us. Thus do we consecrate ourselves, the living, to carry on the struggle they began. Too much blood has gone into this soil for us to let it lie barren. Too much pain and heartache have fertilized the earth on which we stand. We here solemnly swear: this shall not be in vain. Out of this, and from the suffering and sorrow of those who mourn this, will come—we promise—the birth of a new freedom for the sons of men everywhere.

Amen.

Grainy film clips of the ceremony show immaculately graded and packed sand with perfect rows of white wooden crosses, "with here and there a Star of David blooming," remembered Dan Levin. Marines still wore their combat dungarees as they stood in formation around the cemetery's perimeter until the rifle salutes, taps, the prayers, and the hymns were finished. Then they swarmed across the sand to find the graves of lost buddies.[24]

From the island, Rabbi Gittelsohn's words were typed and mimeographed, and many Marines sent copies home. One such copy reached *Time* magazine, which published excerpts in July 1945. Quotes from the sermon in newspapers and magazines and broadcasts by Robert St. John and Fredric March reached many stricken American families. One grieving mother wrote Gittelsohn, "Our son . . . sleeps there with his buddies . . . He was killed February 20 . . . . I wish I might read all of your sermon—it would

---

[24] Camera footage of the ceremony can be seen at USMC 101863: 5th Div cemetery dedication on Iwo Jima (P-2290; 5D-16-32; R-1-4), U.S. Marine Corps Film Repository, Moving Image Research Collections, University of South Carolina, Columbia.

Combat correspondants SSgt Bob Cooke and Sgt Dan Levin
and Capt John W. Thomason, 4th Marine Division, Iwo Jima, February 1945.
National Archives and Records Administration

be like a service in honor of the boy we love so well. May I have a copy, please?"[25]

After he returned to his congregation in 1946, Rabbi Gittelsohn spoke at a service for Gold Star families in the New York area, seeking to direct their sadness and grief: "Somewhere there's a miner's son just the age of your boy who never had a decent chance in life because his father was killed in a mine accident and he himself has had to slave in the mine ever since. Do something for him, and you keep your boy alive. Somewhere there's a Negro who can't be the artist or scholar he wants to be because his skin happens not to be the exact shade of yours or mine. Spend the rest of your days achieving justice and fulfillment for him, and you keep your boy alive. Somewhere there's a Jew, a young Jew like your son, who has miraculously lived

[25] Gittelsohn, *Here I Am—Harnessed to Hope*, 141.

through the horror of Holocaust. Keep that young Jew alive, bring him into Palestine where he can rebuild his life with dignity. Thus you will keep your son alive."[26]

During the next half century, Gittelsohn became a major figure in American Jewish life and president of the Central Conference of American Rabbis. His words at the 5th Division Cemetery were often recalled, and on the 50th anniversary of the battle, less than a year before his death, he repeated many at the national ceremony at the Iwo Jima memorial.[27] Rereading the words of his own sermon decades later, however, he confessed, "How easy it would be . . . to succumb to bleak despair. So many promises and pledges! So much firm determination to promote justice, to rectify wrongs! Where has it all gone?"[28]

In his memoir of the battle, Dan Levin reflected, "Once I went into the Marines I left the question of our war's transcendent meaning to others. Let them make the overriding ideal statements, so that these heroes' deeds (and mine) would be placed within a moral universe. . . . I . . . could quietly go on with the business of falling, one among many, rifle pointed ahead, shielding the simple rose of freedom with my heart." Hearing "the slight young chaplain" that day, Levin wrote, "I was vaguely thrilled." The chaplain was speaking of the war, the future, and the "moral universe."[29]

---

[26] Gittelsohn, Here I Am—Harnessed to Hope, 122.
[27] "50th Anniversary Commemoration of Iwo Jima," CSPAN, 19 February 1995, 52:45. Rabbi Gittelsohn can be heard speaking near the end of the video.
[28] For his doubts, expressed in 1988, see Here Am I: Harnessed to Hope, 137-39.
[29] Levin, From the Battlefield, 97. On the following pages, the former combat correspondent recalled how the chaplain's "words barely floated over me, and my attention moved in and out. I was composing a dispatch in my head, and paragraphs of my story and of his speech must have shuttled in and out, like alternating presses." For Levin's interpolation of Chaplain Gittelsohn's sermon with his story, see From the Battlefield, 97-101.

His themes—to overcome racial and religious prejudice, to focus on providing a decent living for all Americans, to engage in the world—animated public policy in the decades after the war.[30] Chaplain Robinson helped me understand that I was drawn to Gittelsohn's sermon because it so well expressed my own American beliefs—beliefs that the war had clarified—beliefs my parents had absorbed during the war and passed on to me.

Writing about Chaplain Gittelsohn's sermon in *The American Interest*, I went out on a metaphorical limb. "I make this claim," I wrote, "of all the words that aimed to capture the meaning of America's role in the Second World War and to chart the way for the postwar future, this is *the* speech for textbooks, anthologies, classrooms, recitations, YouTube, memorial ceremonies, and movie scenes."[31]

I propose, but you decide. Read of the war, the naval chaplaincy, and Chaplain Gittelsohn's own meditations in his book, now brought to a wider readership by the Marine Corps University Press.

---

[30] In 1955, *Better Homes and Gardens* magazine asked eight former chaplains who had served in the Pacific theater, "Has 'foxhole religion' really lasted?" Gittelsohn told the magazine, "I believe many men realize now . . . that the highest purpose of life is cooperation with God in order to help realize in peace the ideas for which we fought in war. . . . mature religion means recognizing that life is a creative partnership of man with God . . . rather than allowing God to take the entire responsibility." Henry Lee, "Has 'Foxhole Religion' Really Lasted?," *Better Homes and Gardens*, September 1955, 259.

[31] Donald M. Bishop, "Iwo Jima and 'The Purest Democracy'," *American Interest*, 23 December 2019.

ABBREVIATIONS
AND ACRONYMS

AGCT	Army General Classification Test
AUL	unauthorized leave
AWOL	absent without leave
CHC	Chaplain Corps
GI	government issue; also a loose reference to American military servicemembers
LST	landing ship, tank
MCI	Marine Corps Institute
MPs	military police
MRE	meals, ready-to-eat
MOS	military occupational specialties
OCS	Officer Candidate School
Seabees	U.S. Navy construction battalion forces
USMCR	U.S. Marine Corps Reserve
USNR	U.S. Naval Reserve
USO	United Service Organizations
WAVES	Women Accepted for Volunteer Emergency Service
WRA	Winchester Repeating Arms
WRI	War Resisters' International
YMCA	Young Men's Christian Association

Pacifist

TO PADRE

INTRODUCTION

What Not to Expect

This is not a *war book*, at least not in the usually accepted meaning of the term. It is not an account of battle; it is not the adventures of heroes, though I suspect that more than one quiet hero will be found on its pages. Neither is it a biography of the author, nor a confession of personal religion. To expect any or all of these things in the pages that follow would be unfair alike to reader and writer.

I have had two purposes in writing these chapters. One, to trace something of the cataclysmic changes that almost overnight converted a people of peace lovers and pacifists into a military machine of deathly efficiency. Two, there is a warm—beautiful and ugly—thrilling but depressing story to be told from the memories and files of the chaplain. He has an unparalleled, unequaled opportunity to observe ordinary human beings under far from ordinary circumstances at close quarters; to see what makes them tick; to discover what makes them laugh and cry; and to observe their heartaches and sorrows, their problems and worries, their sadness and joy. I have learned more about human behavior in 24 months as a chaplain than in an equal number of years as a student of psychology. It is this story—these

Rabbi Roland B. Gittelsohn.
Jacob Rader Marcus Center of the American Jewish Archives, Cincinnati, OH

experiences—that I want here to tell. In a sense, these pages will offer a parade of human emotions at their best and worst, the same emotions that have always governed life, though magnified now under the microscope of war.

The stories that follow will speak for themselves. Perhaps it should be said, however, that in some ways they do not represent anything like a fair cross section of life under arms. There comes a time in every chaplain's life when he sinks down in confused amazement and is tempted to ask: "In heaven's name, are there no more *legitimate* babies being born! Are there no husbands and wives who are permanently, faithfully in love?"[1] The answer, which is apparent of course the moment the question is asked, is that by and large the chaplain plays host to men who are in trouble. If he confers consciously with 10 people a week who come to him with marital difficulties, he passes unwittingly several hundred a day who are happy and well adjusted. It is necessary for him, and the readers of these pages, to apply some such corrective as this to the stories recounted here.

The chaplain's experience is a rich one—rich both in sorrows and its joys. Mine is neither distinct nor usual. This is a story that could be written by any one of us. It tells of an experience that—granted the ghastly premise of a necessary war to begin with—no one of us would have wanted to miss. I think it would not be immodest or inaccurate to say that we shall—most of us—return one day to our civilian congregations considerably changed. We shall be better ministers, priests, and rabbis, because we have been chaplains. The events that are changing us are too interesting and gratifying to be hoarded for ourselves. They should be shared with others. This is my main motive in offering a volume of this kind.

Roland B. Gittelsohn
Lieutenant (Chaplain Corps), U.S. Naval Reserve

---

[1] Emphasis in original.

PART I

Pacifist No More

CHAPTER ONE

I Don't Believe It!

If my usually unreliable memory serves correctly, the Sunday concert of the New York Philharmonic orchestra was about one-third finished. We were driving lazily down a Long Island highway, paying considerably more attention to the music than to the truck farms we were passing.[1] Suddenly, the music was annoyingly interrupted. At first, we thought something had gone wrong with our car's radio; a twist of the dial restored our confidence on that score. Then we suspected that the station's transmitter may have been blown off the air; the announcer's voice reassured us about that. But no fiddling of the dial or voice of an announcer could dissipate the real cause of our annoyance that Sunday afternoon. It was not just a concert that had been interrupted—it was our lives. It was the civilization of our generation that had gone "off the air." For the words we heard, even while we were yet seeking the cause of the disturbance, were these:

---

[1] There is much confusion about the term *truck farm*. For some, it references a farm close enough to urban centers that its produce may be transported by truck to the city. However, the word *truck* also refers to garden vegetables intended for sale in the markets.

"Ladies and gentlemen, we interrupt this program to bring you a late news bulletin. Japanese planes have attacked the United States Naval Base at Pearl Harbor."[2]

It would be difficult to reconstruct exactly how I reacted. I can remember the music. I can recall my feeling of near petulant annoyance when the music stopped. And I can hear the announcer's voice as clearly today as I did then. But my sensations immediately after the bulletin had been read are hazy and confused . . . like the troubled memory of a jumbled dream just after the dreamer has awakened. The one thing I do remember is a foolish, irrational, wishful refrain that ran through my head until I stopped it with fatigue: "I don't believe it!" I am not sure whether I actually voiced the words or not. But I do definitely recall clocking them more than once as they raced past the grandstand of my consciousness. And even after the concert had continued, even after we had asked and been asked scores of times what details were available, I still remember protesting to myself: "I don't believe it!"

If I had been the only one to react that way, my wishful incredulity would scarce be worth comment. Because I was not the only one, and because in a sense my disbelief was a small part of our generation's disbelief, it may be important to chart not only the reasons for my foolish skepticism, but also the course of my subsequent changes. There were many reasons—none of them simple. Trying to remember them now, after all the tortuous changes of the past 36 months, is like trying to remember the exact pattern of the waves at a spot the ship has passed long since. But it is important that we try.

---

[2] For examples of live radio broadcasts at the time, see " 'This Is No Joke: This Is War': A Live Radio Broadcast of the Attack on Pearl Harbor," History Matters, G. Robert Vincent Voice Library, Michigan State University, 01:57.

Sailors stand amid wrecked planes at the Ford Island seaplane base,
watching as USS *Shaw* (DD 373) explodes in the center background,
7 December 1941. The USS *Nevada* (BB 36) is also visible
in the middle background.
Official U.S. Navy photo 80-G-19948,
now in the collections of the National Archives

Reason number one—overconfidence. As one who had
bitterly opposed every naval appropriation since his first high
school debating days, I was convinced that the United States,
and especially the United States Navy, had built up (unneces-
sarily?) a defense well-nigh impregnable. Pearl Harbor *had* not
been attacked, because it *could* not be attacked.[3] It was as simple
as all that! More than once, as British Prime Minister Neville
Chamberlain's sinister umbrella pointed its way to inevitable

---

[3] Emphasis in original.

storm clouds in the future, I felt inwardly happy that the monies I had called wasted were appropriated and the ships I had not wanted were built.[4] As I look back now, it seems to me that what I was doing was resting securely behind an argument well lost. But apparently the argument was not well enough lost. Whatever the reasons for 7 December 1941—and experts will speculate about that long after the war has been won—the indisputable fact is, we were not as strong, as ready, or as prepared as most of us thought. I might have believed that Sunday afternoon that some lesser place had been attacked. But Pearl Harbor? Impossible! Might as well say that the German fleet had sailed into Hampton Roads, Virginia.

Reason number two—call it flabby liberalism of the nineteenth century brand. Call it foolish optimism. Call it anything you like, but I refused to believe, up to and including that day on 7 December 1941, that the Japanese were any more warlike than me. Arguments to the contrary often infuriated me. I blamed them on the kind of press that had so largely forced us into the Spanish-American War.[5] Threats that the Japanese planned to attack us were dismissed as propaganda for a larger navy. Fears that the Rising Sun had evil designs against us were impatiently written off as xenophobia, 1941 style. Let the Japanese alone, and they will let us alone. Do not arm against them, and they will not arm against us. Be careful not to arouse their suspicions, and they will not offend our sensibilities. On some such road as this lay the path of peace in the Pacific. The Japanese were exactly like us, a people who wanted peace, but could be teased or

[4] Douglas McCollam, "The Umbrella's Shadow," *Foreign Policy*, 13 October 2006.
[5] George W. Auxier, "Middle Western Newspapers and the Spanish American War, 1895–1898," *Mississippi Valley Historical Review* 26, no. 4 (March 1940): 523–34, https://doi.org/10.2307/1896320.

taunted into war. They would not attack unless we made them afraid of *being* attacked.[6]

I did not say or think this out in the first sudden shock of that frightful Sunday afternoon. But I had been thinking and saying it for years before. And it would be foolish to deny that it had more than a little to do with my spontaneous refusal to believe.

The reader who has glanced with suspicious curiosity between the lines of reason number two will not be surprised in the least by reason three for "I don't believe it." From the minute that I was old enough even to think that I could think, until sometime in the late fall of 1940, I was a pacifist. Not just a peace lover who misunderstood or misused the word, but a complete pacifist—a complete, convinced, literal, unreasonable, dogmatic, unchangeable pacifist! If there was one absolute in my personal credo, it was the absolute of pacifism. I belonged to the War Resisters.[7] I took the Oxford Pledge.[8] I vowed never to aid or bless any war of any kind. I told my friends that I was prepared to spend the next war in prison. I argued with my father that submission to the worst evil was better than resisting it by force,

---

[6] Emphasis in original.

[7] War Resisters' International (WRI) is a secular pacifist organization founded in 1921. As an antimilitarist organization, WRI declared: "War is a crime against humanity. I am therefore determined not to support any kind of war, and to strive for the removal of all causes of war." "About War Resisters' International," WRI-IRG.org, accessed 6 November 2019.

[8] At an Oxford Union debate in 1933, British students passed a motion that "this House will not in any circumstances fight for King and Country." In April 1935, thousands of American students signed a parallel pledge or oath not "to support the United States government in any war it may conduct." See "The Oxford Union King and Country Debate in 1933," Churchill College, Cambridge, Archives Center; and "The Student Movement of the Thirties: A Political History," Center for Socialist History, Archives, accessed 9 February 2021.

and in the mirror of what I thought was logic, I mistook my own unreasonableness as his. I read Harry Emerson Fosdick's magnificent sermon "Apology to the Unknown Soldier" regularly from my pulpit, and felt as if Dr. Fosdick had written it especially for me.[9]

I remember showing some of my youth discussion groups the collections of horror pictures published after the First World War in an effort to condition them as irrevocably against war as I was—or as irrevocably as I thought I was. I recall arguing for pacifism with a fellow guest one night in the home of a very close friend, arguing close to the point of anything but pacifism in my personal belligerence. I remember with contrite horror that shortly before the Battle of Dunkirk (1940), France, I made the public statement—with full knowledge as a rabbi of what Nazism meant to my own people—that so firm was my conviction against war that even if the alternative were to allow Adolf Hitler complete control over all Europe, even that would be preferable to our entrance into the war. Now, as I remind myself of that statement, my conscience blushes almost as deeply as the reddened, angry face of one congregant, a veteran of two wars, who that night literally held onto the sides of his seat to keep from jumping up in the midst of my sermon.

Such was the impassioned fervor of my pacifism. True, I no longer felt that way even before the attack on Pearl Harbor. But my conversion was still in process, and even that part of it that was by then complete, was still too stiff and shiny to fit me comfortably. The four months after Dunkirk were mental-

---

[9] The full text of Fosdick's 12 November 1933 sermon at Riverside Church in New York City is in the *Congressional Record–Senate*, 16 June 1934, 11971–73. See also Robert Moats Miller, *Harry Emerson Fosdick: Preacher, Pastor, Prophet* (New York: Oxford University Press, 1985).

ly the most uncomfortable I have ever lived. The foundation, or at least a substantial part of the foundation for my deepest spiritual convictions, had been rudely yanked out from under me, and I spent that summer painfully suspended between two worlds but actually at home in neither. Not more than a week after Dunkirk, a distinguished friend, a college professor who is now a major in the Army, could still shock me into fury by saying: "The quicker we get into this war, the better for us and for the world." But by the following October, I was shocking my congregants equally by renouncing—albeit blushingly and uncomfortably—the pacifism I had thought a part of my very self.

By the last month of 1941, I was no longer the pacifist who preferred Hitler's rule of Europe to U.S. involvement in war. The former possibility was by then too likely to be tossed lightly off the tongue. But it would be foolish to pretend that the deep conviction of years had been entirely rejected. In fact, if any one element could be singled out as the greatest accounting for my disbelief, it would have to be this: the ghost of an absolute pacifist rode with me that Sunday afternoon, and before I could speak, or even think clearly, he heard the announcement of Pearl Harbor, and he it was who rushed in to say: "I don't believe it!"

Today, I believe it. Today, I am a chaplain in the United States Naval Reserves.[10] The president of the youth group, who gasped with me in 1937 horror pictures of the last war, became a lieutenant in this one and was killed last November in France. What happened to our convictions—the change that has occurred in our lives—is the story of a generation. As such, it de-

---

[10] Between 1915 and 2005, the Reserve element of the U.S. Navy was called the Naval Reserve. On 29 April 2005, President George W. Bush signed a memorandum for the secretary of defense redesignating the Service as the Navy Reserve based on the 2005 National Defense Authorization Act.

serves to be told. What have we experienced in this war? What have we learned about ourselves and our nation? What does to-day's war presage for tomorrow's peace? What was wrong with our pacifism of pre-Dunkirk vintage?

Important questions, these. Important and profound. But suppose we seek to answer them simply and directly in the "first person." America is made up of first persons and will be saved or lost by first persons. Your experiences and adventures may differ from mine, but chances are that in our heartaches, our anxieties, our conclusions since the war began have been pretty much the same. So, suppose we seek to answer the big questions through the story of one man who, for a foolish, fleeting moment at the end of 1941, refused to believe what has since become the most compelling, disturbing factor in his life.

CHAPTER TWO

To Be or Not to Be

If the months immediately following Dunkirk were mentally the most uncomfortable of my life, the days during which I tried to decide whether to enlist as a chaplain were the most difficult and disturbing. In the former instance, it was a philosophy that had to be remodeled; in the latter, it was both a philosophy and a personal way of life. As difficult as that double adjustment had to be, however, in one respect I was fortunate. I experienced a kind of preview nearly a year in advance of the soul-searching storm and stress destined for me. My closest friend, Rabbi Jacob Philip Rudin of Great Neck, Long Island, New York, became a chaplain in the United States Naval Reserves 11 months before I did.[1] He too had been a pacifist. During the months of his struggle with himself, at a time when he was probing his conscience to its bottom-most depths to determine his future

---

[1] Rudin was born in Malden, MA, and received his bachelor's degree from of Harvard College in 1924. In 1928, he was ordained at the Jewish Institute of Religion, which awarded him an honorary doctor of divinity in 1981. He enlisted in the U.S. Navy Chaplain Corps during World War II and saw duty in the Pacific and in the Aleutians. For more on Rabbi Rudin, see "Jacob Philip Rudin Papers, 1920–1959," manuscript collection no. 142, Jacob Rader Marcus Center of the American Jewish Archives, Cincinnati, OH.

course of action, we met many times and used each other as sounding boards. We mentioned every conceivable argument both for and against becoming chaplains so many times that one session might almost have been a carbon copy of another. I realized much later, however, that there was a fundamental difference in our approaches at that time. Jack Rudin's insight was much keener then than mine. To him this was, in the month following Pearl Harbor, an issue that was deeply, immediately, and intensely personal. It was a decision that had to be made at once. I was still arguing more or less as a matter of theory—from a point of view that was detached—toward a decision that would have to be made some day, not necessarily then.

Six months later, when the issue suddenly hit me as intensely as it had affected my friend before, when I began to rehearse and rehash the pros and cons for myself, not for rabbis in general or at large, I found myself with the strange feeling that "this was where I had come in." These were arguments that I had heard before. By the time I faced the issue for myself, the ground, in a sense, had been prepared for me.

Of what did that ground consist? What were the arguments that guided me from stubborn pacifism, through painful doubt, to the donning of a uniform I had been positive I would never wear? Understanding something of these arguments and reasons should make it easier to evaluate not only my changed views on war and peace, but also my successes and failures as a chaplain.

Primarily, there were four thoughts that kept pounding away in my consciousness during those difficult days. Two were at least partly the result of my being a Jew; the others were more general, and probably played a part in the thoughts and decisions of every person who entered the chaplaincy.

As a Jew, and especially a rabbi, I was immensely proud of

the part my people had played not only in this war, but in every struggle of American history. I knew that a coreligionist of mine had raised the money without which George Washington might never have led his revolutionary army to victory, and that Jews were to be found in Washington's forces far beyond their tiny proportion of the civilian population in those days. I knew that in the Civil War, Jews fought in the thousands on both sides. I remembered that in World War I, at a time when we constituted some 3 percent of this nation's population, we supplied close to 5 percent of its people in service. And when I read in this war of Meyer Levin and Ira Jeffrey; of Commander Solomon Isquith, captain of the USS *Utah* (AG 16) at Pearl Harbor, and Sergeant Irving Strobing, who tapped out the last feeble message before the fall of Corregidor, I knew in my heart that once more the Jew was doing their full share in defense of this beloved America.[2]

But how about myself? The Jew meant me too, not just these others. I had as much for which to thank America as anyone. My grandfather and father had fled from the oppression of Czarist Russia. America had opened its arms to them. What was I doing to repay the country for the blessed gift of birth under the Stars and Stripes? Every quota for Jewish chaplains that had been announced by both the Army and Navy since Pearl Harbor had been abundantly filled. Was that in spite of me or because of me? This was the type of question I could not help but ask myself. And the only inevitable answer to this type of question was the first reason for my decision.

[2] Cpl Meyer Levin served as a bombardier on a B-17 Flying Fortress. Ens Ira Jeffrey served on the USS *California* (BB 44), which was moored in Pearl Harbor the day it was struck and sunk by the Japanese. Cdr Solomon Isquith was the senior officer aboard the *Utah*, barely surviving its destruction. Sgt Irving Strobing was an Army radio operator in the Philippines.

The second reason, likewise stemming from the fact that I was a Jew, was the fate of my people since the rise of Hitler. The strongest word in any language is too weak, the most frightful description too feeble by far, to tell the story of Jewry in the last 11 years. The most fiendish persecutions of the Spanish Inquisition and of Cossack brutality pale beside the measure of Nazi fury. Pierre van Paassen coined the perfect title when he referred to the Jewish people in this war as "the forgotten ally."[3] Together with the Chinese, we have the honor of being fascism's first and oldest victims. When war first came to England and France, we Jews were near the close of our seventh year of war. The unspeakable brutalities perpetrated on the Chinese by their fellow Orientals had been directed in exact duplicate against us by the Nazis.[4] Long before Pearl Harbor, we Jews had suffered a thousand Lidices.[5]

It was against such a background, in the perspective of such misery and sorrow, that many of us had to decide the issue: to be or not to be a chaplain. Daily, as I opened a new dispatch of the Jewish Telegraphic Agency and read of a new blood bath,

---

[3] Pierre van Paassen (1895–1968) was a Dutch-Canadian-American journalist, writer, and Unitarian minister. See Pierre van Paassen, *The Forgotten Ally* (New York: Dial Press, 1943).

[4] See, for example, *The Nanjing Atrocities: Crimes of War* (Brookline, MA: Facing History and Ourselves National Foundation, 2014).

[5] Lidice was a small town in the former Czechoslovakia located about 12 miles (20 kilometers) from Prague. German forces destroyed the town and murdered or deported everyone in retaliation for the 1942 assassination of Reinhard Heydrich, a prominent Nazi official and head of the Gestapo who was also acting Reich protector of Bohemia and Moravia. The operation to kill Heydrich by soldiers of the Czech army-in-exile was portrayed in the Czech-British-French epic film, *Anthropoid*, directed by Sean Ellis (Los Angeles, CA: LD Entertainment, 2016), 120 min.

the question asked itself: And what are *you* doing about all this?[6] Helping to arouse people to the real danger? Not enough! Raising money for relief, and stimulating the purchase of war bonds? Insufficient! Others can do this much, as well as you and without you. The fate of minorities for generations, the very right of Jews and Chinese and Czechs to live and breathe, depends on the outcome of a war in which you will either play a part that is immediate and direct or be a good cheerleader on the sidelines. Which will it be?

So much, then, for the motives that had compelled me, especially as a Jew. In turning now to reasons number three and four, it would not be unfair to say that they are factors that affected every potential chaplain of every faith or creed. All of us felt, in one way or another, that the tormenting question in our individual mind was a reflection of the greatest test religion had faced at least in our generation. Let me put the matter as simply and bluntly as I can. Thousands of young men and women, men and women for the most part at an age of relative indifference to the voice of faith, were feeling a need for religion, many of them for the first time in their lives. Every report from a chaplain already in the field, every letter from a member of my congregation already in the service, testified to that need.

When everything else on which these boys and girls had thought their lives were based—home, friends, parents, and vocations—had suddenly and rudely been snatched away from them. When many of them were lost, confused, and bewildered, then, perhaps for the first time, they turned in their need to the synagogue or church. And rightly so! If religion has no message

---

[6] The Jewish Telegraphic Agency is an international news agency and wire service serving Jewish community newspapers and media around the world. Emphasis in original.

of strength and inspiration for young men and women in such a moment of need, when and how will it ever play a role in their lives? Religion—Judaism and Christianity alike—is "on the spot" in this war. If religion has nothing to offer our soldiers and sailors now in their moment of greatest need, they will have nothing to offer religion, indeed, no use at all for religion, when the war is over. In short, I saw the boys and girls on my own temple's honor roll in one of two future capacities. They would be either the board members and enthusiastic congregants or the indifferent absentees 10 years from now. And I could, in some small measure at least, determine which they would be by either bringing them or denying them the message and comforts of Judaism.

Finally, there was a fourth, but by no means least consideration at hand. If the choice before me represented a test of religion at large, in a much more deeply personal sense, it meant a test of faith in my own life. It almost seemed as if everything I had been preaching to others for seven years suddenly came home to roost. My most eloquent sermons seemed to step out of their tomb in my files, point a finger at their creator and ask, "Did you mean us, or were you just fooling yourself?" I had preached that it was not material comfort or ease that mattered most in life; it was the moral and spiritual values that were most important. I had said that it was better—if need be—to die for a good purpose than to live for no purpose. I had insisted in democracy, as in religion, the most important goal was the greatest good for the greatest number, that our individual lives take on cosmic meaning and significance only when we devote them to the whole of humanity. I had proclaimed that no man had a moral right to live in comfort while so many others suffered unspeakably, that no man could face his conscience unless he were truly and honestly sacrificing for the common good.

I scolded some of the businessmen of my congregation for thinking of themselves at a time when history hung in the balance. And from the hills and valleys of my own conscience, there came back the resounding echo: "How about yourself? Do you expect these people to follow what you preach or what you practice?"

The answer had been given centuries before by our Jewish sages: *Lo ha-midrash [hu ha-]ikar, eleh ha-ma'aseh* (Not study [or theory] is the essential thing, but action).[7] The choice before me, the choice that seemed so desperately difficult and involved, was after all a simple one. Either I practiced what I had preached, and thereby earned the right to preach again, or I would never again be able in good conscience or faith to say the things I had.

One more word here is of the utmost importance. It could not be exaggerated in a thousand pages, far less than these few brief sentences. I did not enter this debate wrestling with the angel alone, neither was my final decision just my own. Indeed, I doubt seriously whether I could have found the strength to do this thing on my own. From beginning to end, from first suspicious stirrings to final firm decision, my wife was with me. With unique insight that women often have, she knew what my choice would be before I knew it myself. But more important by far, she gave me the strength to begin this thing, and at every moment of weakness and discouragement, it was she and her love who have given me the will to continue. Too much has

---

[7] This quote has been edited to conform to modern Hebrew standards. It is a quote from the *Mishna*, specifically the book known as *Pirkei Avot* [Ethics of the Fathers] from chapter 1. The basic principle that it illustrates is that what is important is not the explanation but that actions speak louder than words. The *Mishna* is the 63 tractates in which Rabbi Judah set down the Oral Law, where Jewish law is discussed and organized by subject matter.

been said in praise of chaplains in this war, too little about their wives. Our wives could have kept us at home had they loved us less and their own immediate comfort more. Instead, they helped us go. Whenever I receive a letter of tearful gratitude from some parent or wife, I feel like shouting back across the ocean's deep: "It is not I who have brought you this comfort. It is Ruth and I together. Thank her, not me!"

Such, then, was the stuff from which my decision had to be made. At one time, I might have convinced myself that my obligation to my wife and two children was of equal importance, or that the civilians whose children had gone off to war also needed me to sustain their morale. I might once have assured myself that there were few enough of us on the home front who could seek to direct public opinion in and out of Congress in such manner and direction that the peace would not be lost in Washington, DC, before the war could be won in Germany and Japan. But in the early spring of 1943, all this was fading more and more into the background. And the important, inescapable, unforgettable things were these: that I had no right to take pride in what Jews were doing to help win the war unless I were directly doing something myself. That the blood of 2 million slaughtered Jews in Europe was calling out insistently to my blood. That religion had no claim on tomorrow if it failed the challenge of today. That I could not in good conscience teach others a way of life that I was not willing and ready to practice myself.

Dunkirk had found me a pacifist—disturbed but still convinced. Pearl Harbor had jolted the last of my uncomfortable pacifism. By the beginning of 1943, my conscience had completed the cycle and had compelled me to apply for the right to wear the uniform of a chaplain in the U.S. Navy.

CHAPTER TWO

CHAPTER THREE

Recipe for Chaplains

One of my close friends in civilian life expressed profound amazement when he heard that, after accepting a commission in the Chaplain Corps, my first duty would be to attend the Naval Training School for Chaplains at the College of William and Mary, in Williamsburg, Virginia.[1] "What?" he exclaimed. "Do you mean to tell me that after you spent five years in a seminary learning to be a rabbi and seven years in a congregation practicing your profession, the Navy has to send you to school for eight weeks to learn it all over again?"

No one who understands the tremendous gap between life as a civilian clergyman and life as a chaplain could be in the least surprised that both the Army and the Navy have established

---

[1] The Naval Chaplain School opened in February 1942, to train the many civilian clergy who were commissioned as chaplains in the Navy as it expanded during the war. First located at Naval Station Norfolk, VA, it moved to the College of William and Mary in Williamsburg, VA, in 1943. The wartime school closed on 15 November 1945. New chaplains now train at the Naval Chaplaincy School and Center at Naval Station Newport, RI. The Navy created a film showing chaplains training at William and Mary, see *Navy Chaplain*, produced for the Bureau of Personnel, U.S. Navy (Burbank, CA: Pathe News-Warner Brothers, 1945), 16 min.

schools for the indoctrination of chaplains. It would be neither unfair nor inaccurate to say that the average civilian minister, priest, or rabbi is a man who has grown soft physically, who is very much accustomed to doing things his own way, who is more at home giving orders than receiving them, whose experience has been rather narrowly confined to his own little denomination, and who would rather not have to identify a cruiser from a destroyer or a transport from a tanker. To transform such a man into one who is physically conditioned for hardship, mentally prepared to obey even orders that he dislikes, broadly conversant with all major religious groups, and thoroughly acquainted with all types of ships and crafts, is no simple task at all. Take it from one who had trouble being thus transformed. There are times, as a matter of fact, when a corps of Harry Houdinis might have better results than a faculty of instructors. The amazing thing is not that schools of indoctrination are necessary, but rather that so much can be done to so many in such a short time.

The guiding genius of the Naval Training School for Chaplains was Captain C. A. Neyman, who conceived the school in the first place, planned the curriculum, and served until the summer of 1944 as officer in charge.[2] A faculty of about a dozen chaplains, more or less, served under his supervision. For the most part, the instructors were men who had seen either overseas or shipboard service. They included both regular Navy and Reserves. At the time of my indoctrination in the early summer of 1943, the chaplain who escaped from the ill-fated USS *Hornet*

---

[2] For more on his work at that time, see Capt Clifford M. Drury, *The History of the Chaplain Corps, United States Navy*, vol. 2, 1939–1949 (Washington, DC: Bureau of Naval Personnel, 1948).

(CV 8), the chaplain who served on the USS *Wasp* (CV 7) when it was sunk, and two of the first chaplains to serve with the Marine Corps in this war were members of the staff. Obviously, any curriculum directed by men of such experience would not fail on the side of being too academic or theoretical. To make doubly sure of this, after three weeks of classroom instruction, each student was sent out for two weeks of field duty with an experienced chaplain at a Navy shore station near Williamsburg. Then three more weeks of class work before orders to his first active duty station. Such, in its broader outlines, is the recipe for the making of a Navy chaplain. Now, what are the specific ingredients?

More than once during the eight weeks' instruction itself, there were moments when we students lost sight of our larger goals, snowed under by a mass of detail. Looking back, however, from the vantage point of both time and experience, it seems clear that the Navy was trying to accomplish three things with us down at Williamsburg: first, making us physically sound and hard; second, making naval officers out of well-nigh hopelessly unmilitary civilians; and third, providing us with the tools of our future trade.

It is a good thing the members of the 300-odd congregations whose clergyman were at William and Mary in the summer of 1943 could not see their spiritual leaders at the end of their second week of instruction. Theirs, truly, was a ministry of pain. What aches! What suffering! What groaning and moaning! What an adventure in anatomy! We discovered the outraged presence of muscles where we least suspected them. We reached the point where we could neither cough nor sneeze nor turn over in bed sans soreness and pain. And beneath the loudest, most eloquent outbursts of complaining that the Tidewater Ba-

Raising of the flag in commissioning ceremonies at
Williamsburg, 24 March 1943.
*Capt Clifford M. Drury, The History of the Chaplain Corps,
United States Navy, vol. 2, 1939–1949, 60*

sin of Virginia has ever heard, we loved it! It was more fun than
a month of Sunday school picnics.

We began our physical conditioning with a series of strength
and endurance tests to be repeated at the end of the course as
a measure of progress. From then on, there was one form or
another of physical drill for two hours a day, five days a week.
There were calisthenics and baseball and an obstacle course.
There was a weekly session of swimming that included life-
saving and abandon ship drills. Many a theological paunch hit
the water in a manner most unbecoming the dignity of the clergy. Incidentally, we got a hearty laugh when, during the summer,
a national news magazine published a spectacular article about
our training in which our breathless congregants back home
read how their hero-clergymen were swimming through burning oil. The only burning oil that any of us saw at Williamsburg
was on the training film screen. True, we were taught the proper
strokes to use in case of burning oil, but our efforts were limited

Student chaplains exercising on the obstacle course
at the Chaplains' School, Williamsburg.
Capt Clifford M. Drury, The History of the Chaplain Corps,
United States Navy, *vol. 2, 1939–1949, 60*

in realism by a well-sterilized, comfortably heated college swimming pool. Rounding out the schedule of physical drills were afternoons spent in military marching and several long-distance runs on a two-and-a-half-mile cross-country trail, 90 percent of which always seemed to be uphill.

By actual tests, our class was something like 35 percent improved in strength and endurance by the week of our graduation. I doubt if any other achievement gave more student chaplains a keener sense of personal accomplishment. For one thing, most of us, being pulpit athletes, were proud as peacocks at so obvious an improvement in a field hardly our own. For one thing, all of us felt finer and fitter when we graduated than we had for years. But even more important was the obvious connection between this physical fitness and the work we were to do. One of our instructors, Chaplain Merritt Williams, was awarded the Purple Heart during our term at school for injuries sustained during the sinking of the *Wasp*. Another, Rear Admiral Edward B. Harp Jr., had to spend 39 consecutive sleepless busy hours at his battle station on the *Hornet*, a small, stuffy, below-decks aid station without ventilation. A third, Frank Sullivan, told of walking once across 14 miles of steaming, malaria-infested jungle trail to meet a boy who was near the breaking point and felt he had to see the chaplain. It did not take too much insight to perceive the connection between the experiences of these men and our aching muscles. Dead chaplains are of no use whatsoever to anyone. And we could see quite clearly that sometimes the difference between a chaplain dead and a chaplain alive might well be a few turns around the obstacle course and another round or two of knee bends.

The story is told at the Naval Training School for Chaplains—told so frequently and vouched for so vehemently that it probably never happened—of the embryo chaplain from a small town who had picked up his uniforms at the very last moment before leaving for Williamsburg. While packing his crisp new uniforms in his trunk on the last afternoon home, he was horrified to notice that the tailor had carefully provided shoulder board straps on the khaki and white uniforms, but had apparently forgotten them on the blues. Since chaplains are ordered to report to the school in blue uniform, that deficiency posed quite a problem. It would hardly do to make a bad first impression on Chaplain Neyman by being out of uniform. So, the zealous neophyte put his handy mother-in-law to work, sewing loops on the shoulders of his blue uniforms, and at midnight he boarded his train, unusually well marked. The only thing that is alleged to have saved him from ridicule and embarrassment is the fact that, after dozens of eyebrows were raised incredulously on the train the next day, a kind Navy chief called the poor fellow aside and mercifully informed him that since the blue uniform carries one's stripes and insignia on the cuffs, it is not necessary to be redundant with shoulder boards.[3]

Very few of us were as unworldly as that young fellow, or as naive as the one who strutted proudly into the school one day faultlessly attired in the uniform of a chief petty officer. But complete frankness dictates a confession that the difference between the petty officer and chaplains was at first largely one of degree only. As a group, each beginning class at the school is just about as unmilitary a conglomeration of homo sapiens as the eye has ever seen. The first time I wore my Navy uniform, I felt like half policeman and half theater usher. On my first afternoon in Williamsburg, I saluted an apprentice seaman and walked by a commander with glorious abandon. And vanity compels me to insist that I was no exception. In short, task number two of our course at William and Mary was to wave the magic wand of indoctrination over us and transform us from civilians to naval officers.

Perhaps the major portion of our time was occupied that way. We were given a course in the 845 pages of the *U.S. Navy Regulations*.[4] We were taught by lecture, by example, and by our

---

[3] See "Uniforms of the U.S. Navy, 1942–1943," and "Uniforms of the U.S. Navy, 1943–1944," Naval History and Heritage Command, 19 September 2008.

[4] See "80.2.2, Directives," General Records of the Department of the Navy, 1798–1947, Record Group 80, 1804–1958, National Archives and Records Administration, Washington, DC.

own mistakes the proper way to prepare official Navy correspondence. We heard lectures on ranks and rates in the Navy and on the various types of ships used by the Navy. We were introduced to the field of naval history. We, who had been preaching sermons throughout our professional careers, were taught that an altogether different kind of sermon must be delivered, sometimes in an altogether different kind of manner, if we expect our altogether different type of congregation to listen. Closely related to the field of preaching was the whole matter of Navy lingo. On my first visit to the Office of Naval Officer Procurement in the Third Naval District, I noticed, on the 18th floor of a skyscraper in lower Manhattan, a sign that read "Don't Throw Butts on the Deck," and for a moment I almost convinced myself that I could feel the ship swaying.

Let no skeptical reader minimize this matter of lingo. The chaplain who does not speak the language of the Navy might just as well stop wasting his time in the Navy. To a busy sailor, the difference between a landlubber and a salt is often the difference between one who "walks along the floor, near the wall, then climbs up the stairway through the ceiling to the next floor," and one who "walks along the deck, near the bulkhead, then climbs the ladder through the over-head, to go topside." Sailors are very apt to lack either the time or the inclination to translate a sermon as they listen. The padre who likes his congregation to be awake, does well to speak their language in the first place. So, he does not eat dinner prepared in the kitchen; he has chow that is cooked in the galley. It is not sugar that he puts in his java, it is sand. He does not pack their clothes away, he stows away his gear; and when he needs it later, he breaks it out. When he hears that someone "drew a dead horse," he does not wrinkle his nose before anticipated odors; he knows that someone simply drew advance salary from the Navy before shipping to an overseas station.[5] The first week or two at school constituted a process of endless translation. It was almost like learning a new language. Soon, however, the language of the Navy became so much a part of ourselves that I feel sorry for our civilian congregations when we return.

Another essential part of remodeling us into naval officers was the teaching of Navy courtesies and customs. The first time I boarded a ship was an experience I shall never forget. To make matters even worse than they might otherwise have been, it was a British carrier. As I plodded up the gangplank, I felt as if I was walking on the biggest, clumsiest feet in the Navy—incidentally, no small distinction. It seemed that every person on the dock below was gazing intently and precisely at me to see if I knew what to do. Three-fourths of the way up, if I could have run back down without becoming, in very fact, as ridiculous as I already felt in my imagination, I would have done so. At the top, I saluted the national ensign with a hand bearing at least a dozen fingers, then tripped affectionately into the arms of the officer of the deck, mumbling incomprehensibly words that neither he nor I could recognize. There is one right way—and an undetermined number of wrong ways— to board a ship. Part of our faculty's job at Williamsburg was to teach us the right way.[6]

Likewise, they had to teach us the technical organization of both a ship and a shore station, the identity and relation-

---

[5] For example, see *The Amphibians Came to Conquer*, FMFRP 12-109-I (Washington, DC: Headquarters Marine Corps, 1991), 82.
[6] See *OPNAVINST 1710.7A, Social Usage and Protocol Handbook: A Guide for the Personnel of the U.S. Navy* (Washington, DC: Office of the Chief of Naval Operations, Department of the Navy, 2001).

ship of the various officers, the proper place of a chaplain in the Navy scheme of things, whom to salute, and when and how and why. Unless the chaplain knows how to abide by the courtesies that are expected of him, and unless he understands the proper channels through which to proceed, his usefulness to the men he serves is much less than it should be. So, the teaching of customs and courtesies is not just a matter of "tone," a kind of Emily Post at sea. This, like most of the other subjects we were taught at school, is a means of improving the chaplain's efficiency as a chaplain and of maximizing his services to the men who need him.

Quite the same thing can be said of our third field of instruction: the tools of our trade. In a sense, the chaplain is expected to be a jack of all trades. For anything that no one else aboard knows about, for any help that no one else is able to give, men turn to their chaplain. Therefore, the chaplain who wants to retain the confidence of his men most know a great deal about many things. He must know the mechanics and set up of insurance, allotments, family allowances, and medical care. He must understand the proper way to prepare either a will or a power of attorney. He must be intimately acquainted with the policies and procedures of both Navy relief and the American Red Cross. He must have at his fingertips some basic knowledge of mental hygiene and personal counseling. He ought to know a little about library work in case he is asked to take care of the ship's library, something about obtaining and projecting movie films in case he is the recreation officer, and much about materials and methods for group singing in the event that he is called on for that.

All this is somehow crowded into the curriculum at Williamsburg. Plus, they teach the proper handling of official wedding and funeral services, and the Navy way of rigging for church, and conducting divine worship. Plus, many other subjects, too many to be mentioned here, are quite enough to give every student chaplain at one time or another a feeling of bewilderment and frustration.

Before leaving this discussion on the tools of our trade, a sort of postscript is in order. A surprising number of Americans do not know that the Marine Corps has neither doctors nor chaplains nor hospital corpsmen of its own. Which means that a certain number of Navy personnel in each of these fields is ultimately assigned for duty with the Marines. I had the honor of being the first Jewish chaplain ever assigned to such duty. The relationship between the Navy and Marine Corps is one of the most fascinating and involved connections in human history. Someday, a curious scholar will earn his PhD by exploring all its hidden possibilities. I remember very well the opening sentence of Chaplain Jack F. Robinson's lecture on the Marine Corps at Williamsburg: "Gentlemen, the Marine Corps is a component part of the United States Navy; the marines, however, frequently get the relationship reversed."[7]

The important point to be made here is that duty with the Marines requires a very special kind of preparation and training. When I was at Williamsburg, our preparation along this line consisted of exactly one lecture. Since then, there has been considerable improvement. Now, the faculty at Williamsburg includes several chaplains who have had extensive overseas combat experience with Marine units in the field and who are

---

[7] For more on Robinson's time at the school, see Capt Clifford Merrill Duty, (CHC, USNR), *History of the Chaplain Corps*, pt. 2, *1939–1949* (Pensacola, FL: Chaplains Corps, Department of the Navy, 1994).

equipped to transmit the benefit of their knowledge and experience to students at the school.

It would be a sad mistake to close this description of what makes a Navy chaplain without adding a word concerning the most unusual phase of the whole training process. Nothing but a war could bring 300 clergymen—Protestants, Catholics, and Jews—to live together intimately for a period of two months. Speaking for myself, I can honestly say it was one of the most instructive and inspiring experiences of my life. During the seven professional years prior to my acceptance of a commission, I daresay fully 90 percent of my contacts with the clergy were with rabbis, that is to say, almost exclusively with clergymen of my own faith. My contacts with Christian ministers, while friendly and cordial, were limited rather narrowly to an occasional interchange of pulpits, a joint religious service now or then, or an infrequent community problem or occasion that brought us together. Much the same must be said of my Christian colleagues. Their contacts with rabbis were at least as restricted as were mine with ministers and priests. In fact, a substantial proportion—would I be exaggerating in supposing perhaps even a majority—of the 50 men who graduated with me from Williamsburg had never before in their lives spoken to a Jew for more than a fleeting second, face to face, until they came to know the two of us in their class. Bear in mind that, as of the date this is being written more than 2,000 clergymen have gone through this unique experience in preparing for the Navy alone, and it will be easy to see that this is scarcely the least important result of our training.

I lived with three roommates during my six weeks of life on the campus at William and Mary, two during the first half and another after our return from field assignments. They were, respectively, a Presbyterian, a Southern Baptist, and a Roman Catholic. If they learned half as much about my faith as I learned of theirs, they will never regret an experience that to me was priceless. Every night before securing, while they knelt for their bedtime prayers, I, in the same room at the same moment, laid on my sack reciting to myself the watchword of Judaism, "*Shema Yisrael, Adonai Eloheinu, Adonai Echad*; Hear O Israel, the Lord is our God, the Lord is One." In what other land could that happen? Under what other circumstances *would* it happen?[8]

I doubt if any town in America has witnessed more clean, honest, intelligent, searching curiosity about religion than the little town of historic Williamsburg since the Navy chaplains took over. We asked questions of each other so fast and furiously that our biggest problem was finishing one answer before the next question was fired. I remember, as some of the most fascinating bull sessions of my life, several evenings on which I was the lone Jew, sprawled out indelicately in a room with seven or eight Protestants and Catholics, all of whom were firing questions at me concerning Jews, Judaism, and Zionism.[9] And on more than one occasion, the direction of the questions was reversed.

But the interplay of three major religions in a living democracy was not limited to our personal and informal relationships. It was a conscious and deliberate part of our schooling. Every class, for example, hears lectures on both Catholicism and Juda-

---

[8] Emphasis in original.
[9] Zionism—the Jewish nationalist movement for the creation of a Jewish national state in the ancient homeland of the Jews (*Eretz Yisrael*, "the Land of Israel")—originated in Eastern and Central Europe in the latter part of the nineteenth century based on the ancient attachment of the Jews and of the Jewish religion to the historical region and its hills called Zion.

ism, given respectively by chaplains of the Catholic and Jewish faiths. I witnessed the first Catholic mass of my life in the form of a "dry mass," demonstrated and explained by Catholic classmates.[10] Most of my colleagues, in turn, saw a Torah and an ark for the first time in their lives.[11] Men belonging to each of the three groups were told, clearly and concisely, what they could do to comfort and sustain a dying sailor or Marine of a faith other than their own. And since Catholic and Jewish men are the ones most apt to be without a chaplain of their own in an emergency, the holidays, festivals, prayer books, and procedures of these two faiths were carefully and skillfully explained. In addition to holding our own Sabbath service each week, the Jewish students made a practice of attending the daily Protestant devotion at 0640 each morning. Of the 12 members of each class who were invited to conduct these Protestant daily devotions, during my entire stay at Williamsburg, one was always a rabbi!

No words of description can be more than pale facsimiles compared to the living thrill of having experienced such an adventure. No bitterness of superiority or competition. No missionizing. No salesmanship. Just an honest effort to understand each other based on an equally honest determination to help each other. Did we succeed? May I offer, in testimony to that question, the words of one of my roommates on the day we finished classes: "I wouldn't hesitate to entrust the religious train-

---

[10] Dry mass is used for instruction. According to the Catholic Archdiocese of Military Services, a dry mass lacks one or more of the elements required for a valid a celebration of the Eucharist, or communion (e.g., no priest, no intention to consecrate, no valid bread or wine, or no formula of consecration).

[11] Here, Torah refers to the hand-inscribed Hebrew scroll of Genesis, Exodus, Leviticus, Numbers, and Deuteronomy. The ark refers to the ornate cabinet inside the synagogue where the Torah is kept.

ing of my Christian child to a rabbi like either of you in this class."

This, then, is the stuff of which Navy chaplains are made and the manner in which they are prepared for their tasks. There is no easy, universal formula to be followed. No two chaplains can be trained exactly alike, because no two chaplains have exactly the same job. But within the framework of the almost infinite variety to be found in the chaplaincy, the Naval Training School for Chaplains sets the general direction to be followed, and it established a flavor and a tone that carries through the entire Chaplain Corps.

It would be difficult to overvalue the preparation we received at Williamsburg. Above all else, perhaps, it changed us—in language, in habits, in dress, and in thoughts—from civilians to naval officers. I know how immensely important that change is, because for the better part of a year before leaving my pulpit I had served as a temporary civilian chaplain at Mitchell Field, Long Island. The attitudes and responses of the chaplains there were always of the utmost in courtesy, but there was no mistaking the fact that I was not one of them. At best, I was a welcome outsider. As a trained chaplain in uniform, the response is altogether different. Not long ago, an officer in my Marine congregation told me how he resented the gratuitous advice offered by a civilian official at an affair for men in uniform. "It wasn't so much the words as such that annoyed me," he concluded, "it was the fact that a civilian was speaking them. It would have been perfectly all right if you had said the same thing. You're one of us."

Perhaps that is as good a way as any to summarize the purpose of the Navy's eight-week seminary: to make the men feel

Chaplain Gittelsohn and many of his classmates would join Marines
during their Pacific battles. Here, Chaplain Gittelsohn leads a service
on Iwo Jima, February, 1945.
Official U.S. Marine Corps photo

that we are "one of them." It will be interesting to see how far
we succeed in that direction, as we turn ourselves now to some
of the actual experiences of the chaplain in the field.

PART II

What Makes Morale?

CHAPTER FOUR
Your Friend Away from Home

If chaplains the world over could vote on the most misunderstood word in the English language, I daresay 80 percent of them would choose the term *morale*. The average person seems to assume that morale is made up of one part free cigarettes, one part beer, and one part sweater girl.[1] This is not meant to detract in the least from the importance and value, respectively, of either cigarettes, beer, or sweater girls. But combined, enlarged, even tripled, they do not make morale. Morale is something greater and vaster than any or all of the ingredients commonly associated with it. The chaplain ought to know, for in a very real and genuine sense, it can be said that his chief business, in the Army and Navy alike, is the building and preserving of morale. So much so, that having followed through my own personal experience the nearly incredible transformation of pacifist to padre, I can think of no better way to trace the fascinating work of the chaplain than under the heading of his efforts in the quest of that elusive, intangible, indispensable goal—morale.

---

[1] The term *sweater girl* was made popular in the 1940s and 1950s to describe Hollywood actresses such as Lana Turner, Jayne Mansfield, and Jane Russell, who set the trend of wearing tight, form-fitting sweaters.

The official Navy definition of morale comes much closer to the truth than the unspoken but self-evident definition of most civilians: "The measure of determination to succeed in the purpose for which the individual is trained or for which the organization exists."[2] There you have it in a nutshell, stripped of all excess verbiage and glamor, reduced almost to the technical coldness of a college textbook, but true none the less. Sailors and Marines who are fully determined, beyond all distraction or doubt, to succeed in the purpose for which they have been trained—namely killing the enemy while remaining alive themselves—have high morale. And anything that increases that determination is a contribution to their morale. But having agreed to that concept, the larger and more important question still remains: What is it that creates and sustains such determination? More specifically and immediately, wherein can the chaplain help to increase that determination?

The first answer to this question is simple enough as to be missed altogether: just by being available. Just by being a kind of professional friend, on whom the men can depend when they are in trouble, and to whom they can go as they would to their own parents. During the first weeks of my active duty as a chaplain, I unconsciously assumed that every man who came to my office brought with him some specific question or problem. So, I would welcome him, offer him a chair, a cigarette or a piece of candy, find out where he came from and whom we knew in common, then expansively ask: "Now then, what can I do for you?" I learned my mistake after a few such questions were answered by embarrassed silence or equally embarrassed improvising. I

[2] *Bureau of Navigation Manual, 1925* (Washington, DC: Government Printing Office, 1940), 262.

learned that men do not always know themselves what problem brings them to the chaplain, that sometimes, indeed, they have no well-defined problem as such. They just need some quiet place where they can feel at home, some understanding person to whom they can talk. Many is the time that every chaplain has a visitor who needs nothing more than to sit down and "shoot the breeze." The United Service Organizations (USO) very aptly calls itself "your home away from home."[3] The chaplain in this, his first capacity as a builder of morale, might with equal validity be called "your friend away from home."

A boy who is now overseas with me affords a perfect example of how important it is at times to have a listening ear available. I had first met him nearly a year ago at boot camp. Months later, we were thrown together again briefly at a camp for advanced training. At neither time, however, did I have the opportunity of becoming acquainted with him beyond just learning his name. It was after we had both gone overseas in the same division that he came to me after services one Friday night and asked when he could see me in my office. An urgent tone in his voice gave me the impression that some specific problem was bothering him. So, we made an appointment for early the next morning.

The following day, I spent very nearly two fascinating hours with the boy. I learned much about him. His parents had been divorced before his fourth birthday. Reading between the lines of his somewhat reserved story at this point, I gathered that his father had been "no good." His mother—apparently a most capable and unusual woman—had given birth to six children, of

---

[3] The United Service Organizations still describes itself in these terms. See "About: The Organization," USO.org, accessed 8 November 2019.

whom only this boy and a sister 15 months his junior had survived. From the time of her divorce, the mother supported both children without help from anyone. The father had married a second time, and when he died six months later, left not a single penny for either child.

The boy himself had worked at a dozen different kinds of jobs continuously from the age of 7 to 17. Beginning with his 14th birthday, he had managed to take care of his own clothes and personal expenses. When he was 16, and his sister not quite 15, their mother passed away. Her very fine influence on the boy is obvious to anyone who really knows him. He enlisted in the United States Marine Corps precisely on his 17th birthday. I have met no one his age in the Corps who knows better how to take care of himself, or who has a clearer view of what he wants, both now and at war's end. Even now, in the midst of extensive preparations for combat, he is taking several courses at the Marine Corps Institute in order to complete his high school education.[4] Later, he expects to enter college and to become either a civil or chemical engineer.

And what was the urgent problem about which he came to see me that Saturday morning? A thoughtless person, listening in on our conversation, might have concluded that he had no problem, that he was just wasting a chaplain's time. But anyone with a measure of insight could have seen how badly he needed

---

[4] Founded by then-Col John A. Lejeune, the Marine Corps Institute (MCI) developed correspondence courses for Marines in all kinds of military occupations specialties (MOS). Courses were available in infantry strategy and tactics, leadership skills, MOS qualifications, personal finance, mathematics, and other subjects. Completion of MCI courses was generally required for promotion to the next Marine enlisted rank. MCI was deactivated in 2015 and reestablished as part of Marine Corps University's College of Distance Education and Training.

someone to listen and to understand. Here was a fine boy, a boy unusual in both ability and ambition, who had never in his life really had or known a father. He needed someone not only that one morning but regularly who would serve for him in the stead of a father. Someone whose very listening would reassure him that he would one day be able to carry out all those fine hopes that he might be ashamed even to mention to one of his buddies. In short, he needed a friend away from home. I dare to hope he found one.

Men sometimes come to the chaplain with the tiniest, apparently the most insignificant requests. Dozens of boys have asked me to compose a telegram for them on the occasion of a death in the family, to help them send flowers home, or to suggest the right gift for the right girl at the right time. One Catholic chaplain whom I know was even asked once to write a love letter. The boy knew how he felt toward the girl all right, but "shucks" he "wasn't ever much good at fancy words anyway." So, would the padre mind if the boy just told him how he felt and let the chaplain choose the right words?

Are these little things really important, really helping to win the war? This sending of telegrams and writing of love letters? Well, that all depends, I suppose. If they can make some boy or boys feel less stranded and alone, give them just something of the feeling that here in this one room in the midst of strangeness and confusion is a friend—a man who welcomes them always and who considers every concern of theirs a concern of his own. Is it hard to see the relationship between that and these boys' "determination to succeed in the purpose for which they were trained?"

Sometimes, of course, the need for a friend away from home is more obvious, or at least more specific. Men come in to tell the chaplain all about the girls they love, and they ask whether the chaplain thinks they ought to be married before going overseas. I remember one man whose first marriage had ended in divorce more than five weeks prior, who, after much hemming, hawing, and beating around the bush, asked the chaplain if he thought it would be wise to marry a girl he had known for all of three weeks! Another boy spent a whole evening in my office on a much worthier mission. He was just back from two years overseas. As soon as he received his overseas furlough, he would be on his way home to marry his sweetheart. But neither of them knew much about the so-called "facts of life." So, he came to the chaplain to get all the information he could about marriage, in general, about birth control and sex in particular. Here he was in the office of one who five minutes before had been a complete stranger, asking him now the most intimate questions he had ever asked anyone.[5] To whom else could he turn for this kind of friendship?

I almost think that in these words is the key to this first role of the chaplain as an available friend: To whom else could he turn? In civilian life, there were parents, perhaps there was a teacher, an uncle, an old scout leader or camp counselor. In military life, there is often only the chaplain for this kind of thing. No one else has both the interest and the time. That is why death messages are normally delivered by the chaplain. And even when such messages reach a man directly, without going through the chaplain's hand, usually a man's first thought is to

---

[5] Gittelsohn would later write *Consecrated Unto Me: A Jewish View of Love and Marriage* (New York: Union of American Hebrew Congregations, 1966); and *My Beloved Is Mine: Judaism and Marriage* (New York: Union of American Hebrew Congregations, 1969).

turn to his chaplain. Then, more than at any time, "a feller needs a friend."

I shall never forget one experience of this kind. A boy of 19 came in to see me at about 2100 one night. We will call him Carl, though of course that was not his name. I could tell the moment he walked in with a friend that something was wrong. But he, his friend, and I had smoked through half our cigarettes before Carl so much as spoke a word. Then, as he opened his mouth, he suddenly gushed forth with a full minute of anguished, convulsive crying. Finally, with the aid of his friend, he managed to give me, punctuated generously with semicolons of tears, the thing that brought him to my desk. Carl's brother Fred, three years older than himself, had been a hero to him as long as he could remember. In fact, Carl had joined the Marine Corps on his 18th birthday mostly because Fred was a Marine. And he had been gloriously happy, for six days ago, he had been transferred to a replacement battalion, which meant that he would soon be overseas, fighting the same fight that Fred was fighting, perhaps even the same battle. That much of the story Carl was able to tell me himself. But no more. The rest I learned from the crumpled telegram that he handed me when he just could not speak another syllable. It read, "Just received wire. Fred killed Makin Island. Be brave. Love—Mother."[6]

Do not for a single second underestimate the morale val-

---

[6] On 17 August 1942, 221 Marines of the 2d Marine Raider Battalion, commanded by LtCol Evans Carlson, landed on Makin to take the island back from the Japanese for use as a base during future attacks on the nearby Japanese-held Marshall Islands. The raid was successful, though at the expense of 21 lives. See Maj Jon T. Hoffman, USMCR, *From Makin to Bougainville: Marine Raiders in the Pacific War* (Washington, DC: History and Museums Division, Headquarters Marine Corps, 1995).

ue of just having the chaplain around as an available friend at a time like that. Carl and I talked a long while that night. At first, his thoughts were primarily on how he could keep from shipping out with his battalion; it was difficult to tell whether Fred's death had frightened him or had just made him desolately lonesome. Whichever it was, he wanted very much to get home. I did not discourage him; I had no right to. We just sat there and talked. We spoke of why Fred had joined the Marine Corps in the first place, and why Carl had followed him. We talked about the kind of home they had, about their parents, about the sort of life they were fighting to defend. We commented on how much every American who enjoyed freedom in the future would owe to boys like Fred, how Fred would go right on living in other people's happiness. And when we finished, Carl did a strange thing. Of his own accord, he rose and said, "Chaplain, I'm not so sure now that I want to go home after all. Maybe the best thing I can do for Fred's sake is to get over there and continue his fight just as fast as I can. I want to sleep on this tonight. If I don't come back in the morning, you'll know I'm going on out with the battalion."

Postscript: Carl did not come in the next morning. I have not seen him since. His battalion shipped out a few days later.

Well, is there any need to say more about the morale a chaplain can build just by being your friend away from home? One boy who came to see me a number of times before he left the country had no parents, no brothers or sisters, no uncles or aunts. No one closer in this world than a cousin who lived in Spokane, Washington. Oh yes, and a chaplain whose door was always open whenever the boy needed a friend to talk to. And 2,000 other chaplains, more or less, in this man's Navy. So that wherever he might be sent on the face of God's Earth, he can be sure of finding nearby an open door or a raised tent flap behind, which is another "friend away from home."

I shall never be able to think or write about this phase of the chaplain's work without thinking of Pete. I met him one morning at the Marine Corps base in San Diego, the boot camp where new recruits receive their initial weeks of training. He was about as lonely, homesick a specimen as I had seen in a long time. One of the doctors had asked if I would have a talk with Pete—a sort of last fling before giving up. The boy had been desperately unhappy since arriving at the base. Since the second day, as a matter of fact, he had been in the dispensary. With a body that was amazingly close to perfect, with no evidence of the slightest disease or disorder, Pete was "suffering" from one of the widest assortments of evils and ills in the history of humanity. I took him out of the ward and sat down with him in the corner of a recreation room. There, I told him of other young men who had been just as discouraged as he at the start but had finished their boot training with enviable records. I tried to help him see that he had been coddled and sheltered all his life by his mother and that his frustrations and fears were perfectly natural under the circumstances. And above all, I emphasized that this was to be but the first of as many intimate talks as he wanted. I promised that he would not have to fight this thing through alone. I would stand with him to the finish, and I would help whenever and however I could.

I wish that I could somehow project on this page the transformation that came over that young man's face. As we stood up to leave the recreation room, he held out his hand and his face literally shone as he said, "Gee, Chaplain, it's great to know I have a buddy here who will help me." For the first time, Pete felt that he was not completely alone in a new environment that seemed both strange and hostile. Because he felt that way, he fooled the doctors as well as himself; he finished his boot training successfully.

Carl and Pete and hundreds of others like them are scattered now all over the Pacific. Some of them would be amazed to know that I remember their names, let alone their stories and their problems. But they would not be surprised in the least to hear it said that the chaplain's first gift of making morale is just being a good friend. They know.

CHAPTER FIVE

Your Life—In Three Minutes

No man who carried 60 pounds of excess weight on their back would be apt to win honors in a 100-yard dash for speed. Nor would any man who carried the immeasurable burden of mental worries, anxieties, or fears be apt to excel in their "determination to succeed in the purpose for which he was trained"—read, morale. The Army, Navy, and Marine Corps go in every extreme of caution and doctors by the tens of thousands help them, to keep out those whose physical handicaps would prevent them from doing a creditable job of fighting. All three branches of the Service were alarmingly late, however, in exercising anything like an equal amount of care in the cases with mental handicaps and defects. And even after they had commenced to awaken from their lethargy on this count, the shocking scarcity of trained psychiatrists in this country was a further discouragement. As a result, every military unit of size today has in it some few men whose minds and central nervous systems are by no means equipped for the life they face. Some of them were mental misfits even as civilians; others have commenced to crack only under the stress and strain of military life. Some are either permanent problems or will at least require a long period of treatment before being normal again; others are as strong as you and I but are temporarily confronted by problems and decisions that are too much for them. They need help over an immediate bump if they are to continue the journey ahead.

There is little that a chaplain can do for those who are either psychotic or neurotic, except to see that they reach the attention of a doctor who is qualified to help them. But there is an enormous amount of help the chaplain can give those who are momentarily floored by a problem bigger than themselves and who will be of little use to themselves or anyone else until that problem has been solved. And such help is a second contribution, a very considerable contribution, to that "determination to succeed" that we have been calling morale. Every time a chaplain has helped to remove the heavy weight of worry or anxiety from one mind, he has thereby helped make a more effective soldier, sailor, or Marine.

Every chaplain I have known has commented at one time or another on the refreshing and immediate candor of men in the Service. In a sense, all the camouflage and subterfuge of genteel civilian life are shed. Perhaps because the age group among service men is a fairly young one, perhaps because these military people have no time for circumlocutions and guessing game, or perhaps because the relationship between chaplain and men is one of understanding confidence, very little time is wasted. When civilians come to their pastors for personal guidance there is usually a threshold of embarrassment and hesitance that must be crossed. When military men come to their chaplain, sometimes they will not even wait to sit down before plunging into their stories. Within three minutes, they have told everything important in their lives, and by the end of five minutes, nothing has been spared. In short, there is a forthright directness that makes it that much easier for chaplains to know their men, and therefore very much more probable that they can help them. Were it not for this, the chaplain, whose contacts with any one person are necessarily limited both in frequency and length, would be unable to contribute as much as he does the to lifting of oppressive worries and anxieties.

One type of situation in which chaplains are frequently of great help in uplifting morale is in cases of emergency or need at home. When a man is far removed from both his family and his accustomed way of life and learns or even suspects that something has gone wrong with their loved ones at home, he is apt to become depressed or even desperate. Even if he manages to suppress the almost irresistible urge to go "over the hill," to "beat it" home now and pay the penalty later; so long as his mind is filled with worry, he is not apt to be much of an asset even in terms of sheer fighting efficiency.[1]

A man came into my office one morning with a story that challenged the term *grim*. The nervous gymnastics of his fingers and the dark, pitted circles under his eyes bore eloquent witness to his frame of mind. Two years ago, his young wife had died of tuberculosis. He showed me her picture and that of their little girl, who was two at the time of her mother's death. The immediate cause of his visit to me was a telegram from somewhere in Tennessee, advising that the little girl, now finishing her fourth year of life, was critically ill—a victim of both tuberculosis and pneumonia. She was not expected to live. And here was her father in the Marine Corps, thousands of miles away, without per-

[1] In this instance, the term *over the hill* does not refer to one's age but rather being absent without leave or deserting your post.

mission to leave camp and without the money for a trip even if he had permission. If tears were wings, he would have been half way to Tennessee by the time he finished his story.

What could the chaplain do in a case of that sort? Several things: first, and perhaps most important, help the man think and plan straight. The human mind is a curiously inefficient and treacherous paradox. When we need it most desperately, it goes off on its widest, wildest tangents. So, this man in his trouble was thinking impulsively and hysterically. He needed someone to supply a measure of calmness and coolness. First, the American Red Cross must be asked to investigate the facts and verify the emergency at home. That done, the same agency would be ready to extend a loan.[2] Then the man's commanding officer must be contacted, the emergency of the situation laid before him, and his permission secured for a furlough. Then a half dozen Army and Navy air fields had to be contacted to see if, by some kind chance of fortune, there might be a flight east that day. Unfortunately, there were none.

Next step, contacting the railroad offices to discover fares, connections, and schedules from San Diego, California, to Tennessee, then rushing through the papers and loan for quick departure. Then we had to get out a letter to be carried along, stating the emergency and requesting that every consideration and priority be given a Marine father who had already suffered his portion of tragedy, who was rushing desperately home in a race with the angel of death. The finish line: the bedside of a four-year-old little girl.

Seven hours after the man first walked into my office, he

---

[2] While the American Red Cross may have provided this service at the time, loans for family emergencies today are provided by Army Emergency Relief, the Navy-Marine Corps Relief Society, and the Air Force Aid Society.

was walking out of the Camp Elliott gate.[3] The 15 days of his emergency furlough were tense and anxious days for me, even though a dozen other cases of similar importance immediately kidnapped my energies. I could scarcely wait to see the man again, within minutes of his return to camp, and to learn from him that his little daughter had miraculously pulled through. It would be a long hard struggle yet, but the doctors had assured him she would be all right.

Any need to dwell on what those 15 days had done for that man's morale? Or to describe his touching expressions of gratitude? For a time after his return, he worked at the salad counter in our officers' mess. Daily, he waited for me to reach out for a salad, rushed up to grab it from me as soon as he saw my choice, then made me wait while he went back to the galley to prepare me a fresh one, anywhere from two to four times the normal size. Not only did the officer's mess make no profit on me, but for three weeks I ate salad until I felt like a rabbit. But my gastronomic reward was nothing compared to the heart-warming gratification that came to me every time I looked at my own two kiddies and thought of him.

Not every morale-decreasing burden that came to the chaplain's attention, however, is as dramatic or spectacular as that. Often, men are torn between conflicting loyalties within their families. Unless or until such conflicts are resolved, many a bull's-eye will be missed. One day, as duty chaplain, I called in a man for whom we had received an urgent telegram, indicating that his mother was desperately ill. I thought his case would fall

---

[3] Originally named for Comdt George F. Elliott (1846–1931), Camp Elliott was created to improve conditions in an overcrowded Army/Navy/Marine Corps training area and opened in 1940. After the war, the camp would become part of what is now known as Marine Corps Air Station Miramar.

into the usual patterns—a few tears at immediate receipt of the message, a request for American Red Cross verification, a conference with the commanding officer to secure a furlough, and perhaps the need of arranging a loan. There are more surprises in a chaplain's day than in Pandora's box. When I had established a bond of understanding sympathy with the man, he literally opened to me the floodgates of his life. His father had died when he and his sister were mere babies. In all the years since then, his mother had served and slaved in a manner that would keep them everlastingly her debtors. But she had also developed a possessiveness that threatened to make their lives unhappy carbon copies of her demands. When the sister had fallen in love and wanted to marry, her mother had reacted with such violent unreasonableness that the affair had to be dropped. When the boy had proposed to a lovely girl, his mother tried every trick—legitimate and illegitimate—in the bag of a psychotically possessive mother who senses a threat to her monopoly of affection. Finally, when the boy, unlike his sister, married anyway, he was literally if unbelievably thrown out of the house, denounced to the local draft board as a slacker by his own mother, and told that she never wished to see him again.

Since then, she had repented and was now trying as frantically to see him as she had once determined to banish him. The present telegram was merely an incident in a long series of either pretended or imagined illnesses that were being exploited as devices. With all that had happened, the man still felt that he owed his mother a great deal and did not want to cause her any unnecessary pain. But, he also loved his wife. She felt, understandably, that she had been wronged. She refused to go through more of the same humiliation, especially since she expected a baby in the spring. To say the least, it was a befuddled, distracted, and bewildered Marine who told me this amazing story. Character: excellent. Confusion: enormous. Morale: zero.

It took a number of talks with the chaplain to help him straighten himself out. To understand that he owed two definite but very different obligations to these two women—his mother and his wife. To see that the ideal situation would be one in which he could discharge his obligation in full to each, without detracting in the slightest from the other. But to recognize also that, in his case, something less than the ideal would have to prevail. And if, regrettably, it should be wholly impossible for him to give equal priority to both claims, then his mother, by her own mistakes, had made it necessary for her needs to come second and the wife's first. But over and above all else, it was necessary to help this man see that in no sense was he to blame, and in no way should he punish or reproach his own conscience. I doubt if removing a tumor could have provided a greater sense of relief. Forget, if you choose, the pangs of misdirected conscience now removed. Forget the long-term effect on the happiness of a grand young couple. Remember only that a distracted Marine was made into a purposeful Marine; a bewildered Marine made into one "determined to succeed." That, if you please, is morale.

Sometimes, the family problems that keep our boys from top efficiency are even more complicated and more difficult to solve. And sometimes, the demands of a man's conscience and the requirements of the military clash in a way that seems insoluble. I remember spending a great deal of time with a young boy from somewhere in Illinois. He was already in a replacement battalion when his commanding officer sent him to me. The policy of the training command at his camp was not to grant furloughs of any kind or for any purpose once a man was in a replacement battalion. But this boy had a problem that was quite beyond the possibility of solution without a furlough. His father, a shell-shocked veteran of the last war, had been a dangerously heavy drinker for years. So much so that, in his passionate quest for drink, he had endangered the health and welfare of his family. Before the boy had come into the Marine Corps, his father had promised to take decent care of the family, and for a time had seemed to keep his promise. But now, letters from home indicated that he was worse than ever. He had sold the sewing machine and refrigerator for drink, and he threatened to strip the house of every piece of furniture. He beat his wife and three younger children mercilessly, until one day his wife was taken to a hospital, her condition was diagnosed as cancer of the back or rib, and she was given a maximum of six months to live. With that on his mind, a 19-year-old boy was about to be sent overseas.

Because there were children of 15, 11, and 9 years involved, respectively, and because the commanding officer was not only a major but a human being, an exception was made. The boy was sent home to make arrangements for housing his brother and sisters and to see his mother, most likely for the last time alive. The time available was so short that we even had to send him a wire to rush back a day before his furlough ended. And he came back on time, without complaint, a better Marine with finer morale, because the Marine Corps had played ball with him when he needed a little kindness and consideration. Chalk up another victory for morale. Not just for a good time or pleasant diversion, but for good old honest-to-goodness "determination to succeed."

The most pitiless pirate of privacy on Earth is a barracks.

More than one sensitive soul has found the surrender of his personal life the hardest adjustment of all in making a transition from civilian to soldier, sailor, or Marine. To live in a barracks or on a ship is often like hanging your most intimate emotions on a clothesline for all to see. This is a very real worry even for many normal men; for those with special problems of adjustment, it is sometimes pathetic. For there are certain types of serious personal problems that can be fairly well camouflaged in the privacy of civilian life, but which are exposed nakedly in the enforced intimacy of life in camp.

Such, for example, was the problem of the occasional adult bed wetter. The average civilian may even raise his eyebrows in surprise that there is such a problem. But the Navy knows that it occurs frequently enough so that every enlisted man, before being sworn in, must sign a statement that among other things he has never in his adult life been a bed wetter. Not just because of the obvious physical difficulties involved, but because psychiatrists are agreed that in more than 9 cases out of 10, such behavior is a symptom of some mental or nervous disturbance.

One of the most pathetic cases I can remember was that of the 18-year-old Marine who came to me three times before he could summon the necessary courage to tell me that bed wetting was driving him frantic. On two occasions, he came to the office while I was busy with someone else, sat down to wait in the outer room, lost his nerve, and had disappeared by the time I was ready for him. Finally, when it would have required more strength to keep his uncomfortable secret than to tell it, he returned. He told me, after a dozen false starts and new beginnings, that the most oppressive anxiety of his life had been this inability to outgrow the infant habit of wetting his bed. All his life he had been kidded for it. Now, he simply could not take it anymore. Had he been asked to sign a statement denying the existence of any such weakness? Yes, to be sure, but he was anxious enough to get into the Marine Corps to perjure himself. His father was a veteran of the last war, all his friends were already involved in this war, and he was determined to do his share too. He did not want someone else to carry his part of the burden. He felt and expressed a measure of patriotism that made me proud of him. Anyway, he had hoped that this radical change in his mode of living would help him overcome his trouble.

Instead, life in a barracks had made things not better but worse. Fortunately, he had a squad room leader with more than the average amount of understanding. And he emphasized tearfully that his bunkmates were really leaning over backward in an effort not to embarrass him. But there was a limit to what they and his own conscience could stand. And that limit had been reached and passed. Even when he managed to hide the visible evidences of his discomfort via daily laundering, there were telltale odors each morning. Now, he had reached the point where he was literally forcing himself to remain awake all night as the only possible insurance against accidents. He spent all day in the field on infantry drill and all night in sleepless anxiety, where at best he could have an hour of stolen napping in place of evening chow. Multiply that by seven days a week, four weeks per month, and you have a fair notion of the problem that poor boy faced. His body refused to allow him to remain in the Marine Corps; his conscience would not entertain the notion of accepting a discharge.

Altogether, it took something like six or seven weeks even to begin the task of helping him. To assure him that his illness was no more his own fault, no more a source of legitimate shame, than if he had suffered from weak eyes or tuberculosis. To show him that remaining in the Corps was thwarting the vary patriotism he wanted so to demonstrate; that if he continued this way, he would be of little use either to his country or himself. To convince him that it was not necessary to wear a uniform or carry a rifle in order to do one's share toward winning the war; that his own father, working in a war plant, was also a soldier; that he himself, surveyed from the Marine Corps, could contribute more as a worker than his present condition would permit as a Marine.[4]

No amount of ink and paper can portray the depth of that unhappy boy's anguish, or the extent of his relief when he could finally reconcile his conscience to a medical discharge. And it is not too much to claim that his release from active service, paradoxically enough, meant an improvement in his own morale, in that of the men who would otherwise have had to serve with him, and in the war effort at large. Another battle with conscience had been won.

After a certain amount of intimate experience in the business of trying to help troubled human beings, one is tempted to say of conscience what William Ellery Leonard once said of a mother's love—it is the greatest blessings and the greatest curse in life.[5] Another case, typical enough to be important, of conscience as an obstacle rather than a stimulant to morale, is that of the boy who had literally forced his mother to sign his enlistment papers when he was only 16 years old. Her great-

---

[4] Based on the context, the term *surveyed* here likely refers to gathering facts documenting that an individual's service is no longer required, so the Marine may be discharged.

[5] Neale Reinitz, *William Ellery Leonard: The Professor and the Locomotive God* (Lanham, MD: Fairleigh Dickinson University Press, 2013), 78-79.

er wisdom told her it was a mistake. But he had begged her, urged her, pleaded with her, even threatened her until at last both her resistance and her judgment weakened and she signed.

Almost from the moment that her permission had been granted and her son had enlisted, she began a steady decline in health. Small-town neighbors began writing the boy angry letters, telling him what he had done to his mother and alarming him beyond reason. Apparently, there was more than a little cause for alarm since the American Red Cross check indicated a possibility of cancer. When the boy came to me, securing a furlough for a visit home before shoving off was by far the lesser problem. That issue was just a matter of mechanics. But far more than mechanical was the task of getting his conscience squared away. He blamed himself entirely, could never forgive himself in the least. He kept repeating over and over again that he hated himself for killing him mother, that if anything happened to her, he would be unable to live with himself.

The task of helping him, aside from arranging a last visit hone, was three-fold. One, he had to be shown that though enlistment at age 16 may have been a mistake in judgment, his motives and intentions were unimpeachable. Two, it was essential for him to see that he could do nothing for his mother from the medical point of view. The one thing he could do for her and for all mothers was to help win a speedy victory. Three, if, God forbid, his mother did have cancer, he could in no way blame himself. A condition like that must have originated long before his enlistment. Needless to say, it is easier by far to catalog the necessary steps in retrospect than it was, slowly, painfully, patiently, to remove an intolerable burden of guilt, so that the "determination to succeed" might not be smothered.

Sometimes these battles of conscience border more closely

on the specifically religious side of men's lives. I once spent an uninterrupted half day with a boy who could not force himself to destroy human life. To be sure, the armed forces in this war have made finer and fairer provision for conscientious objectors than they did in the last war. But exemption is allowed on this basis only to those who belong to religious denominations and sects whose essential faith prohibits the bearing of arms.[6] This boy belonged to no such church. His problem was a purely personal one, and therefore all the more difficult to solve. He had always wanted to be a doctor, indeed had been on the threshold of a premedical college course when he became subject to the draft. Unable to continue immediately with his long-range plans, he volunteered as a Navy hospital corpsman. In one form or another, war or no war, he was determined to save life not destroy it. But it happened that at that particular moment men were needed far more urgently for the Marine Corps than a hospital corpsman. So, he found himself in khaki instead of blue, a carbine slung on his shoulder, an ammunition bolt clamped around his waist, and an intolerable burden strapped to his conscience.

There is such a thing—any chaplain can affirm it—as a human being who is almost constitutionally incapable of killing. This boy came clearly under that heading. Still, he was in the Marine Corps, there was no possibility then of transfer to Navy hospital duty, and his nerves were badly battered, to say the least. The

---

[6] Based on the 1940 Selective Training and Service Act, conscientious objector status, including some form of service unrelated to and not controlled by the military, was granted solely on the basis of membership in a recognized "pacifistic religious sect." For more modern laws, see Title 32, National Defense, Chapter XVI, Selective Service System, § 1630.16 Class 1-O: Conscientious objector to all military service (1987).

chaplain's only alternative, therefore, was to help him adjust to the unpleasant inevitable. How could that be done? Primarily by urging him to understand that sometimes it is necessary to destroy, precisely in order to save. A forest fire can be stopped only by building a backfire against it. The killing of millions tomorrow may at times be prevented only by the destruction of thousands today. Suppose, as an armed Marine, he were to kill a Japanese soldier who would later have murdered 10 Americans. Had he saved 10 lives any less clearly than by dressing the otherwise fatal wounds of 10 Americans who had already been shot? Or suppose he found himself—as well might happen—the only able-bodied person guarding a dozen wounded patients against a Japanese sniper who aimed to destroy them. Which would be the greater saving of life, his avowed purpose and desire: to allow that sniper tree hunting? Or by opposing, to kill him and thereby save 12 innocent lives? In time of war, who was to draw a clear, unmistakable line between saving and destroying life?

Such questions as these had never before occurred to him. Now, the problem had been set in an altogether different perspective. Still, no tailor-made solution, to be sure, but at least a beginning had been made. At least the raw materials of a possible solution had been placed before him to do with as he pleased.

Perhaps this is the best place, in connection with a different type of personal problem, to speak a needed word on the subject of men, women, and morals. That war nearly always results in a lamentable loosening of moral principles and patterns is too obvious to require further exposition here. That men in uniform often hold too cheaply the morals of the women they meet is a fact far older than any individual now living. The modern "wolf" hails from a long line of more or less distinguished predecessors. Sometimes, we Navy chaplains who serve with Marines and therefore wear their uniform joke that we are actually sheep in "wolves" clothing.

But any of us who has tried to square away lives that seem to be all but hopelessly fouled up knows that there are times and cases in which the serviceman is the injured rather than the injurer. There is a feminine of the species in the wolf world also. There are women in every sizable Navy town who marry anywhere from two to five different sailors under a variety of assumed names just to collect government allotments from all of them. There was the girl, within my own immediate experience, who persuaded a young Marine to marry her because he was the father of her unborn child. Six months after the baby was born, the hapless young father brought me an unbelievable letter from his "wife." The baby was not his at all. She had known it at the time, but had been desperate for financial and legal support. Furthermore, she had known all along who the real father was, and she had now decided that he was also the real object of her worthless affections. So, would her husband mind granting her a divorce, so that she could proceed to marry the lucky culprit?

Another boy all of 19 years in age once came to me with a similar and equally nauseating story. Nearly a year before, he had come home to New Jersey on a furlough from duty in the Canal Zone.[7] While home, he had evidently indulged in one or two sexual indiscretions. Shortly after returning to his duty sta-

---

[7] The Canal Zone was created on 4 May 1904 under the terms of the Hay-Bunau-Varilla Treaty of 1903. In return for annual payments, Panama granted to the United States the sole right to operate and control the canal and about 5 miles (8 kilometers) of land on each side. In accordance with the Torrijos-Carter Treaties of 1977, the Canal Zone ceased to exist on 1 October 1979. Within the former Canal Zone, lands and properties were transferred to Panama on an agreed schedule during the next 20 years. Panama gained full control of the canal in 1999.

tion, a letter from the young lady informed him that she was pregnant, and she requested most urgently that he return immediately to marry her, which he did. On the strength of her letter, he was granted a second furlough—this one an emergency—and without any attempt at further investigation or examination, he proceeded to marry the girl. He spent upward of 48 hours with her before returning to the canal.

Eleven months had passed. Nature was apparently absent-minded; no baby had appeared. An examination insisted on too late by the boy's family established the fact that there never had been a baby. When the boy came to me, despite repeated frantic pleas on his part, his wife had refused to write him so much as a postcard in five months. One possible reason might have been that she was a very busy girl indeed. She had gone through a bank account of nearly $1,000 signed over to her at the time of their marriage, had sold his car for $700, and had made more than a sizable dent in that amount too. It was hard to decide whether to be angrier at the girl's shamelessness or at the boy's stupidity.

This last case will suggest that the chaplain is not a worker of miracles and that often he is helpless in the desire to improve morale by removing heavy burdens of worry. But more often than not, at least some small measure of assistance proves possible. One of my most richly gratifying experiences as a chaplain occurred while I was stationed at Camp Pendleton, California. I found myself one morning sitting across the desk from a face burdened with utter distraction. It belonged to a Chicago man who had been married long enough to have a three-year-old daughter whom he loved intensely. At the beginning of his career in the Marine Corps, he and his wife had exchanged letters daily. Though he had continued the practice, her letters began to arrive with more frequent and longer delays—first four a week, then two, then one. At the time in question, he had received no word from her at all in nine days. Each mail call had come to mean intensified agony for him. Even when she had written, however, her letters had been completely devoid of any affection or love. To make matters distressingly worse, his sister had written that his wife had been keeping company with other fellows. The net result was a Marine mind utterly unable to concentrate on anything in the line of official duties.

My first effort was to secure a better balanced and more objective picture of the whole situation. So, I wrote directly to the girl for more information. Her answer was immediately and refreshingly honest. She was frank to say she felt no real affection for her husband; she had not, as a matter of fact, for a whole year before he left. He had been most unkind and inconsiderate during the years of their marriage. He had taken her for granted. Often, he had placed the preferences of his sisters and parents before hers. He had gone far on the road to killing all her love for him, and this enforced absence had suddenly and strangely convinced her that she did not need him anymore.

Upon reading to the man his wife's side of the story, I was amazed—and in a sense delighted—to find that he agreed completely. He remarked, "Everything she says is true, chaplain, only she didn't say half enough. I can see now that I was a pretty sorry failure as a husband. It took this experience to show me how deeply I miss and need her. I know in my heart that if only I could see her for a few days, she would see the change in me, and everything would be right between us."

I approached the man's commanding officer from two points of view. First, even in wartime, saving a marriage from disaster, especially where a child is involved, is eminently worth any reasonable effort. Second, even in terms of military efficiency itself, this man would be worse than useless to the Marine Corps in his present frame of mind. In spite of an urgent and immediate need for men, the commanding officer agreed on both counts. The man went home on a 15-day furlough. How right he was, and how richly rewarded the major and I felt for our efforts would be quite apparent from the following letter we received from the grateful wife a week or two later:

> Dear Chaplain Gittelsohn,
>
> I feel I should write and thank you for your cooperation in arranging an emergency furlough for . . . I'm happy to say that all our marital troubles have been straightened out and we have complete faith in each other. I found out . . . [he] was a new man, very sweet and understanding, and had acquired many new virtues. I'm sure he will be in a better frame of mind through all this, thus making him a better Marine. Again, I say thank you, and God bless you!

I have dozens of similar letters in my files. Some of them will be reprinted on pages yet to come. They are, frankly, one of my own greatest sources of the "determination to succeed."

Thus far, we have been thinking purely in terms of building or maintaining morale for the immediate moment. It does not require too elastic an imagination, however, to see that often the chaplain has a rich opportunity to build more than for the moment of war. One Sunday after services at the Marine Corps Base in San Diego, I was approached by a bundle of inferiority complexes. He had been married seven years, had a beautiful wife whom he loved, and two children ages three and one whom he adored. All his life, he had felt insecure, had been especially afraid to meet new people. He told me it had taken a supreme amount of willpower even to approach me for our discussion. He was just about as completely and utterly unsure of himself as any human being I had ever met, even his physical appearance bothered him. At one stage of our talk, he turned to me with tears in his eyes, a tremor in his voice, and said most revealingly, "Chaplain, do you like what you see in the mirror when you shave? I don't!"

Why had such a man enlisted in the first place? Because the same inner fears and frustrations that made him so pitifully insecure also insisted that this was the only way to prove to himself that he was a "man." Now, however, he felt that boot camp was proving, if anything, the opposite. And he climaxed his sorry recital of personal tragedy by saying, "Chaplain, if I fail in this too, I can never force myself to return to my wife and children!"

I could think of only two things to do for him. First, I must try patiently to show him that by concentrating on his weaknesses, many of which were common to all of us, to the utter neglect of his strengths, some of which were uniquely his own, he was rapidly becoming his own worst enemy. Second, I must make the services of a Navy psychiatrist available to him when, as and if he felt he wanted to take that step. Unfortunately, in this particular instance, the man was transferred out of my jurisdiction before a great deal could be accomplished along either line. His case, however, is potentially typical of many in which the possible effect of wise guidance and counseling now may reach from the present far into the future, from the uncertain heartache of one man into the lives of his dear ones. The chaplain can sometimes be an architect of souls while he tries to succeed as a maker of morale. The responsibility is not an easy one.

Here is another example of the same situation. A young boy of 18 years, whom I had never met before, came to see me. With refreshing and disarming frankness, he told me within the three-minute framework that is followed so frequently that before shipping out to this Pacific base, he had indulged in sexual relations with a 19-year-old girl in Los Angeles, California, that she was now pregnant, that he was by his own knowledge as well as her admission definitely not the father, and that he nevertheless felt badly and wondered if there were anything he could do to help her. Our discussion quickly went beyond the immediate problem, however, to the larger one of his sex life in general. I was interested in learning more about the boy. He impressed me as a strange combination of paradoxes. Beneath a surface veneer of blasé gruffness, I could sense a young, slightly frightened, almost tender boyishness. At first glance, he struck me as a kind of Casanova in knee pants. I wanted to know more about him.

Before we were finished, the answer—a large part of it at any rate—was quite evident. A nice young boy of 17 years had, out of the most commendable of patriotic motives, persuaded his parents to let him enlist. Up to that time, he had indulged in no sexual indiscretions. In camp, however, a new world had been opened to him via the Monday morning boastful reports of successful weekend exploits by some of his friends. It was the sort of thing he might have experienced at a later date in some college fraternity house, and it struck him hard. He began to feel that unless he too had a conquest to report, he had failed to establish his virility and manhood. So, he proceeded to correct that situation. The girl in Los Angeles was the third or fourth on his list. He was already, at the mature age of 18, a "veteran."

But that was only half the story, and the least important half at that. Sensing that he was inherently a decent, even lovable kid, and that he was still holding back some part of what had brought him to me, I tried to encourage him: "Well, fellow, do you feel more manly now that you have something to boast about too?"

He said, "That's the funny thing, Chaplain. I found from the beginning that, after I had experienced relations with a girl, I just couldn't get myself to talk about it. So, I still let the others do the talking, and I kept quiet as I had before."

"And how do you feel, now that you've had this new type of experience?" I wondered.

"To be perfectly honest with you, Chaplain, I feel disappointed—sort of letdown. Maybe I wasn't missing as much as I thought I was," he replied honestly.

"There's one other question I'm most anxious to ask. You don't have to answer if you don't want to. When did you have more honest, genuine respect for yourself: before, when you listened to the others; or now, that you know yourself what it's like?"

"You know the answer to that question, Chaplain, or you wouldn't have asked it. I haven't any respect at all for myself now. That's why I came here," he cried.

I tried to show my young friend why he felt disappointed, or as he put it, "letdown." I tried to explain how human beings differ from animals; how sex in our lives is deeply, beautifully bound up with love, with marriage, with a family. How easy it was to cheapen sex by misusing it, and how, by so doing, to deny yourself the kind of all-sustaining love of one woman of which only human beings are capable. And over and above all that, how it was still possible for him to change. True, he had made an unfortunate and mistaken beginning. It would have been better by far if he could have seen all this without learning it the hard way. But the important thing was at least to learn from such experience, even if it could not be erased, and by denying himself a lesser pleasure now, inherit a greater and deeper joy later.

The overwhelming probability is that in civilian life that boy would never have come to an older friend with such a problem. Helping him was as much a job of lifelong planning as it was a challenge to immediate morale. Because he suffered with a pressing personal problem that brought things to a head, there arose a fertile opportunity to teach him one of the most valuable lessons in life.

Others too may be able to gain indirectly from his experience. In many training camps and bases, regular, sensible, realistic lectures on sex, delivered by both doctors and chaplains, are a part of the training program. The story of this one boy, and of others somewhat like him, will be told someday soon, somewhere, to a large group of men or women in uniform. And in that group, there may be 1, or 5, or 50, who never had the courage to ask for themselves, but who needed precisely such a message for their own lives. Someday in the peaceful future, a boy and a girl may fall in love, and together learn life's highest bliss because a chaplain had a chance to speak in the midst of war.

In a sense, each one of the men we have spoken of in this chapter is a sample. As I described each, I could think of many dozens of others whose stories followed the same general pattern, with variations that were only minor. Some men bring their anxieties with them from civilian life. Others first become frustrated and burdened in the difficult transition of putting their souls into uniform. In either case, the chaplain's job is the same: to be a wise and understanding counselor; to "square away" consciences that have somehow become "fouled up;" to help remove those burdens of the heart and mind that become too oppressive and thereby destroy an asset more valuable than the finest of equipment: the spirit and morale of the men who will use that equipment—or misuse it.

CHAPTER SIX

Am I a Man or a Machine?

If life in uniform is no promoter of privacy, neither is it a great respecter of individuality. Two weeks in the Army, Navy, or Marine Corps is apt to make even the most colorful personality a masterpiece of anonymity. The chaplain senses that in his first 12 hours at training school. In civilian life, he was aided somewhat in learning the names of new people by peculiarities and eccentricities of dress. At least as a temporary aid to memory, a yellow necktie can be the clergyman's best friend. Especially in meeting a large number of new people in a singular evening, one can immediately associate their names with differences in dress until their faces come to have meaning. But the first day at Chaplains' Training School is a bewildering process of meeting several dozen strangers with identical shirts, identical neckties, identical caps. To attempt remembering Chaplain Smith as the fellow with the khaki shirt is somewhat less than helpful.

But there is more to the uniformity of the military than mere inconvenience. Men soon feel that they have lost every symptom of individuality, have indeed ceased to be individuals at all. Instead of being Johnny Stewart, whom everyone in town knows, you are the third guy from the end in the second line of the first platoon. You are no better, no worse; no smarter, no duller; no faster, no slower—in fact, you are no different from anyone else. You have no name except, "Hey Mac!" You are methodically rolled through the assembly line of a training course with often no more individual attention than a Fisher body received.[1] The answer to nearly every question you ask is to be found somewhere in a dry formula that has no regard at all for you as a person. Everyone dresses alike, marches alike, gripes alike, and soon thinks—if at all—alike.

This does not mean that our military Services deliberately set out to destroy a man's individuality or even that they approve the process. To the contrary, there have been innumerable instances in which officers have gone far out of their way to allow for individual differences. But a military machine, by its very nature and essence, must tend toward uniformity of every kind. When a nation of peace lovers and pacifists suddenly builds up a gigantic machine of more than 10 million fighters, there is every possibility and more than a little probability that the individual as such may be trampled on in the process.

Very few of us can stand the neglect of being anonymous for long, especially if we are not too happy or well-adjusted to begin with. And precisely here, I think, is the most important single function of the chaplain in the military scheme of things. The chaplain's office is very apt to be the only spot in a camp, outside his own tent, where a man is reasonably sure at all times of being treated as an individual. Indeed, many will tell you

---

[1] The term *Fisher body* refers to the well-known automobile maker founded by the Fisher brothers in 1908 in Detroit, MI. Fisher Body was a division of General Motors for many years, but it was dissolved to form other General Motors divisions in 1984. The name and its iconic "Body by Fisher" logo were well known to the public, as General Motors continued to display the emblem on their door sill plates until the mid-1990s.

that it is almost the only place where anyone will bother to ask their names. Elsewhere in camp, you live—whether you like it or not—by rules that are no respecters of persons. In the chaplain's office, you become once more a man, a person, an individual different from any and every other individual in camp. It would be difficult indeed to exaggerate the enormous importance of this, especially to men of some sensitivity.

One of the worst forms of military anonymity is that of the man who has special abilities that the machine has failed to recognize. I remember one case of a man who came into the Marine Corps from several years of unusual experience as a civilian in a naval supply office. He was 1 of no more than 50 men in the entire country who had expert knowledge of priorities in naval supply work. In the Marine Corps, he had by mistake been slapped into the infantry. He had no particular objection to infantry duty, despite the fact that he was nearly twice the age of most men in that branch. But he knew two things: that he had certain special abilities, and that somewhere the Marine Corps must have need of those abilities. It seemed to him—and to the chaplain—a shameful waste of manpower to ask him to tote a rifle. But his every attempt to apply for a transfer had been thwarted by a first sergeant whose favorite answer to any question was "no." Because the man was reluctant to go over the head of his first sergeant, he came to the chaplain for advice. Because the chaplain could rush in where privates feared to tread, he was able to contact the colonel in charge of the nearest base depot quartermaster's office.[2] The colonel had been looking for

---

[2] For more on the responsibilities of the depot quartermaster's office for the period, see *Quartermaster Base Depot Company* (Washington, DC: War Department, 1944).

just such a man for so long he was about to give up. The "match" was a perfect one. The colonel got precisely the aid he needed, the man rejoiced that he could use his special talents, and the Marine Corps gained immeasurably. The only one who could possibly have objected was the detoured first sergeant, and up to the present moment no one has asked his opinion.

A similar case was that of the young Jewish man with the second-highest score I have ever seen on the Army General Classification Test (AGCT), which is given to every Marine recruit. These tests are somewhat parallel to general intelligence tests, and they are scored exactly the same. The average or normal score is 100. Anything above 120 is unusual.[3] This particular young man boasted a score no less than 142. He came to camp at a time when the Japanese Language School, one of the most difficult types of training in the Marine Corps, was hungering for men of superior intelligence.[4] Again, it was an original, perhaps unavoidable mistake, plus a myopic noncommissioned officer who barred the way, plus a "matchmaker" who was needed. For such a young man to be used in the ranks of the infantry would be the most wasteful kind of extravagance. The major in charge of the Japanese Language School nearly hit the ceiling when he heard there was an AGCT of 142 running loose. Before his blood pressure had settled back to normal, there was one more student standing by for the next class in Japanese.

And so, it happens again and again. On one occasion it is a man who is manifestly unable physically to perform the arduous duties of the infantry, but who has a rich business background

---

[3] "History of Military Testing," Official ASVAB, accessed 12 November 2019.
[4] For more on the program through Military Intelligence, see Joseph K. Yamagiwa, *The Japanese Language Programs at the University of Michigan during World War II* (Ann Arbor: University of Michigan, 1946).

that makes the quartermaster's tongue hang out. Elsewhere, a skilled mechanic is about-facing himself into dizziness at a time when motor transport is desperate for men to service trucks. Or a man who has graduated from the March of Time camera school and the Marine Corps combat photographers' school finds himself pushing a broom.[5] To be sure, the Corps has highly capable classification officers and elaborate systems of filing, all aimed at putting the right Marine in the right job. But occasional mistakes will be made, and in most cases, the authorities are thankful to the chaplain who points them out.

Sometimes, the difficulty can be traced to a careless or over-zealous recruiting officer. Especially in the larger induction or enlistment centers, there grows a kind of intramural competition between the "salesmen" of the Army, Navy and Marine Corps. The prospective serviceman is sometimes offered everything but a chauffeur-driven jeep if they will enter the desired branch. Rash promises are made, sometimes with every good intention of keeping them, but rash none the less. There was the case, for example, of the 34-year-old man who had 13 years of meritorious service as a civilian postal clerk. Letters from his former superiors, bank officers, and public officials testified both to his splendid character and unusual ability. Though his original intention was to join the Army, he was swayed by a recruiting sergeant's assurance that in the Marine Corps, as soon as his recruit training was finished, his experience would net him a rating as technical sergeant, with a specialty in postal work. So, he entered the Corps, groaned and grunted through boot training that was meant for men half his age, completed "Marine kindergarten" with a fine record, was assigned to a com-

---

[5] The March of Time camera school was a six-month course for motion picture work.

bat unit for postal work, and found himself with the rank of
. . . private first class![6]

The promises of the recruiter were worthless. First, he was
in a different and distant city. Second, he had no right to make
promises in the first place. The unfortunate postal worker, realizing intelligently that nothing could be gained by grieving
about the past, immediately turned his planning toward the future. There was a way to rectify mistakes of this kind. A letter to
the Commandant in Washington, DC, prepared in an approved
manner and sent via proper channels, might help. But in this
case, the first proper channel was a young, inexperienced legal
officer who was more impressed by rules than by the individuals
they were meant to serve. For some strange reason, which I do
not understand to this very day, the man's letter was returned,
disapproved. It was, to put the matter with discreet mildness, a
disgruntled postal clerk who came to the chaplain at this point.
The fact that other men, with less experience and fewer recom-
mendations but with better breaks, had secured their sergeant's
stripes did not help much. He regretted his enlistment, he was
sorry he had ever heard of the Marine Corps, and he did not
care, frankly, whether letters reached their destination or not.

Lest it be suspected that chaplains always solve every problem, with a Horatio Alger-type of tenacious success, let it be
said at once that this was one of many cases in which, so far as I

---

[6] It is possible that the term *Marine kindergarten* refers to basic training at
Parris Island or San Diego, CA, meaning the entry-level boot camp. Calling
it "kindergarten" may simply be a lighthearted way of saying "this is just the
beginning" and implies that Marines go on to other, more challenging schools,
including the school of battle.

know, the solution is still unachieved.[7] I cannot say whether this man will secure his advance rating or not; I do not know. But I do know that everything possible was done to make him feel that the United States Marine Corps had not been established 169 years ago for the sole and express purpose of persecuting him. Marine regulations were studied to determine that the legal officer had clearly exceeded his authority in returning the letter, then a new letter was prepared in proper form, the necessary endorsements secured, and the papers sent off to Washington. And when, shortly afterward, our postal friend was shipped overseas before an answer could be received, he left with the assurance that a chaplain back in the states would continue to watch the situation, would anxiously await the Commandant's answer, and would write to him the minute there was any news. Was this important in the building of morale? Well, suppose we let the man speak for himself. His farewell to the chaplain went something like this:

> *Sir, in this whole series of disappointments, you've really made me feel that I have a friend who is interested in what happens to me. Whether I eventually get what I know I deserve or not, I'll never be able to forget that, or to thank you enough.*

Not by any means can every case of this kind be blamed on any one person. Sometimes, men lose their individuality simply

---

[7] Horatio Alger Jr. (1832–1899) was a prolific writer of young adult novels and stories. The protagonist of a typical Alger novel was a penniless young man who caught the attention of a prosperous benefactor through a display of honesty, charity, moral strength, altruism, or gumption. Alger demonstrated how these virtuous children struggled against adversity to achieve wealth and acclaim. Many of Alger's novels were serialized in magazines for young people, and reprint editions are still published.

because of the vastness of the military machine and the many necessary complexities of operating such a machine. The speed with which some are moved about from one camp to another is often a factor in these situations. Here is one of the most noticeable differences the chaplain finds from his former work. In civilian life, people stay fairly well put. An address is an address, not a delusion. In military life, one soon learns to accept as this motto, "Here today, gone tomorrow."[8] There was, for example, the case of the man whose wife had become seriously ill shortly after his induction into the Service, leaving no one to look properly after their four young children. He wanted to put in for a dependency discharge.[9] Twice in a matter of weeks, he had gathered all the necessary papers, had seen all the right people, had secured all the required permissions, and had approached the very threshold of submitting his application. Each time, he had been moved to another camp at the crucial moment. By the time he came to me to initiate the premise a third time, some of the original papers were already outdated and had to be renewed. It is not hard for a man with such an experience to feel, after a while, that he as an individual—his worries, his problems, his fears—have been swallowed by an impersonal machine. Actually,

---

[8] The first known use of the phrase can be seen in John Calvin, *Life and Conversion of a Christian Man* (1549), and given the uncertainty of military service during the Second World War, it may refer to the fleeting nature of a person's lifespan. It may also simply refer to unpredictable transience as servicemembers trained and units deployed, often with little notice.

[9] Military regulations offer guidelines for servicemember discharge that cover the spectrum of issues from disability, mental or physical, to hardship. *Dependency hardship* refers to when the death or disability of a member of a servicemember's (or spouse's) immediate family causes that family to rely on the servicemember for principal care or support. See, for example, *Army Regulation 635-200, Active Duty Enlisted Administrative Separations* (19 December 2016) chapter 6, section 6-3.

neither the machine nor its manipulators are to blame. But the man's morale is apt to suffer nonetheless.

When, added to frequent changes of address over vast stretches of the Earth's surface, you have unavoidably rapid and frequent changes in rules, the result is apt to be something like the story Andy had to tell. He had a bachelor's degree in education, and he had fulfilled most of his requirements for his master's. For several years, he had coached and taught all major sports at a Midwestern high school, where he had turned out more than one state championship team. As raw material for Officers' Candidate School (OCS), he was from every point of view a "natural." But at the particular time of his enlistment, the quota of needed officers was amply filled, so Andy was placed in the infantry. Before he could dot his i's or cross his t's, he was overseas as a private first class.

As a member of a combat unit, Andy was promoted to corporal on what is known as an organizational warrant, which means his promotion was a temporary, localized one, and if he were to leave the outfit that had promoted him, he would automatically revert to his former rate. That, as a matter of fact, is exactly what happened sometime later when Andy was selected from the field to be returned to the states for enrollment in Officers' Candidate School. The return to private first class was not anything to worry about, however, since the former rule that only a corporal or higher could enter OCS had been relaxed. Now, if you want to see how weird the involvement of one poor individual in the machine can become, through no one's fault or malice, hold on tight and read carefully.

Andy sailed for the states on 4 August. On 18 August, 48 hours before he was to land in San Diego, the original ruling was restored; once again, only noncommissioned officers with the rank of corporal or above could be admitted to OCS. This meant that on his arrival, Private First Class Andy could no longer enter the very school for which he had been specifically returned. When his plight was called to the attention of the proper local authorities, they immediately dispatched an inquiry to the Commandant in Washington, asking for further instructions. Andy and several others in a similar predicament were kept in standby status, awaiting a reply.[10] When no answer was immediately forthcoming, and when men were needed urgently for outgoing units, there finally came a day when the anxious candidate could be held over no longer. He watched the mail earnestly, hopefully, but unsuccessfully until the very moment of his departure. Twenty-three hours after he had left, an answer came from the Commandant: he was not to blame for the change of rule while he had been in transit; he was to be given the opportunity he had earned as a candidate for commission.

Here is another of those unsatisfying cases where it is impossible to say just how successful our efforts were. All that I know for sure is that Andy never passed an opportunity to drop in at my office. He felt at home there. He knew that I was treating him as an individual personality and trying to extricate him from a hopeless, impersonal tangle of red tape. He wrote to me after his return overseas. I sent both to him and his overseas commanding officer the full particulars of the Commandant's letter, which gave him what he wanted 23 hours too late. I hope that Andy will yet be returned a second time for a crack at that commission. I would stake my reputation on an all-out prediction that he would make amply good on the opportunity. But

---

[10] *Standby* refers to a preparatory command, where the order to standby alerts a unit or servicemember that they will be receiving their marching orders.

whether he succeeds or not, I have a pretty good idea what it meant to him to have someone take this kind of personal interest in him at a time when life in the Marine Corps must have seemed to him like a Ferris wheel powered by perpetual motion.

You have followed the stories of the expert in priorities and the potentially brilliant student of Japanese, of the postal clerk, the man who needed a discharge, and of Andy, and may be now about ready to conclude that the Marine Corps is abundantly ensnared in red tape. You would be right. You would be equally right if you reached the same conclusion with respect to the Army and the Navy. In fact, men in uniform have a word for when they speak of something being *snafu*, they mean "situation normal, all fouled up."[11] But a wholesome, healthy tonic to easy criticism would be the honest questions: "Under the circumstances, could I or anyone else do better?" This is not meant to be a wholesale exoneration of military red tape any more than it should be construed as a wholesale indictment. There is undoubtedly a good amount of confusion that might have been avoided. There is some viciousness, much pettiness, and even a bit of plain, unadulterated stupidity, which is to say that the military is made up of people, and people in uniform are still people. The same qualities that characterize them in civilian life will show up in one proportion or another when they don uniforms.

But when all that has been said and acknowledged, the fact remains that under the best of circumstances, much of the red tape is unavoidable. Given a Marine Corps that grew in two and a half years from 18,000 to more than 400,000, and an Army

---

[11] First used ca. 1941, this informal U.S. military acronym is "an expression conveying the common soldier's laconic acceptance of the disorder of war and the ineptitude of their superiors." See, "snafu," Oxford English Dictionary Online.

and Navy that expanded correspondingly, the wonder is not that there is some red tape but that the machinery works at all.[12] Even with the ringside seats our generation has had from which to witness the waging of war, most of us still have pitifully little notion of what is involved in the preparation of a single action, or for that matter, the running of a single camp. My respect for the ordinary average buck private increased 300 percent the first time I tried to put back into a reasonable facsimile of an M1 Garand semiautomatic rifle the pieces I had so gleefully taken apart.[13] My understanding of the preparations necessary for battle deepened immeasurably the first time I stood on the flight deck of a carrier and watched the planes being loaded aboard. And my predisposition to become harsh and intemperate in my angry criticism of red tape in the Marine Corps has become more controlled as I have seen more of the overwhelming difficulties involved.

Indeed, precisely here is one of the significant contributions of the chaplain. The chaplain is not a miracle worker or a Mr. Fixit. A clever cartoon shows two American soldiers, obviously stationed in a more backward corner of the Earth, curiously eyeing a native medicine man crowned with a grotesque headpiece. The first doughboy is hopelessly bewildered. The second turns to him and explains, "He's sorta like our chaplain!" We chaplains decline both the compliment and the responsibility. Our tasks, vis-à-vis the heartaches of red tape, are far more modest than the cartoonist saw them. First, we can help the victim of red tape

---

[12] See LtCol Frank O. Hough (USMCR), Maj Verle E. Ludwig, and Henry I. Shaw Jr., *History of U.S. Marine Corps Operations in Word War II*, vol. 1, *Pearl Harbor to Guadalcanal* (Washington, DC: Historical Branch, G-3 Division, Headquarters Marine Corps, 1958).

[13] The term *buck private*, first used in the 1870s, refers to a private in the U.S. Army or Marines who has not attained the rank of private first class.

to see himself as a part of the much larger picture and to realize that in an undertaking so utterly, immeasurably vast, some amount of confusion is simply inevitable. The boy who can perceive that—even though he is actually in no better position than he was before—is apt to feel at least that the integrity of his own personality has been somewhat restored. Second, we can serve, if my colleagues will permit me the phrase, as a kind of military floor walker. Believe me, a camp or training station can be the seat of such cruel confusion. So many offices, so many sergeants major, so many adjutants, and so many questions that so many people cannot answer. My heart has often bled for a new draft of men as I watched their faces during the first hour in camp—masterpieces of pitiful bewilderment! The average boy, caught in a trap of confusion to begin with, has not the slightest notion where to turn for information or help. The chaplain, if he knows his way around, can be of tremendous help as a directory, showing men where to go and how to proceed in their troubles.

Third and last, the chaplain can help men understand that in time of war, the requirements of the Service itself must come before the needs and abilities of any one individual. This is one of the most difficult things to accomplish. Time and time again, men come in to show us how badly they have been miscast. This one, with years of experience as an electrician, is in the infantry. That one, who managed a successful department store in civilian life, is being taught to fire a mortar. And the explanation, plainly and simply enough, is that at this precise moment the Marine Corps, which has more men in maintenance and quartermaster's than it can possibly use, is desperately, urgently in need of more for infantry and mortars. A man can be made to see a situation of this kind either as a mean, vicious plot directed exclusively against himself or as an opportunity for individual growth and for greater service than he could ever have rendered otherwise. In the one case, he will look on himself as a martyr to the machine, and his morale will be low. In the other, he will see himself as a man serving men, and his "determination to succeed" will be great. Often—very often—the difference depends on the chaplain.

The quiet, timid unassuming fellow is usually the one most in need of the individual attention that a chaplain can give. Military life is clearly geared to the extrovert. The man who likes to be part of a crowd, who can "shoot the breeze" far into the night, who slaps backs with proficiency and zeal, seldom has trouble adjusting to life in uniform. It is the quiet kid, the one who does a lot of inward, serious thinking, the one who used to try his hand at poetry now and then—it is he who is apt to feel hopelessly bewildered and lost in a camp without a quiet corner. To him, an understanding chaplain can make all the difference in the world, especially so since the average chaplain is inclined toward being something of an introvert.

The boy with specific difficulties or fears is equally in need of personal attention. The swimming instructor at the Marine Corps base in San Diego was not to be blamed if, in the course of teaching several thousand recruits how to swim, he could not stop to inquire why Charlie absolutely refused to enter the pool. But the chaplain discovered the reason in one minute. At the age of nine, Charlie had fallen into the YMCA pool. He was pulled out with more water inside him than a little fellow was meant to have, and from that time on, he suffered from a dread, an unreasoning fear of being ducked in water. On two or three occasions at the beginning of his boot training, he had bravely tried to enter the pool, but had become violently sick. Swimming was a necessary requirement of training. What was Charlie to do?

The chaplain—or at least this particular chaplain—is the very last person in the world to give swimming lessons. But he could confer with the captain in charge of athletics and with the sergeant at the pool. He could urge them to understand the background of Charlie's terrible fear. As a result, Charlie was faithfully promised that at no point would he be forced to do anything he felt he could not do. Then he was shown—slowly, patiently, step by step—why swimming was so indispensable a part of his training, how men had died needlessly at Tarawa because they had not learned sufficiently how to swim, how his own life might one day depend on his ability to stay afloat.[14] When he was told further of others who had conquered the same fear, and was assured that he would be given individual instruction at the pool, at least half the battle had been won. Three weeks later, the young man who never could learn to swim was one of the happiest fellows at the base. He had passed his 50-yard swimming test!

Before leaving our discussion of the chaplain's work viewing men as individuals rather than numbers, one or two brief observations from the chaplain's own point of view may be helpful. In the process of bending over backward to help his people, it is easy for the padre to be imposed upon. The first thing he must do is be sure of his facts, and be sure that he recognizes and understands the real problem. Sometimes, it is possible to talk

---

[14] See Col Joseph H. Alexander (Ret), *Across the Reef: The Marine Assault of Tarawa* (Washington, DC: History and Museums Division, Headquarters Marine Corps, 1993).

to a boy at length three or four times without discovering the real burden on his mind. There was one fellow for whom I was trying to secure a transfer from one type of duty to another. I worked with him for three and a half weeks. It was only after he had gone over the hill and returned 28 days absent without leave (AWOL), that I discovered the transfer had nothing whatsoever to do with his real problem. He was either afraid or ashamed to tell me that what really bothered him was a well-grounded suspicion that his wife was being unfaithful at home. His only interest in a transfer was to get into an outfit from which it might be easier to secure a furlough to return home for a personal investigation. When he learned that his suspicions were confirmed, transfer or no transfer, back home he went to institute divorce proceedings, to take steps for the custody of his little daughter, and then to come back to camp, where he was ready and willing to take his punishment. How foolish of me to concentrate for nearly a month on a shift of duty that was only a fringe on the real problem.

I recall another man who came in one day with one request, and within 20 minutes he had laid before me a veritable catalog of complaints. His first sergeant picked on him, he could not stand the noise of rifles on the range, he had painful eczema of the hands, his wife was either pregnant or had a tumor, and the doctor at the naval hospital did not know the first thing about treating her. None of which was the real problem at all. The real difficulty was that the man was frantically afraid of going overseas. All these petty things he complained of were simply the pegs on which he had hung his situational neurosis for convenience sake. Obviously, the first step in solving a problem, is to recognize what the problem is.

There are rich rewards and high satisfactions in the work

of a chaplain. There are also heartaches and tears. One grows warmly attached to many of these youngsters in the course of time. To have them leave, to see them sail forth into no one knows what dangers or pains, then later to read their names on a report of casualties, is not easy. More than once, you feel as if these are your own sons. There are immense responsibilities too. It is frightening to realize how many men depend on you, and how little there is for you to depend on yourself. I have had high-ranking doctors, men who were outwardly calm and sure and strong, come to me on the eve of leaving for combat to admit how weak they really were, how unsteady and unsure of themselves. No honest chaplain will deny there are many moments when he needs a chaplain himself. If he is fortunate to be within the United States and to have family with him, his wife and children can be—indirectly but none the less blessedly—his chaplain. If he is overseas and they are far away . . . well, then he has himself to fall back on, himself and whatever faith he has built his life on—himself and God.

CHAPTER SEVEN
Where Do We Go from Here?

All this is essential for the making of morale: having a friend away from home; knowing someone who can help resolve your troubles, your worries, your doubts; being treated as a sacred personality, not a cog in the machine. All this is essential, but not even all this is enough. Most Americans are not professional fighters, they are civilians in uniform. Today, for the first time in its history, that is true even of the Marine Corps. And civilians in uniform, even more than professional soldiers, need to feel themselves a part of something much bigger, need to see quite clearly the goal for which they are fighting.

There is so much in military life today making a man of sensitivity feel alone in the vast universe, that anything which compels him dramatically to see himself as part of a bigger whole is good. In a somewhat superficial yet real way, the military review fits in that category. Even as a pacifist, I noted more than once with manifest discomfort, that a good military band parading down the street set my foot tapping and my spirits marching. Parades were invented by a master psychologist; of that, I am sure. And the effect of a good parade in stimulating the morale of group unity is electric. I shall never be able to forget the first

Parade and review at Camp Elliott, ca. 1944.
Louis R. Jones Collection (COLL/935), Archives Branch,
Marine Corps History Division

time I witnessed some 6,000 Marines at Camp Elliott in full battle dress, parading across the boondocks, led by a Marine band, to be reviewed by General Matthew H. Kingman. I talked to individual boys afterward to see how the review had affected them. Almost without exception, there was a perceptible increase in each one's feeling that he had been a part of something immense and thrilling.

But, this is only a beginning. There are deeper and more fundamental considerations than just the physical in which men need to see they are not alone. Right here is where one of the oldest truths of religion makes its contribution to modern wartime morale. Every faith worth existing has always insisted on the paradoxical truth that the only way for a man to make himself supremely important is to act as if he were wholly unimportant. Christianity and Judaism alike have taught that the man who forgets himself in the service of others is the man whom others can never forget. For the first 33 years of my life, I knew that because I had heard it and read it. Now, as a chaplain, I know it because I have experienced it and seen it. The prophets were altogether right. The Marine who thinks of himself least, and who concentrates on how he can serve others most, is the Marine whose morale is apt to be highest.

You could not doubt that for a single second had you been with me the night that Junior came in to say goodbye. To be sure, that is not his real name, though most of the other fellows in the Field Medical School at Camp Elliott called him that because he was only 17 years old.[1] Actually, he looked even younger than his 17 years. I have seen high school sophomores who might have passed as his older brother. It took Junior nearly seven weeks to cover his upper lip with a light, fuzzy down; then, the other boys destroyed his proudest achievement by shaving it off. All in all, Junior was just about the last kid in the world from whom you would expect much in the way of mature, reasonable thought. That is what makes my experience with him all the more memorable.

Perhaps I ought to explain, before going on, that Junior was a Navy hospital corpsman, assigned to duty with the Fleet Marine Force. Like all Navy doctors and corpsmen so assigned on the West Coast, he was sent to a Field Medical School for further training under Marine combat conditions. At the time of this incident, having completed the eight-week course in saving and preserving life under fire, he had been assigned to a replacement battalion and was about to ship out. On one of his last nights in camp, he and about nine other Marines had gathered

---

[1] For more on the Field Medical School, see Warren A. Beck and Ynez D. Hasse, "Historic California Posts, Camps, Stations and Airfields: Major Navy and Marine Corps Installations during World War II," in *Historical Atlas of California* (Norman: University of Oklahoma Press, 1975).

in my office to shoot the breeze. The conversation had ranged for an hour over every conceivable subject except the one closest to our hearts. Junior had said very little.

Suddenly, out of a clear sky, he interrupted someone else and said—I quote his awkward eloquence verbatim—"Chaplain, tell me . . . suppose a fellow feels that he wants to pray, but he's never prayed before by himself, and . . . well . . . after all . . . I'm not a chaplain, so what should I do?"[2]

I tried to explain to Junior that he did not have to be a chaplain in order to pray. I pointed out to him that every Jewish service has a time of silent meditation, so that each person could voice his own most intimate aspirations. And I assured him that whatever he had on his mind, expressed by whatever words came from his tongue, would be as acceptable to the Almighty as the most polished phrases of the most gifted poet. For a time, that seemed to satisfy him. The group conversation reverted to its former channel.

A half hour later, when the others rose to leave, Junior maneuvered himself to be the last to leave. When he and I stood alone in the room, he said, "There's one thing I want you to know, Chaplain. It isn't for myself I want to pray. I realize how much those guys out there on the islands depend on us. I want to pray that I won't crack up when they need me. I want to pray that I'll be able to use all the things they've taught me here to save lives, without getting too scared."

Though I remember every word of what Junior, in the wisdom of his 17 years, said to me, I confess I cannot recall how I

[2] The term *out of clear sky* dates back several centuries, ca. eighteenth century. This expression compares an unexpected event to a bolt of lightning from a blue sky. The expressions "out of the blue" and "a bolt from the blue" are based on a similar idea, though people often leave out either clear or blue. *Collins COBUILD Idioms Dictionary*, 3d ed. (New York: HarperCollins Publishers, 2012).

answered him, if indeed, I did. All I know for sure is that I was very proud of him then. Yes, proud that he had turned instinctively to religion in the greatest need of his life. But even prouder still that he had recognized the highest meaning of prayer and faith—a selfless devotion to others. When a youngster of 17 years can face Japanese snipers with that kind of prayer on his lips, he has come pretty close to the rock bottom that counts most in life. How many of us, who are several times 17 years, can say that the holiest hope in our hearts is: "I want to pray that I don't crack up when they need me."

I was saddened when I said goodbye to Junior. I had grown fond enough of him to miss him. But I had no worries about his morale, his "determination to succeed in the purpose for which he was trained." On the morale front, he had acquired one of the most valuable assets a man can have—an understanding that he was not an end in himself, a recognition that he, Junior, was part of something vast and historic. That night in my office, Junior had learned what the Reverend Jim Casy learned in John Steinbeck's *The Grapes of Wrath*—that no man alone really has a soul, that each one really has a small part of a greater soul, that no one of us is any good unless his little piece of soul is together with the rest.[3]

The same was even more dramatically true of the hospital corpsman one of my boys told me about shortly after he had returned from overseas combat. The scene was on a Pacific island. The time was the early stages of our first major campaign to push the Japanese westward from island to island. A group of American Marines were spending the night in foxholes, ad-

[3] John Steinbeck, *The Grapes of Wrath* (New York: Random House, 1939), 32–33. John Carradine played the scene in the award-winning film directed by John Ford (Los Angeles, CA: Twentieth Century Fox, 1940), 129 min.

vanced considerably beyond their own front lines. Their task was to serve as security, to prevent the Japanese from infiltrating during the night, and thus reaching our main positions. These boys had been cautioned that under no circumstances were they to leave their foxholes for any purpose or reason. To do so would be to invite immediate fire from their own troops, from the Japanese, or from both. What made their position even worse was the fact that they were surrounded by tall grass. In that grass were three varieties of living species: Japanese, wild pigs, and Americans. Because the slightest motion of the grass could be any one of three, every Marine was ordered to assume it was the first and to act accordingly. Hence, the utter need for every one of our boys to stay put.

The night was still young when a Japanese mortar shell struck one of our foxholes. Its lone occupant was painfully wounded. A corpsman in another foxhole some 40 or 50 yards away could tell from the low, miserable moans he heard. What was he to do? He had been warned under no circumstances to leave his own foxhole. But he also knew that over there a man was badly hurt, and he as a corpsman was in the Navy precisely for that purpose—to mend and save those who were hurt. It did not take him long to resolve the conflict. He wormed his way out of the hole and started the slowest, most painfully anxious trip of his life. It took him the better part of an hour to cross half the length of a football field. Every time he moved an inch or two, he stopped, fully expecting the crack of fire. Meanwhile, the moans of the boy who had been hit continued to guide him.

When the corpsman finally reached his destination, working purely by instinct and touch in the darkest blackness he had ever seen, he tenderly, expertly stopped the flow of blood and bound up the man's wounds. But then he could tell, from the feel of his patient's pulse and the coldness of his body, that loss of blood had left him almost too weak to live. The coolness of the night would probably kill him before the morning sun could bring its warmth. So, the corpsman disregarded his own safety once more, and like a mother animal bringing life and warmth from her own body to that of her offspring, he wrapped himself literally around the body of the wounded man, exposed himself above the foxhole's edge to enemy fire, and lay there the rest of the night, keeping his patient warm enough to live. Today, a fine young American boy is alive, only because of a corpsman's patience, courage, love, and skill.

What does all this have to do with morale? Everything! That corpsman had learned the same lesson Junior was beginning to recognize. He had been able to see himself as an important part of a still more important whole. He was not just a lonely, frightened corpsman. He and the boy who moaned, and millions of others too, were all a part of something greater and vaster than themselves. And they could go on living, only if that something greater could be saved. Otherwise, it would do them no good to live. In a sense, this is the highest morale. And the chaplain, as a teacher of religion, has an incomparable opportunity to help men build it.

Then there is still another phase of morale in its largest meaning. One of the finest ways I know of making men want to fight for democracy is to treat them democratically in the very act of fighting. In the old days, we pacifists used to base part of our unalterable opposition to war on the fact that it and democracy were incompatible. Over and over, we insisted that a military machine had to be a dictatorship, could not be democratic. And we deduced from that the high improbability of reaching the desired end of democracy via the means of military dictatorship. By and large, we were right, far more so than most of us would want to be. But there have been certain notable, even if infrequent, exceptions found in certain units and organizations, where a measure of democracy has prevailed even in the fury of battle. And it is in no sense a coincidence that in precisely those units' American morale in this war has reached an all-time high.

The mere mention of Carlson's Raiders should be enough to illustrate what I mean. If the history of this war is destined to immortalize any one unit of the American fighting forces, it will be the 600 men led by Lieutenant Colonel Evans F. Carlson. Six hundred of the finest physical specimens the Marine Corps could gather—trained to the highest peak of skill—ready for the utmost in death-defying battle. But skill, physique, and courage are not the whole story of Carlson's amazing Raiders.[4] In no small measure at all, their phenomenal success was due to the fact that they lived democracy while preparing to defend it. Officers and men wore the same clothes—lived alike, trained alike, fought alike. If there was any aristocracy in the 2d Raider Battalion, it was an aristocracy of responsibility, not one of privilege. The symbolic keynote of Carlson's philosophy of combat for democracy was that officers cannot sleep on bedding rolls while their men use ponchos. Of such small stuff is morale often made.

I remember meeting Captain Leon Goldberg of Boston, one of the real heroes of our 1944 landings on Engebi in the atoll of Eniwetok. In the 13 March 1944 issue of *Life* magazine, Richard Wilcox told how Goldberg fearlessly led his men from the beach

---

[4] For more information on Carlson's Raiders, see John Wukovits, *American Commando: Evans Carlson, His WWII Marine Raiders, and America's First Special Operations Mission* (New York: NAL Caliber, 2009). Carlson's concepts of leadership were introduced to American filmgoers in *Gung Ho!* He was played by Randolph Scott. *Gung Ho!: The Story of Carlson's Makin Island Raiders*, directed by Ray Enright (Los Angeles, CA: Walter Wanger Productions, 1943), 88 min.

Three U.S. Marines man a machine gun position near a Japanese dugout on one of the islands of Eniwetok Atoll, 18–22 February 1944. A Douglas SBD Dauntless bomber passes overhead.
National Archives and Records Administration, 513201

in a wild dash that took them far beyond the airstrip they were supposed to secure. They finally found themselves clear across the island, where they divided the Japanese forces in two, then did more than their share in mopping-up the remnants. Largely because of this one company, an island that our top military men hoped to take in 24 hours was completely captured in less than one-fourth of that time. When the mission had been accomplished, the battalion executive officer said, "Goddam it, Goldberg's trying to win the whole Pacific war with one company!"[5]

---

[5] Richard Wilcox, "Landing on Engebi: Life Staff Men Share a Moment of Danger with Assault Troops at Eniwetok's Main Base," *Life*, 13 March 1944.

Sitting in my office getting acquainted with Leon Goldberg, it was hard to account for his success, impossible to see how *Life*'s Wilcox could have called him "a ball of venomous fury."[6] He was mild-mannered, slow-speaking, almost timid-looking. In languid, almost annoyingly lazy drawl, he explained his dash across Engebi as you or I might describe a stroll to the corner store. What, then, was the secret of this man's success? What made his men follow him unquestioningly, unhesitatingly, into the grimmest of danger? My conversations with him and with others who had served with him gave me at least part of the answer. First, Leon Goldberg asked no man to do what he himself was not willing to do first. He did not *order* them to proceed across the island; he showed the way.[7] He led by the authority of example, led in such a way that others had to follow. Second, Leon Goldberg had lived with his men through 18 months of training in Samoa. By the time they went into action, he called every one of them by his first name; they called him "Goldy." In short, here was a democracy in miniature. Here was a group of men who knew that democracy was worth fighting for—knew it because they were themselves living democracy then and there. Here, therefore, was a group whose morale would ever be the best.

Along with the actual experience of democracy, as a vital factor in morale, is an apt understanding of what democracy involves. One of the saddest spectacles in the armed forces today is the appalling ignorance, shared by millions of American fighting men, of the essential meanings of democracy and the real objectives of the war. I for one would hate like blazes to stake my country's future on the definitions of democracy one would

---

[6] Wilcox, "Landing on Engebi," 24.
[7] Emphasis in original.

get in an average barracks or tent! It would not be unfair to say that by and large we have been doing a first-rate job of teaching men *how* to fight, without teaching them *for what* they fight.[8] Morale based on that mistake is at best shallow. Too many men are fighting just to kill Germans or Japanese, without realizing that they confuse means with ends.

Here is one respect in which we Americans, with a few notable exceptions, fall woefully behind our allies. The Russians, the Chinese, even the British have a much clearer understanding than our boys seem to have of the world for which they are fighting. Shortly after my outfit had reached its first overseas base, I organized a discussion group of some 15 men, who gathered weekly for an evening of talk and thought about our war aims and peace plans. We began by trying to answer the question: "Why are we fighting?" Here, so to speak, was a hand-picked group of men, a group whose very voluntary presence at such sessions indicated far more than ordinary thoughtfulness. How much greater the shock and disappointment, therefore, to hear such answers as these: "for self-preservation," "my neck or theirs," and "to kill Japanese before they can kill me."

My job with that group, and this nation's job with its soldiers and sailors at large, is to help them see that these may be good enough goals in the immediate fiery height of battle. But before the battle has been joined, and again after the din and fury are finished, "my neck or theirs" is no longer sufficient. Then men need a clear-cut understanding of what they fight against, and what they struggle toward. Then we need a picture of the new world, and a grim determination that we can and will achieve it. In the long run, nothing less than this will make morale.

---

[8] Emphasis in original.

Yet, precisely here is where we have suffered our greatest failure and potentially our most disastrous defeat. For many reasons, this is probably truer in the Marine Corps than in either the Army or Navy. For one thing, the Marine Corps has a considerably lower age group, with a lower level of political awareness. Then again, Marines are by inclination and tradition our professional fighters. The aim of the Corps is to make every man a fighter. This was true even before the Women's Reserve began to replace men in noncombat positions.[9] There has never been any such thing as a permanent clerk, for example, in the Marine Corps. Even a man assigned as clerk or assistant for the chaplain's office is subject to recall at any moment for infantry duty. It is no more than natural, therefore, in a Corps devoted so exclusively to sheer fighting skill itself, that the goals for which we fight are sometimes overlooked.[10]

But they must not be! Sheer physical strength is not enough. Brute force is but a beginning. The biggest, strongest, toughest men are often the first to crack up if we fail to give them an urgent, compelling drive. A chief who had served on one of the minesweepers that had cleared the way for our landings at Salerno, Italy, told me that they had one bully aboard their ship. In the months of preparation and training before they actually hit combat, every man in the crew suffered doubts and fears except this one. He was positive. He was sure. He was the biggest, strongest man on board. He laughed at the others in their moments of weakness and doubt. And they, while they hated and despised him, envied him too.

---

[9] See Col Mary V. Stremlow (USMCR), *Free A Marine to Fight: Women Marines in World War II* (Washington, DC: History and Museums Division, Headquarters Marine Corps, 1994).

[10] See "Our Values," Marines.com, accessed 14 November 2019.

They need not have. For when action finally came, when the Germans at last began to drop their hailstones of dynamite on a helpless little minesweeper, it was precisely he, the strong one, who cracked up so pitifully they had to tie him up and carry him below decks. We risk exactly that on a larger and more dangerous scale, if we give our men only arms and strength and force, but deny them the vision and understanding that alone can give them victory. "Not by strength and not by might, but by my spirit, saith the Lord."[11] Here is not only good religion, good faith. Here also is good fighting morale for a nation at war.

Perhaps the oddest part of this picture is that it should be so true in a Marine Corps whose Evans Carlson pointed the path so progressively. For Carlson's Raiders not only lived democracy as a regular feature of their training, but they studied the nature and meaning of democracy. They met in regular sessions to discuss the goals of the war, the social systems of other nations, the liabilities and assets of democracy at home, how to win the peace as well as the war, and half a hundred other topics of the same sort.[12] Much of what the Army and Navy have done subsequently along this line is patterned on the pioneering of Carlson. Many of us, incidentally, have not by any means given up hope that the Marine Corps too may yet give more time to this sort of thing. On more than one base or post, the chaplains especially are seeking to introduce some measure of integration or orientation into the training program.

The Army has done much more along this line. Nearly every large unit has its orientation officer, whose job it is to instruct soldiers in the meanings of the democracy they defend. Some of

---

[11] Zecharia 4:6.
[12] Wukovits, *American Commando*, 56–58.

the printed materials published for the use of these officers and their instructors border on the truly excellent.[13]

Now and again, one meets an inspired officer who is awake to the task. An Army dentist whom I know well is doing this kind of thing in Trinidad and Tobago in the Caribbean. A pharmacist's mate who used to instruct in the Field Medical School at Camp Elliott succeeded admirably. With almost every class, for example, he would use a lesson on the administration of blood plasma to point out the essential equality of all races, religions, colors, creeds and bloods.[14] Or in speaking of some great scientific discovery, he would go out of his way to emphasize how the various immigrant groups that came to America have contributed to the sum of its culture, both in science and in the arts.

Does this sort of thing pay dividends in actual combat, or is it merely the idle speculation of untested theory? My own personal conviction after watching, through the hell and fire of Iwo Jima, the very men whose morale I had sought to affect for nine months before Iwo Jima, is that we have here a fact more urgent and real than even the most sanguine of us had suspect-

---

[13] See, for example, *Digest* 1, no. 6 (May 1944); and the seven documentaries made by Army LtCol Frank Capra, *Why We Fight* (1942–45).

[14] Gen George C. Marshall, a product of his upbringing, had early concerns about African American troops and transfusing their blood to white soldiers, though he would later reverse his position. See, for example, Morris J. MacGregor Jr., *Integration of the Armed Forces, 1940–1956* (Washington, DC: Center of Military History, U.S. Army, 2001); and *"A New War Weapon to SAVE Lives": Blood Plasma—A Lesson Plan from the Education Department* (New Orleans, LA: National World War II Museum, 2017). It is worth noting that the first use of refrigerated fresh blood, rather than blood plasma, for transfusion to Marine combat casualties was during the battle of Iwo Jima. The blood was rushed across the Pacific from blood banks in the United States. See Douglas B. Kendrick, *Blood Program in World War II* (Washington, DC: Office of the Surgeon General, Medical Department, U.S. Army, 1964).

ed. During our division's first combat operation, many men excelled in unbelievable courage; of that, more in a later chapter. But there were only two who, almost every time I saw them in combat, complained bitterly that they were not being allowed to do enough or risk enough. One was Pharmacist's Mate Frank Polokoff—a member of my discussion group—who has perhaps the finest grasp of political reality of any enlisted man I have known. The other—Emanuel Hochberg—is a man closer to age 40 than 30, who understood and felt the utter urgency of world events so sharply that long, before our own country became embroiled in the conflict, he volunteered as a member of the Republican Army in Spain. Neither Polokoff nor Hochberg is a youngster, anxious for juvenile thrills. Both are married men of mature responsibilities. Both were busy on Iwo with necessary jobs. But both were dissatisfied, because they saw in sharp focus the goals for which they fought.[15]

No effort to build morale can be successful without recognizing the enormous validity of "where do we go from here?" For what are we fighting? What *is* the American way of life?[16] What kind of world, what type of society do we want? These are big questions—big and challenging. Very few fighting men will find complete answers. But the mere asking of questions, the churning of ideas, the stimulation of clear, honest thinking about goals, will be our most valuable aid in winning a war to attain those goals.

---

[15] This paragraph was originally included following the concluding paragraph of the chapter. It has been moved per the intent of the author to allow for a logical flow of ideas.
[16] Emphasis in original.

CHAPTER EIGHT

This Is It, Boys!

There has probably been more nonsense, more rubbish, more pure poppycock written about men in battle than about any other subject. The plain unvarnished and perhaps unheroic fact is that generalizations about this are at least as inaccurate as generalizations about most things. No two men react exactly the same in combat. Perhaps the closest we can come honestly to observations that apply to all or nearly all are the following instances. First, everyone fears combat. Some briefly, some from the moment they enter boot camp. Some openly, some in their own hidden hearts. Some deny it, some more honestly confess it. But *all* fear it.[1]

Second, large numbers of men seem to suffer almost from temporary amnesia during the immediate, intense fury of battle itself. The writers of scenarios and scripts have made much of the frontline soldier who is charged to a new height of military efficiency by visions of home and loved ones. Beautiful, but at least in a considerable number of cases, it just does not work that way. Most men faced with death and destruction forget

---

[1] Emphasis in original.

A Marine relieves another on the beach at Saipan as they crawl under enemy
fire to their assigned positions, June 1944.
Official U.S. Marine Corps photo

everything—home, wives, children, parents, even selves—forget
everything except the one desperately immediate task of killing
the enemy before he kills you. Gaining 50 yards here becomes
the whole aim of life. Knocking out one pillbox there is for the
moment the complete object of living. For an urgent hour or
day, nothing else matters, nothing further counts.

Third, the hours just before attack are probably the most
frightful any man could experience; hence, they are necessarily
the hours when a chaplain is needed most. In a sense, everything
the chaplain has done before to build morale is aimed at this—
an increase in men's determination to succeed at the approach
of zero hour. And so, on the carrier before the planes take off,
in the briefing room after the pilots have received their final

instructions, on the hushed, darkened transport just before men start going over the sides, the padre faces his grimmest and gravest challenge. Himself frightened, himself facing the same dread dangers as they, the chaplain must give his men the spiritual rations that will see them through whatever is in store for them.

Of what are men most afraid just before facing the enemy? The best, briefest answer I have seen to that question was written by a Marine lieutenant who was fated shortly to give his own life on the bloody beaches of Saipan in the Northern Mariana Islands. A few days before boarding the transport that was to take him on the longest journey of his life, he wrote me this: "I do believe that the fear of death does not bother men so much as the thought that perhaps they shall never again be able to see the people and things they love, and do the things they enjoy."

What can the honest chaplain offer to men with fears like these? When they need him most, and he feels the weakest. What can he say? Instead of beating about many bushes and talking *about* the subject but not directly *on* it, let me give you here, for better or for worse, an actual precombat sermon much as I have given it more than once to men who were facing combat.[2] In cold, printed words, it cannot be the same as when spoken to a group of men who surcharge the very air they breathe with tenseness and strain. If you can picture such a group, can somehow sense the desperate, longing needs of their minds and hearts, here is what one chaplain would say to them:

> Men, this isn't going to be a sermon, at least not in the usually accepted meaning of the word. For one thing, I'm going to talk now much more briefly and rapidly than most of you are accustomed to hearing

---

[2] Emphasis in original.

me. This isn't the time for lengthy talks of any kind. We stand much too close to combat to indulge in the luxury of length. This is a time for brief, crisp instructions, followed by immediate, snappy action. I'm going to try, therefore, to keep my words tonight appropriate for the occasion.

Furthermore, I propose to be just as practical as I know how. Your line officers wouldn't think of sending you into action, as they will very shortly, without giving you in advance the weapons and ammunition you'll need for military success. But there's another kind of weapon, a second type of ammunition, that you're apt to need just as badly as the first. I mean the kind of weapon that can keep you going when you think you've reached the end of your rope. That's the kind of preparation I want to give you tonight. And by way of giving it, there are four things I'm anxious to say.

First, in the difficult days that lie ahead of us, wherever you are, however you feel, don't forget one of your most valuable weapons, your Jewish religious services. The United States Marine Corps thinks religion is important enough in actual combat that it sends a considerable number of chaplains, one of them a Jewish chaplain, with each and every division. As far as may be humanly possible, I promise you that even in combat I shall get around to see as many of you as I can. But don't wait for me. Every one of you has a small Jewish prayer book of his own. Use it. When the Sabbath comes, and if your military position permits, get together with or without me. Meet wherever you can. Meet in groups of 10, or 5, or 2. If necessary, pray just by yourself. But the important thing is: pray! Don't deny strength and hope that can come from joining your fellow Jews in the division and throughout the world in Sabbath worship!

And don't think for a single foolish moment that I'm speaking just theory. I know of Jewish men in American Samoa who, without even having a chaplain, used to walk or hitchhike as far as 20 miles each way to join in weekly prayer. I know of men who never even knew the meaning of prayer before, who have told me that prayer was the only thing that kept them going in some foxhole when they thought they were finished. I know a doctor in the Marine Corps who attended one of my services stateside the night before he sailed into combat, and who later wrote me this: "I can't tell you how much solace and peace of mind my few hours with you meant to me. It's difficult putting into words the feeling one experiences the eve of departure for places and experiences unknown, and not without their dangers: . . . I felt as though something substantial had replaced that unknown void." Men, my first weapon for you tonight is to learn from the experience of others, to take advantage of the same strength they've known.

My second suggestion is, I think, equally practical. As you go from this base into combat, don't ever be ashamed to admit to yourself that you're afraid. Any man of any rank who tells you he isn't afraid of combat is either a liar or a fool. I've talked to some of the real heroes of this war, to Captain Leon Goldberg, for example, whose work on Eniwetok with the 22d Marines was so heroic and outstanding that Life magazine saw fit to give a whole column to the story of his deeds. Life's correspondent called Captain Goldberg in combat "a ball of venomous fury." But Leon Goldberg wasn't ashamed to admit to me that on the assault transport and in the landing craft he was anything but "a ball, of venomous fury."[3] He was, as he put it himself, "scared stiff." Don't you be ashamed to admit that either. The first way to fight fear is to acknowledge it!

The second way is to realize that every one of us has a reserve of courage and strength that he usually doesn't even suspect in himself. Not just Leon Goldberg, but every man I've ever talked to who had been in combat, said the same thing. No matter how frightened he was in advance, no matter how worried about his probable behavior under fire, when the important moment came, he was somehow stronger than he dared even hope to be. You and I have such reserves of strength in us too. You can call that strength God, as I do. You can give it any other name you like. The important thing is, it's there. And when you need it most, it will help you!

Weapon number three tonight is a simple statement, and perhaps for that very reason unmistakably true. You can be the most important

---

[3] Wilcox, "Landing on Engebi."

THIS IS IT, BOYS!

man in this division!⁴ I'm not exaggerating now, and I'm not talking to some group far away from here. I'm speaking directly and only to you fellows who are gathered here with me. You, you, you, and you can be, in all literal fact, the most important man in this division, barring none! I know there have been times when you've felt yourself lost—a tiny, insignificant cog in a tremendous, overpowering machine. There have been times when it didn't seem to make much difference whether you did your job or just doped off. If you've felt that way before, men, don't make the mistake of thinking that it's true now. Any one of you, without exception, may find himself in the next 24 or 48 or 72 hours in a position where the fate of a company, the lives of a battalion, the success of a campaign might well depend on you.

Does any man here think I'm exaggerating? The history of this war is proof that I'm not. Every one of you knows now the classic story of General Mark Clark's secret landing on the coast of North Africa, to make final plans and preparations for the first of our great amphibious operations in the European theater.⁵ I doubt whether any man in history has ever faced a more unnerving strain. Suppose General Clark—one man—had lost his nerve? Suppose he had weakened. Suppose he had turned back when

---

⁴ Emphasis in original.
⁵ Capt Godfrey B. Courtney, "General Clark's Secret Mission," *Life*, 28 December 1942.

going forward was what we needed? You know the answer as well as I. We might never have landed troops in North Africa. We might even have lost the war! At the very least, our final victory would certainly have been delayed by months, if not years. All because of one man!

Someone here is thinking to himself: "Sure, but he was a general. Do you expect us to be generals?" The answer is: "No. I just expect you to be men!" Mark Clark succeeded, not primarily because he is a general, but because long before he pinned stars to his shoulders, he was a man. And other men without stars have proved equally that you can be top man in this outfit. On Guadalcanal, at a moment when the final outcome swayed so uncertainly in the balance that it still makes my blood run cold to think of it, a Marine mortar outfit somehow lost contact with its command post. There was urgent need for mortar fire immediately on a specific target. Nothing else could save the situation. The entire campaign might well depend on getting word at once to a mortar outfit that was "lost."

At that exact moment a boy younger than many of you, an enlisted man, as a matter of fact not even a signal man, remembered that years before as a Boy Scout he had studied signaling. Quickly, he made himself flags with whatever crude material was available. Unhesitatingly, he stepped out, fully exposed to enemy observation and fire, and began to wave his flags in a pattern that had meaning. He was hit. He lost consciousness, but not before he got his message through. . . . When that boy huddled on a transport the night before he hit the beach, just as we're doing now, he had no thought or expectation that he would be the most important person in his outfit. But that's exactly what he became! Without his brave, inspiring courage, God, alone knows when we would have secured the island or won the war.

Do you want one more example to prove that even the least of you has a hidden reserve of strength that can make him the most important Marine in our division? All right, let me give it to you in words written to me by one of my closest young friends from my civilian congregation back home, Lieutenant David H. Hornstein.[6] Lying on a hospital bed in France, after an Army surgeon excavated pieces of shrapnel from his body, David wrote me this:

> I'm here now only because one of my men
> (according to our peacetime standards we
> might have called him lazy, immoral and
> no-account) crawled over open ground
> covered by enemy fire to where I had
> crawled behind a stump, and cut away my
> clothes and bandaged my wounds. He had
> just finished bandaging me when they shot
> him dead, right between the eyes, and he
> dropped with his head on my thigh. I lay

---

[6] U.S. Army Lt David H. Hornstein of Rockville Center, NY, was later killed on 28 November 1944 by a sniper's bullet in the Vosges Mountains of France as he was rejoining his unit with the 315th Infantry Regiment of the 79th Infantry Division.

for 45 minutes until it was dark enough for me to crawl behind cover where the medics could get to me. I owe my life to that man. He didn't believe in what I did, nor were his standards the same as mine, but when the cards were down he came through. He must have thought something of me, for he was a rifleman and didn't have to come to me; it wasn't his job. He just yelled, "The lieutenant's hit pretty badly," and crawled over. Three minutes later, he was dead, having given his life for mine. I hope it wasn't an unworthy sacrifice.

Did you hear the initial description of that man—lazy, immoral, and no-account? But when the cards were down, he came through! Tomorrow, men, the cards may be down for one of you. Come through! Come through the way I know you can. Your life—all our lives, a battle, an invasion, a whole campaign—might depend on that. You can be the most important man in this outfit.

And now we have just a moment or two for the fourth and last thing I want to say tonight. As we go from here into combat, men, we become members of the most honorable fraternity on Earth, the fraternity of those who have suffered and sacrificed so that humanity could move forward instead of backward. From the days of our ancient Jewish prophets through the lives of countless rabbis who became martyrs for kiddush

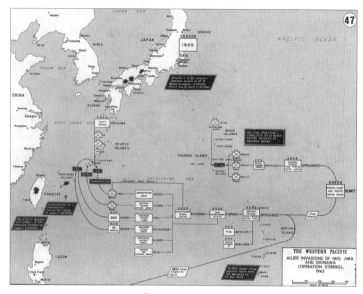

Map of Iwo Jima landing, 1945.
Thayer Soule Collection (COLL/2266) at the Archives Branch,
Marine Corps History Division

hashem *(sanctification of God's name), and from*
Socrates who died for his devotion to truth to the
people of Lidice who died for our right to be free,
humanity never gained liberty for either body or
soul without someone suffering for that liberty.[7]
Tonight, you and I become members of that frater-
nity. Tonight, we become one with the brave un-
dergrounds of Europe, with Yugoslavia's Josip Broz

---

[7] *Kiddush hashem* refers to a religious or moral act that causes others to rev-
erence God, especially religious martyrdom in times of persecution, derived
from rabbinic expositions on Leviticus 19:2 and 22:32. For Socrates, see Plato,
"The Apology of Socrates," trans. Benjamin Jowett, adapt. Miriam Carlisle et
al., Internet Classics Archive, 2004.

Landing ship, tanks (LSTs) arriving at Iwo Jima, February 1945.
*Thayer Soule Collection (COLL/2266) at the Archives Branch,
Marine Corps History Division*

*Tito and French General Charles de Gaulle, with
the staunch, strong people of London and Moscow,
with the Jews of Palestine who helped save Suez
and North Africa. No higher honor will ever come
to any of us.*

*As we go forth to battle, let's not forget that,
men. Thank God, we're able to contribute our
share without the heartbreaking worries so many
others have had. We know that our wives, our children, our parents, our sweethearts are safe, that no
enemy can touch them. We know where they are,
and how they are. And we know that final victory
for them and for us is very near at hand.*

Go out there and do your job! You're an expert

at it. There isn't a man in the world better trained to do your job than you. You've done it perfectly a hundred times already. You know it, forward and backward. You've been trained to do it with your eyes closed. Go out there now, and do it with your eyes open.

I want to close tonight with a story that is told about one of our Hasidic rabbis. A disciple came to him and said: "Rabbi, I've been searching everywhere for the Messiah, but haven't found him. When will the Messiah come to usher in the day of perfect happiness and peace?" "The Messiah will not come as you expect him to at all," answered the rabbi. "There is a little spark of the Messiah in every human being. When all of us unite, when each one uses his little bit of Messiah together with everyone else's, then and only then will perfect peace be secured."[8]

Men, you and I have—each one of us—a spark of Messiah within ourselves. This is our chance to use it. This is our chance to act as if the whole of future civilization depended on us alone. Let's use this chance, and use it well! Ye'varechecha Adonai v'yishmerecha; May the Lord bless you and keep you. Ya'er Adonai panav eleicha v'ichunecha; May the Lord let his countenance shine upon you, and be gracious unto you. Yisa Adonai panav eleicha veyasem lecha shalom;

---

[8] Charles M. Leaming, *The Key to Fulfillment of Bible Prophecy* (London: Tate Publishing, 2006), 42.

*May the Lord lift up his countenance upon you,
and give you the gifts you need—the gift of courage, the gift of strength, the gift of peace.*

Amen.[9]

---

[9] The Priestly Benediction: Numbers 6:24–6:26.

CHAPTER NINE

Dear Son . . .

Civilians too have problems of morale, especially civilians whose sons or husbands are in the armed forces. To suppose for one foolish moment that because the chaplain is in uniform while they remain in *mufti*, therefore the strengthening of their morale on the home front is no concern of his, would be a gross miscalculation.[1] Every chaplain spends no small proportion of his time making contacts and writing letters that are aimed primarily at the home front. He does this, first, because no worry or problem of any human being can be foreign to him, and second, because he necessarily understands the very direct and immediate relationship between the morale of Private First Class Johnny Jones in Company C, and the morale of Jones's mother or wife back in Indiana. I think my colleagues would for the most part agree with me that worries about home—real or imagined—rate among the very foremost of causes for poor morale in the military.

---

[1] The term *mufti* typically refers to plain clothes worn by a person who usually wears a uniform; but in this case, it refers to those on the home front in civilian clothes.

If these pages have half succeeded in telling the story I have wanted them to, that should be clear already beyond doubt.

A letter sent to me one day by a civilian rabbi whom I know is a perfect illustration of how the spirit of those at home affects morale among our fighting forces. The letter asked whether I could arrange an emergency furlough for a member of the writer's congregation who was then under my jurisdiction. There was a serious family situation at home requiring the man's immediate and personal attention. I interviewed the man himself, asked the American Red Cross to investigate the home side of the case, and came up finally with this picture. Cause: a nervous, anxious wife, who had failed to adjust to the unpleasant but inescapable reality that her husband had to leave her for military service. Whenever she felt lonely, or wherever there was a serious problem facing her, she felt herself utterly broken and lost. She just could not carry on. At frequent intervals, she would telephone her husband long distance and complain to him in tears about her plight. Consequences: a Marine whose eyes and voice and hands all testified too eloquently to the low state of his morale. Determination to succeed? After one of those calls from his wife, I doubt if he had left even the determination to live! Here was a problem that clearly had to be tackled on the home front. Both the civilian rabbi and the girl's relatives had to be called on for help. No chaplain, or better yet, no chaplain's spouse, whose own home and family life have been temporarily broken by war could fail to feel the utmost sympathy for that poor girl. Notwithstanding, she had to be shown unmistakably how unfair her behavior was. Her husband's task would be difficult enough even if each of them shared a proper portion of it. For her to evade her own share, and thus to increase his, would break him completely.

Another and an all-too-frequent instance of the intimate connection between a man's morale and his family's may be found in the many types of foolish letters that people at home send to men and boys in the Service. How many heartbreaking times does a conference in the chaplain's office begin with a man walking in and barely damming a flood of tears as he throws a letter down on the desk and says, "Chaplain, read this!" What the chaplain reads may be the stupid accusation of a jealous sister that the man's wife was seen walking down the street with a fellow. Or the unjustified complaint of a mother that his wife is not treating the children the way she should. Or a series of silly reports about colds and running noses and stomach aches and a whole host of minor ailments nine-tenths of which were cured and forgotten before the letter was even postmarked. Chaplain William A. Maguire with whom I served for nine pleasant months in San Diego, never faced a civilian audience without emphasizing the importance not only of writing, but of sending the *right kind* of letters to men in uniform.[2]

It would be hard to imagine a more startling example of this than the mother who wrote to her Marine son that his father had not been well, that one side of his face had been badly swollen for weeks, that the doctor was sending him to the hospital for X-rays, and that she was afraid they might show cancer of

---

[2] Emphasis in original. Capt William A. Maguire received his bachelor's degree from Seton Hall University in 1910 and master's from Catholic University in 1911. In 1915, he completed his theological studies at University of Lovain (Belgium) and was ordained a Roman Catholic priest on 15 July 1915. He entered the U.S. Navy as a chaplain on 17 July 1917. During World War I, as a lieutenant and the chaplain aboard USS *Christabel* (SP 162), he received the Navy Cross for heroism on 17 April 1918. Chaplain Maguire was present at Pearl Harbor aboard the USS *California* (BB 44) the day the Japanese attacked. See Donald F. Crosby, "Catholic Chaplains under Fire: Pearl Harbor, a Half-century Later," *Crisis*, 1 March 1992.

the face. There were two things obviously wrong with such a letter. First, the doctor had said no such thing; the mother was advancing her own amateur diagnosis not his. Second, even if he had, there was certainly no need *before* the diagnosis was confirmed, and probably no justification even *after*, to forward such alarming information as this to her son.[3] Even if the worst of her fears were confirmed, what on Earth could he do about it except worry himself insane? To make matters worse, for several days after receiving her first letter, the boy received no mail at all. Finally, we asked the local American Red Cross to check. They did. The father's face was not swollen anymore. The doctor had discovered it was a simple case of gland trouble and had administered the proper treatment, whereupon the swelling had subsided. Believe me, it took much longer for the shock and worry created in the boy's mind to subside. Many times a month, the average chaplain faces problems that differ from this in degree rather than kind.

How can he help in such cases? In two ways. First, by writing at once to the offending parent or wife, explaining politely but firmly, diplomatically but unmistakably, what they are doing to their son or husband. Second, by inviting them, if they do have genuine worries, to share them with the chaplain, to call on him for help, and if there is unfortunate news that simply must be brought to the man himself, to allow the chaplain to bring it at the proper time in the least painful manner.

I would not, for a single instant—because of the particular cases with which this chapter has been opened—want to leave the impression that such problems as these are always imagined or that the folks at home are in every case to be blamed. Quite

---

[3] Emphasis in original.

the contrary! Their worries are often real; their troubles are frequently heartbreaking; their need for help is apt to be desperate. One of several ways in which the chaplain can often help them is by serving as an interpreter between them and the military. Anyone who doubts that the American people are deeply and inherently a nation of peace lovers, not militarists, need only read an average week's mail from home in the chaplain's office. By and large, as a people, civilians in America do not even speak the same language as the military. Before the war, unbelievable numbers of Americans did not know the difference between a captain and major. Even now, life in the Army, Navy, or Marine Corps is an esoteric secret to anxious parents and wives at home. No wonder they cannot understand some of the things that happen.

The chaplain can help them understand. When a worried mother wants to know why her son, whose predental course at college was interrupted by greetings from the president, cannot indirectly continue this training by serving as a dental corpsman in the Navy, the chaplain can explain.[4] He can explain in terms of the Navy's overall needs at the moment and in terms of her son's most effective immediate contribution toward winning the war. When a misunderstanding parent berates an innocent Navy corpsman son for volunteering to serve in the Marine Corps or asking to be placed in an overseas unit, the chaplain can in the one case explain that the boy did not volunteer but was chosen, or if the facts are correct, can help the parent real-

[4] During the Second World War, those drafted for military service received an order from the president, which began "Greetings!" The order designated when and where the individual would report for service. See "Order to Report for Induction," National Museum of American History, Smithsonian, accessed 30 December 2019. For more on how the draft worked, see Carl Zebrowski, "Your Number's Up," *America in World War II*, December 2007.

ize that such conduct in the midst of war merits praise rather than blame. When a mother who is ill—not critically so—scolds her Marine son by mail because he has made no effort to come home to see her, while his Army brother has, the chaplain can advise her that there may be many reasons for such discrepancies. One boy may be closer to home. He may be at the moment in a casual status, where his training is completed and his next duty not yet assigned. His brother, on the other hand, may be in the midst of an urgent training schedule, in a most essential type of duty, or in a replacement battalion that is on the verge of sailing. The fault, in any case, is most certainly not his. In short, the chaplain, who in most cases as a civilian in uniform is suspended somewhere between the dual worlds of the military and the civilian, can help interpret each to the other, thereby strengthening morale at home on which morale at the front so largely depends.

Most cases of this kind involve parents whose only crimes are great love for their boys and equally great ignorance of what a military machine is or how it runs. Occasionally, however, one comes across a mother or father who never means maybe.[5] I will never forget the pampered boy who was explaining to me that he had been assigned to a type of duty for which he did not consider himself particularly well suited. When all other arguments had failed, his pièce de résistance, in manner and voice quite stern, was: "My mother won't like that at all!" Or the mother who walked into our offices late one afternoon and announced with vocal trumpets that she had come in person from Kentucky to San Diego to tell the general that he was not treating her boy right! Or the foolish mother who, when her son got into

---

[5] Today, these parents would likely be considered *helicopter parents*, or overly involved in the life of their child.

a series of scrapes clearly his own fault, wrote an angry, impassioned letter to his general, insisting that the Marine Corps be run *her* way.[6] But these cases, however amusing, are fortunately not typical.

Far more usual is the instance in which simple, good, decent, kindly people just do not know what it is all about. For example, the young newly married wife of 17, who had lost faith in her husband and had written that she wanted a divorce, because he had promised to make out an allotment in her favor, but 10 days had passed, no money had come, so she was sure he had lied. Where apparently his word might not be accepted, the chaplain could be presumed to be speaking the truth when he wrote, explaining something of the machinery for setting up allotments and the necessary delay of several weeks between application and check. One cannot resist the temptation of wondering, incidentally, how long such war marriages will last, based as they too often are on no more substantial confidence than that. Will there always be a chaplain handy to patch things up?

Needless to say, there are worries and problems at home that go far beyond mere misunderstandings. Some parents have not received mail from their son for weeks. He may have been off on maneuvers, he may be on his way into combat, or, sad to relate, he may have been just plain neglectful. A chaplain feels quite at home as a booster for consciences.

One of the cruelest things about war is the way it breeds gossip and rumor—what we in the Navy call scuttlebutt.[7] Short-

---

[6] Emphasis in original.

[7] The term *scuttlebutt* comes from a combination of "scuttle"—to make a hole in the ship's hull and causing it to sink—and "butt"—a cask used in the days of wooden ships to hold drinking water. Originating circa the 1800s, the nautical term is said to come from the sailors' custom of gathering around the scuttlebutt to gossip.

The 4th and 5th Marine Divisions move inland, Iwo Jima, 1945.
*Thayer Soule Collection (COLL/2266) at the Archives Branch,
Marine Corps History Division*

ly after he had left the states, my friend Chaplain Leon W.
Rosenberg of the 4th Marine Division was reputed to have been
stabbed to death by a Japanese prisoner.[8] The story was told by
so many people, in such great detail, that few dared to disbelieve
it. I happened to be one of the few. Because I knew that sooner
or later the scuttlebutt would reach Rosenberg's wife and baby
in New York, I set about to ascertain the truth, via the most
direct route I knew: a letter to the alleged victim himself. As I

[8] While the story may have been false, Rosenberg was in fact wounded on Ti-
nian during the course of his service. He was 1 of 46 Navy chaplains awarded
the Purple Heart for action during World War II. See Clifford M. Drury, *The
History of the Chaplain Corps, United States Navy*, vol. 2, *1939–1949* (Washington,
DC: Bureau of Naval Personnel, 1948), 159.

suspected, the story from beginning to end was sheer fantasy. At the time of the alleged stabbing, Rosenberg had not yet left the three-mile limit, had not even seen a Japanese prisoner.

Unfortunately, this sort of thing happens all too frequently. War breeds rumors just as stagnant water breeds mosquitoes. The more anxious and unsettled men's minds become, the more gullibly do they grasp at even the most improbable and fantastic rumors. I know one wife of a Navy doctor who has heard, at various times in the past three years, that her husband was shot, that he was imprisoned, and that he went down with his ship. As I write, the three-time "victim" is on shore hospital duty, living in San Diego. Such is the miserably unkind but, I suppose, inevitable scuttlebutt bred by war. The chaplain can do several things to help immunize parents and wives against this sort of thing. He can caution them in general not to let their excited imaginations and tattered nerves run away with them; he can answer any specific inquiries they may have; and he can investigate the facts and tell them the true status and condition of their loved one.

But there are problems of homefront morale more real and puzzling even than these. For example, the case of the Marine who had succeeded in enlisting before even his 16th birthday. He had been so desperately anxious to play his part in the war that he had managed to secure a false birth certificate, and had come into the Corps under an assumed name. In the course of time, his frantic parents discovered his whereabouts. By then, he had completed his boot camp training and was one of the happiest Marines I have ever seen. Regularly, at least once a week, he came to my office to repeat how very much he loved life in the Marine Corps. And regularly, at even more frequent intervals, came urgent letters to me from his mother, pleading tearfully that I do something to get him released. Let no one who has not faced such a conflict suppose that it was simple or easy situation to handle! Both the boy and his parents had well-defined rights.[9] The chaplain could not ignore the claims of either. Yet, here was a situation in which clearly either parents or boy would have to be bitterly disappointed. Since a discharge would in any event be impossible unless the boy specifically requested one, and since despite numerous letters from home and many talks with the chaplain, he fully intended not to make any such request, that way out was firmly closed. The parents would have to be won over. The only purpose to be served by repeated protests from them would be a decrease in their boy's morale. An easy task? Indeed not. A simple decision for the chaplain to make? Far from it! You may be sure that more than once he lay awake at night, wondering if he had done the right thing, trying to put himself as a parent in the place of these other parents. There are times when every chaplain is tempted to pray for a portion of King Solomon's wisdom.

In other situations, it is easier to perceive more specific and immediate results in the building of civilian morale. One morning when I was still stationed some 12 miles outside San Diego, a nurse, the wife of a Marine officer, phoned me from the city. She sounded most urgent, and wanted to know whether I could see her immediately if she took the next bus to camp. For the next hour, I wondered again and again what serious problem was bringing her out. When she finally arrived and introduced herself, my curiosity was even greater for apparently her only

---

[9] For more on underage enlistment, see Joshua Pollarine, "Children at War: Underage Americans Illegally Fighting the Second World War" (master's diss., University of Montana, 2008).

need was one that could have been handled as well over the phone. Her husband had shipped out early that same morning. She would be leaving by car in a few days for Oregon, and she wanted to know how she might contact prospective passengers to ride with her. I wondered why the tone of urgency, why the uncomfortable bus ride of 12 miles for that? Then I realized, as she sat before me talking, that this practical problem was only an introduction, an excuse, if you will. She was a nurse who had specialized in the psychiatric care of children, a girl of both cultural and spiritual distinction. Her husband too was a psychologist; his preparations for a graduate degree in that field had been interrupted by war. They loved one other deeply, and obviously had a great deal in common. Every minute of their married life had been a thrilling adventure in companionship. There just were not enough hours in the day or days in the week for the two of them to share all the interests they had together. And now, he had gone. The moment they had dreaded—refused to accept as real—was here. She felt the horrible emptiness of being alone. And she needed someone who could listen wisely and understand sympathetically.

When she left, after an hour and a half of conversation, I found myself evaluating our talk. Why did she need a chaplain? Why had she turned instinctively to a man she never saw before, rather than to one of the many friends they had made in San Diego? I think I knew the answer. Only a man whose background was religion, but who also wore the uniform of her husband, could help her. Only one who knew the empty loneliness of her heart, because one day soon he would feel the same hollowness within himself, could give her reassurance and strength. I would not have had the moral right to face her, and to say the things I did, if I had not stood ready to experience the same thing myself. Here, if anywhere, lies the greatest asset and largest opportunity of the chaplain above all others, in maintaining the morale of civilians whose dear ones have left them.

There is an almost irresistible urge to go on like this endlessly, to describe case after case in which the chaplain and only the chaplain could offer badly needed help on the home front. One more case at least deserves to be included before we turn to another type of aid to those at home. For a period of several weeks, I was bombarded by letters from the parents and uncles of an exceptionally fine boy who was in my camp. Even the first letter convinced me that their worry was legitimate. In brief, they had had a son older than this one. About a year or two before, their first born had died, directly or indirectly a result of suffering from dementia praecox.[10] No one could blame them for being more than normally apprehensive about the second boy, who had been very close to his brother. The immediate cause of their letters to me was the fact that on his last furlough they noticed—or thought they noticed—that he was melancholy, introverted, not at all his old self. What to do was beyond them. With the ghastly memory of their older son still painfully fresh, they dreaded the fear that this boy might not be

---

[10] The influential German psychiatrist Emil Kraepelin (1856–1926) considered dementia praecox and manic depression two different forms of psychosis. Kraepelin considered dementia praecox, which is now known as schizophrenia, as a biological illness caused by anatomical or toxic processes. To Kraepelin, schizophrenia was a progressive neurodegenerative disease, which automatically resulted in irreversible loss of cognitive functions. In contrast, manic depression was an episodic disorder, which does not lead to permanently impaired brain function. In 1911, Swiss psychiatrist Eugen Bleuler redefined Kraepelin's idea of dementia praecox as schizophrenia. See H. E. Lehmann and T. A. Ban, "The History of the Psychopharmacology of Schizophrenia," *Canadian Journal of Psychiatry* 42, no. 2 (March 1997): 152–62, https://doi.org/https://doi.org/10.1177/070674379704200205.

mentally strong enough to withstand the strains and shocks of imminent combat. Still, there was always the possibility, which they recognized themselves, that their fears were unjustified, and to create unwarranted doubts in the mind of the boy himself might be as dangerous as to ignore the matter altogether. The chaplain was the only one to whom they could turn their aching, anxious hearts.

I had several long talks with the boy, without revealing directly my primary purpose. I was convinced for myself that he was normal, that he liked the Marine Corps and wanted to stay in it. I maneuvered also for a psychiatrist to meet and speak to the boy informally, without his knowing the whys and wherefores of the "coincidental" meeting. I also consulted one of the boy's uncles, who happened to live about 500 miles from camp, and shared my tentative conclusions with him. The net result of all this was a long letter to the parents in New York, explaining in detail all that had been done, assuring them that from all the available evidence, and in the unanimous opinion of all three of us, the boy was normal and their fears ungrounded. No parent will need persuasion that here was a major contribution to civilian morale.

One more kind of help that can be given to families at home is in the sad but inevitable case of tragedy affecting the serviceman. That letters of condolence from chaplains, in cases of men killed in action, can be a very real help to the survivors should need no proof. Though the chaplain may feel a woeful sense of inadequacy in such instances, somehow whatever words of comfort he is able to write down mean a very great deal to the bereaved. They are particularly anxious to learn from the chaplain any and all details concerning the manner of their loved one's death, where he is buried, and the nature of the funeral or memorial service. Along with whatever such details there may be, it is also my own practice to send them a copy of the special prayer read as part of the service.

But not all such occasions are the results of combat action. Tragedy is no respecter of convenience; it often strikes at the very worst possible time. A young Jewish captain in the Marine Corps sailed from the states about two months after his marriage. His wife remained behind for a few days with relatives in San Diego before proceeding to their home in Chicago. If I recall correctly, she was 20 or 21 years old. She arrived at the home of cousins about 2000 one evening, sat and talked with them until nearly midnight, retired without even unpacking her bags, and the next morning was found dead in bed! Her newlywed husband was two days off the coast, on a troop transport headed west. That the chaplain in San Diego could have a radio dispatch sent to the man and to the Jewish chaplain who was with him, and that the latter could do his best to soften the painful blow, is not the immediate point of relating the story. Perhaps of equal importance is the fact that the cousins in San Diego as well as the parents in Chicago had someone on hand who could handle for them the many practical problems pertaining to shipping the body and effects back East, and who could offer them whatever comfort and consolation might be possible in their unspeakable, almost unbearable grief.

Sometimes the true stories reaching a chaplain beggar description and more than challenge fiction. I have found myself more than once in the midst of a very real situation that, before my military experience, I might well have attributed to the excessively fertile imagination of some novelist. There comes to my mind now one of the most uncomfortable afternoons of my life. I was stationed still at Camp Elliott. We had experienced a

pitifully tragic accident the night before. A battalion in training was out on an amphibious landing operation. The surf was
heavy. Something went wrong with one of the landing craft.
Twenty or 30 men were catapulted into the surging sea before
they were close enough to reach the shore easily. Most of them
made the grade, but two drowned, their bodies washed out to
sea.[11] With the awful shadow of that horror still weighing freshly
on my mind and heart, the very next afternoon I received a telegram addressed to one of the boys drowned the night before. It
was from his fiancée in Chicago. Briefly, it informed him that
she was leaving Chicago that very day, would be in San Diego
the following Saturday, and wanted him to have a minister or
chaplain ready, since she was coming for the express purpose
of marrying him. The young lady's evident and understandable
happiness practically shone on the inanimate yellow blank. And
the dread knowledge of what lay in store for her filled my heart
with what must have been the coldest heaviness I have ever felt.
For several moments, I felt as if my emotions had been para-
lyzed and my will frozen. What could I do—what could anyone
do for that poor girl?

Little enough, indeed. But at least something. First, we tried
to reach her home in Chicago. By the time we had pieced together bits of information found among the boy's personal effects,
had ascertained her address and waited nervously for the call to
clear, we reached her sister 30 minutes after her train had left
the Chicago station. For her, 2,500 miles stretched between the
highest happiness she had ever known and the deepest, dark-

---

[11] For more information, see "Casualties: US Navy and Marine Corps Personnel Killed and Injured in Selected Accidents and Other Incidents Not Directly
the Result of Enemy Action," Naval History and Heritage Command, 2 October 2019.

est doom of her life. I stared at her picture, a snapshot found in her sweetheart's wallet. I wondered: What kind of person is she? What wonderful hopes does she carry across the continent? Where and how can any human being find the strength to tell her what the sea has just done to those hopes?

Our first inclination among the chaplains was to have one of us, accompanied if possible by an understanding woman, meet the girl at the train on Saturday. My wife volunteered to help. Then we realized that there was nothing we could do in San Diego on Saturday that could not be done sooner, and therefore more mercifully, somewhere along the way. We must have contacted at least a dozen chapters of the American Red Cross and Travelers Aid along the route of her journey.[12] It was not until the next day, however, that we finally learned she had been taken off the train somewhere in Iowa; the news had somehow been broken to her, and she was on her way back to Chicago—on her way back, at least for the moment, from light to darkness. After that, our only hope of helping was in the form of letters to her and to the boy's parents and family. Yes, we had indeed done pitifully little. But the replies we received gave us assurance that even that little bit had meant much to civilians who had been trapped by the backwash of war.

This picture of the chaplain's relationship to the home front would be nowhere near complete if it failed to include at least a small sampling of evidence in the words of the civilians themselves. A chaplain's letters from the parents and wives of his men are the richest reward they have. Speaking for myself, I treasure dozens of such letters, no one of which would I ex-

---

[12] Travelers Aid is one of America's oldest social welfare movements, supporting the needs of travelers since 1851. For more information, see "History," Travelers Aid.org, accessed 2 December 2019.

change for a thousand dollars. There have been many moments when I needed a chaplain myself—when I had been caught temporarily in a trap of red tape, when I missed my family miserably, when I was unable to accomplish something of urgent importance—and wondered however briefly, whether it had after all been worthwhile to do this thing. I have one never-failing cure for such moments of discouragement. I break out my file of letters from the families of my boys. I read a few of them again. I let this boy's father or that man's wife tell me for the 10th time what it means to them to have a chaplain of their own faith out here with their son or husband. And then I feel happy again. I say to myself: "This is good! This is the widest opportunity for service you'll ever have in your life. If your son were old enough to be in combat, this is exactly what you would want for him. Until the war is ended, and all this sorrow ceases, you wouldn't want it any other why than this!" Sometimes I wonder if parents, in thanking a chaplain for the little they have accomplished for them, even begin to suspect how much, how *very* much, they have done for him.[13]

How much imagination does it require to picture the feelings of a mother who writes: "These few words are to express my heartfelt thanks and appreciation for your kind letter. I cannot in my sincerest effort convey to you the hope and courage your message has brought me at this time of great anxiety." Or the deep gratitude of the anxious father who begins: "Chaplain, your letter seemed to us like a godsend, surely more than a coincidence. We had not heard from Harold for more than three weeks. We were plainly and literally frantic. Your reassurance must have been a direct answer to our prayers." Sometimes par-

---

[13] Emphasis in original.

ents themselves are even afraid to trust their emotions to paper, and ask a brother or sister to bridge the gap between the gratitude they feel so warmly and the expression they find so difficult. One sister made me realize how much even a simple form letter could mean at home:

> It is with deep thanks and profound gratitude that I write this letter today acknowledging your kind note informing me of my brother's attendance at our High Holiday Services.
>
> I do not know if you can quite realize how happy it made our family circle to hear from you, as we had long awaited some notice from our brother as to the chaplain we might contact if the need arose.
>
> It is therefore a great comfort to us to know that we may feel free to write you, Chaplain, and inquire from time to time as to Nathan's well-being. Though he writes frequently now, and thank God is well and safe, to have the assurance that there is another way we may "double-check" at a future date makes all of us so much easier.

It is in connection with these letters from loved ones at home that the chaplain realizes anew almost daily how much abler he is to help because he wears the uniform and lives the life of the boys themselves. No one who has never suffered from pain can sympathize fully with the man who cries out in his pain. No one knows the meaning of hunger until he himself has been hungry. No minister, priest, or rabbi—however rich his experience, however deep his understanding—can know the frustrations and fears, the dread uncertainties and sorrows of long separation from those we love the dearest, unless he has felt that hollow loneliness himself. The chaplain who reads a letter such as the following before a picture of his own wife and children, whom he misses across 7,000 miles of space and with 7,000 tons of loneliness, understands the heart that wrote it:

> My dear Chaplain—Tonight, upon arriving home from work, I found your letter awaiting me, telling me of the honor you bestowed on my beloved husband, Harry, by his having read part of the service during the Jewish Holydays.
>
> I am sure that Harry attends almost every one of your services, as he writes and tells me about them. Thank you for that kindness.
>
> I hope the two of you are good friends. When Harry was at home, he was a serious person who looked upon me as his understanding and good friend. Now, you are the only one he can look to for understanding and guidance. So, for both our sakes, please try to be as close to Harry as you can be. I hope with God's speed both of you and all the other fighting servicemen will soon be home with their loved ones.
>
> The separation for both of us, I know, is only one of millions of couples, but being married to a good man for nine years and now to be separated is really a little hard to take, Chaplain Gittelsohn, so please try to comfort him. God bless you and your family and loved ones, because there are men like you who are over there to carry on our Jewish faith in God. Thank you for sending me the letter. I want you to know that you too are now added to my prayers. I remain your friend.

Yes, I have more than a slight suspicion of what you mean. This separation is indeed "really a little hard to take." If I, by being here, have made it the least bit easier for you and others to take, I am grateful—deeply and genuinely grateful for one of the richest privileges I have known.

I have saved for the last example one of the most eloquent letters of all. Children and people who are not using their native tongue can often achieve an awkward kind of eloquence that reaches down to one's very heart of hearts. The immigrant mother who wrote me the letter that follows has three sons in the Service. In another letter, she told me what she called the "wonderful news" that her second son had just been fitted with an artificial leg to replace the one shot off in Italy, and she added, "thank God it was his leg, not his life." I wonder if I could be as wonderfully brave under the same circumstances. To correct the grammar or edit the expressions of such a woman would be sacrilegious:

> Dear Chaplain—I received your most welcome letter
> today informing me about you seeing my son Irving
> at services. Of course, Chaplain, you can imagine
> how I felt after reading your letter and assuring me
> Irving is well. There are no words in the dictionary
> that can define, any words that can say or take the
> place of thanks in my heart to you. I feel in my
> heart as a Jewish mother that with such men as you
> with our boys that God will hear our prayers and
> he will bring that day sooner than we all expect
> it and all will be at peace once more and reunited
> with families and friends. I pray and hope, Chap-
> lain, that one day I will have the honor to meet you
> in person and to have you in my home and to give

Marines take shelter on the beach, Iwo Jima, February 1945.
*Thayer Soule Collection (COLL/2266) at the Archives Branch,
Marine Corps History Division*

*you as I say what seems so little to me, the thanks
in words, although I'll never be able to express the
real thanks in my heart that is deep.*

*Thanks very much for your offer of doing any-
thing for me or Irving. Yes, help him for me, Chaplain to keep his spirits up for his mom as I am doing
that same thing for him. Now, it's my time, Chaplain, and it's from way down in my heart please
do not hesitate or be bashful for a minute to write
to me for anything you would like special sent to
you. I have two more sons, Chaplain, my eldest in
the Navy and one in the Army, so you see I have
something really to pray for. The ending of this war*

and I know the end will come. Well, I will sign off for now, Chaplain. Again, I really cannot express my deep thanks and appreciation for your letter to me it meant so much. I remain
Yours Very Sincerely,

P.S. Please excuse writing mistakes and blots as I am kind of sleepy and tired.

PART III

Religion in Uniform

CHAPTER TEN

Atheists and Foxholes[1]

I can picture some anxious reader, at this point if not before, wanting to jump up and interrupt me with something like the following,

> See here, now, doesn't the chaplain, who is above
> all a teacher and preacher of religion, have any du-
> ties or experiences that are specifically and clearly
> religious? You've written of letters and conferences,

---

[1] This chapter title is shorthand for "There are no atheists in foxholes." Although its origin is uncertain, U.S. army chaplain William T. Cummings may have said it in a field sermon during the Battle of Bataan (1942). However, scholars have been unable to find a firsthand witness to the sermon. See Col Carlos P. Romulo, *I Saw the Fall of the Philippines* (Garden City, NY: Doubleday, Doran, 1942); Donald F. Crosby, *Battlefield Chaplains: Catholic Priests in World War II* (Lawrence: University Press of Kansas, 1994), 26; and Fulton J. Sheen, *Fulton Sheen's Wartime Prayerbook* (Manchester, NH: Sophia Institute Press, 2003), 2. Other sources credit LtCol Warren J. Clear (or the anonymous sergeant he spoke with there), who was also at Bataan, or LtCol William Casey. See LtCol Warren J. Clear, "Eyewitness Epic: The Heroic Defense of the Philippines," *Reader's Digest*, July 1942. The phrase is often attributed to war correspondent Ernest T. Pyle; however, no such source published prior to Pyle's death in 1945 is known. It was also quoted by President Dwight D. Eisenhower in remarks broadcast from the White House during a 7 February 1954, American Legion Program. With slightly different wording, the statement appears much earlier in press reports dating as far back as the end of the First World War.

of war aims and morale, but how about religion?
In picking up a book by a chaplain, I certainly ex-
pected to read something conclusive on the subject
of faith.

Forgive me, dear reader, you *have* been reading of religion and of faith.[2] By any definition or standard that I can accept for myself, nearly everything we have talked of so far is religion. If a boy can be given courage to face the grimmest kind of danger, and his folks at home be helped to the strength their lives depend on, I am sure you will agree that is a vital phase of religion, whether we have used the technical term or not. If men can be made to feel that their little lives are of urgent importance, and can be filled with a crusading zeal to live and fight (and maybe die) for others, what word will cover that except religion? In short, the crux of the matter is this: religion is a part of life not apart from life. Religion is a reality that the chaplain expresses every waking moment of his day, not at specified and localized times.

We Jews have an old Talmudic legend that illustrates the indivisibility of the so-called sacred and the so-called profane. Our rabbis were talking once about the respective merits of the body and the soul. Which is of greater importance? They gave their answer in the form of the following parable. Once a blind man and a lame man combined efforts to steal some fruit. What for either of them would have been impossible, became for both of them together simple. The blind man whose legs were strong lifted up the lame man whose eyes were sharp. Directed by his vision and carrying him on his own strong shoulders, he went

---

[2] Emphasis in original.

forth into an orchard and the lame man picked the fruit. Who could determine, asked the rabbis, which of the two was of major guilt? Alone, neither could have sinned. Together, they were indivisibly and equally to blame.[3]

Even so with the body and the soul. Even so with the religious and the secular. They are not separate compartments of life. They belong inseparably together. Religion is the leaven in the bread of life. Without leaven, the bread is not bread. Without the finished product, the leaven is something quite other. The chaplain, of all people, cannot separate his activities and interests into two separate spheres. I remember one particular class back at Naval Training School for Chaplains. The instructor had been lecturing on the way in which a padre aboard ship could help the medics in the heat of battle. When he had finished, one member of our class protested vehemently. "I didn't come into the Navy to administer first aid," he said. "That's the job of the doctors; my job is religion. Before battle, during battle, and after battle, religion is the only thing in which I'm interested." The best answer to his protest was the unanimous disagreement of all others in the room. Though it was not expressed in exactly these words, the rest of us might have summarized our thoughts by saying, "Since when have the saving of human life and the softening of human pain been outside the scope of religion?"

The fact that only one of these chapters speaks specifically of religion as such must not be thought to mean, therefore, that only the same proportion of a chaplain's time is concerned with religious matters. Unless the term *religion* be thought of narrowly as meaning only theology, that fact is manifestly not so.

---

[3] *The Talmud: Selections from the Contents of that Ancient Book, Its Commentaries, Teachings, Poetry and Legends also Brief Sketches of the Men Who Made and Commented Upon It*, trans. H. Polano (London: Frederick Warne, 1877), 278.

Marines, wounded in the battle for Iwo Jima, shelter in a Japanese concrete air raid shelter that was not completely destroyed in the three-day bombardment and aerial attack preceding the landing.
Thayer Soule Collection (COLL/2266) at the Archives Branch, Marine Corps History Division

The aim of this chapter is rather to discuss certain types of activity that come more technically under the heading of religion. For example, from time to time, men the Service have serious problems that stem directly from their religious beliefs. As with the problem of the religious conscientious objector—as distinct from the type we have already spoken of, whose objection did not stem from religious belief—who did not raise the issue at the time of his induction, either because he was anxious to perform his patriotic duty or perhaps because he just did not know his rights in this respect, but who finds now that he cannot in good conscience and faith face the thought of killing another human being. Though obviously no clergyman of such conviction would ever be a chaplain, still the chaplain, whatever his faith, is very apt to be the only man in an outfit who is professionally able and personally inclined to help such an unfortunate person.

The same type of problem is presented, at least in areas behind the actual zone of combat, by Seventh-day Adventists, whose Sabbath day is not that of the majority, or by Christian Scientists, whose faith differs some from that of the majority. I have myself never met a chaplain who was either a Christian Scientist or a Seventh-day Adventist.[4] But by the same token, neither have I ever met a boy of those persuasions whose religious sensibilities were not carefully considered and whose religious needs were not earnestly met by whatever chaplain, of whatever faith, he met.

Under the heading of such technical religious problems would come the plight of the Orthodox Jewish boy who had never in his life eaten food, particularly meat, that was not kosher.[5] In my life as a chaplain, I have naturally come into close contact with thousands of Jewish men. Thinking back now, there have been only two who were totally and utterly unable to adjust themselves as to diet. One, a Navy corpsman, the other,

---

[4] The first Christian Science naval chaplain, Richard Davis, was commissioned in January 1918; see Kim M. Schuette, *Christian Science Military Ministry, 1917–2004* (Indianapolis, IN: Brockton Publishing, 2008), 14. The first Seventh-day Adventist Navy chaplain was Robert Lee Mole, commissioned on 23 March 1953. Another Seventh-day Adventist chaplain, Barry C. Black, commissioned in 1976, became the chief of Navy chaplains, the first African American in that position, in 2000. After he retired in 2003, he was named 62d Chaplain of the United States Senate.

[5] *Kosher* refers to foods that conform to Jewish dietary regulations of *kashrut* (dietary law), coming from the five books of Moses. Among other requirements of *kashrut*, food is divided into three categories: meat, dairy, and *pareve*. *Pareve* refers to foods prepared without meat, milk, or their derivatives, and they can be eaten with both meat and dairy dishes.

an Army dentist, have never eaten a piece of GI (government issue) meat in two and four years, respectively, of military service. But there have been scores of others who, though they finally made an adjustment, did so only at the expense of much inner turmoil and strain. There was one Jewish lad in the dispensary at the Marine Corps base in San Diego whom the doctors asked me to see. They could do nothing more for him. During four weeks of boot training, he had found it impossible to down one complete meal or to keep down even the few snatches of food that managed to pass through his esophagus and his conscience. He was losing both weight and strength. His mental state was deplorable. This was the first time in all his 19 years that he had been forced to eat food that was not strictly kosher.

Short of setting up a kosher kitchen in the Marine Corps, or bringing his mother along to cook for him, what could be done for such a boy? The main thing was to convince him—and only a Jewish chaplain could hope to succeed—that there are times when intent must take the place of performance. If it were possible to observe all the dietary laws to which he was accustomed, well and good. But if not—and here it was clearly not—even the strictest interpretation of Orthodox Judaism would make allowance for a military emergency and would condone conduct that might otherwise be condemned. The battle with his conscience was not easy for that boy, not even with the help of a chaplain who brought him the religious assurance he needed. When we finally brought him to the point where he could compromise at least enough to stay alive, it was a real victory.

But these more technical religious problems are few and far between. The greater part of a chaplain's religious activity is in broader fields, such as in the realm of character training, for example. It would be hard to overemphasize the extent of the chaplain's influence on large numbers of impressionable young men, by very virtue of his closeness to them. There is an intensity about friendships and contacts in the military that one seldom finds in civilian life. Sometimes you get the feeling that men intentionally hasten the process of forming close contacts, that their friendships and the influences they bring to bear on each other ferment and mature more quickly, because they have no time to sit back and wait for more normal processes. I have already commented on the tendency of boys to "tell all" without reticence or inhibition. It has been my observation, and I am sure that of the average chaplain who has some background of previous experience, that regardless of intent or desire, we never get as close to the young people in our civilian congregations as we do to our men and boys in the Service. To be sure, there is much in a military environment that one does not like in terms of building character. But over and against its liabilities, life in uniform has at least this one advantage: that we who are supposed to play a major role in the shaping of character reach much more closely and intensely into the lives we are supposed to shape.

*   *   *

In turning now to formal religious worship, there is one thing I must say that may not meet with common agreement. Still it must be said, because for me it is of the essence of things. It is not true that there are no atheists in foxholes! There are atheists in foxholes, as there are everywhere else! Furthermore, there are a great many men in foxholes who are not really religious; they are just badly frightened. They are as badly frightened, as a matter of fact, that for the moment they are quite willing to take a chance on anything, even the Almighty. Neither is it true that we chaplains have had to build gigantic cathedrals to accommodate crowds. I do not feel that with regard to attendance at services I have either the knowledge or the right to speak for the Catholics. In any event, their percentage of attendance, in the Service as in civilian life, runs higher than that of other groups. But speaking for both Protestants and Jews, it is no disparagement but a simple statement of plain fact to say that it is still only a minority of our men who have been touched by anything remotely resembling a religious experience.

Having said all that, however, and having thus set the record straight, the fact remains that the religious minority is a considerably bigger one than any of us found before in our civilian communities. Take the matter of attendance at worship services. At the present time, I can honestly say that an average of 25 percent of the Jewish personnel in our division attends services on any given weekend. And if it be remembered that numbers of men have duty, or are out on military problems of one kind or another each week, the percentage would have to be more accurately reported as about one-third. As large as I should very much like to see it? Indeed not! But what civilian minister or rabbi can honestly say that as large a proportion even as this of his young people in their teens and 20s worship regularly?

Or take the matter of meaningful *participation* in worship.[6] There is a minimum of solo praying in the military. The service is by the men, for the men, and of the men. I myself have never found a need to form any kind of choir. My whole congregation is the choir. Their musical proficiency is something for which I would rather not vouch. But their enthusiasm, their understand-

---

[6] Emphasis in original.

ing, their whole-hearted singing of unison hymns and responses—ah, that is enough to warm and cheer me every time I hear it! They read the prayers that are marked for congregational reading as if they meant them. And it is no rare or infrequent occurrence to have them break in even on a prayer that the chaplains is supposed to read alone. More than once, I have started to read such a prayer, picked up a few readers at each punctuation mark along the way, and finished with a hearty company.

Or take the matter of personal prayer in moments of crisis and need. That is a sphere in which we have probably suffered our most dismal defeat in civilian religious life. Even men who have learned the art of common prayer together have too largely forgotten or ignored the role of purely personal prayer in the intimate moments of their own inner lives. But here in the Service, I have a number of boys come to me and ask if I would not pray with them before they shipped out. I remember one occasion on which I drove 25 miles to pray with two boys who had called me on the phone to say they were leaving that day and would feel better if they could pray first.

One of the nicest experiences I have had of this kind was the night on which one of my boys came in to tell me that he was happier than he had ever been in his life. He had just spoken to his sweetheart by long-distance wire. From 2,000 miles away, he had proposed and she had accepted. The next day, he was securing sufficient liberty to go to town and buy her ring. But before he left he said, "Chaplain, I'm so very happy tonight that I feel I want to express my thanks. Won't you please step into the chapel and pray with me a few minutes?" That same boy was later badly wounded on Saipan, evacuated to the states, and finally given a medical discharge from the Navy. He wrote to me

U.S. Marines of 2d Battalion, 27th Regiment, wait to move inland on Iwo Jima, soon after going ashore on 19 February 1945. An LVT(A)-5 amphibious tractor is in the background.
Official U.S. Navy photo NH 104130, Navy Naval History and Heritage Command

just a few weeks ago to tell me that he was being married soon and to ask again if I would recite a prayer for him—from 6,000 miles away—on his wedding night.

I could go on, or for that matter so could any chaplain, for many more minutes, giving evidence of the same sort. I could tell of Jewish men such as those in Samoa who walked 5, 10, 25 miles weekly to attend the nearest religious service. I could write of little groups of Jewish men all over the globe who, lacking a chaplain of their own, arranged and conducted services by themselves. I could tell of a group of Jewish servicemen in the Middle East who built the strangest synagogue in 4,000 years of Jewish history. The walls, of discarded canvas, were stretched around pillars of empty gasoline tins. And there they worshiped, fervently and faithfully, every week. I could describe special gatherings on Chanukah, or traditional services for the High Holy Days, or Seder services on Passover, after which grown men found tears their only means of grateful communication. And every other chaplain, of every other faith, could do the same.

* * *

What will be the effect of all this on religious life after the war? That question expresses a major reason for many of us coming in as chaplains in the first place. We felt that in a very real sense religion was on trial, that the attitudes of tomorrow's leaders toward religion and religious institutions would be shaped largely by what religion had to offer them now. How, then, has actual experience in the chaplaincy influenced my own thinking and feeling on this score? While I wish, above all else, to avoid glibness and easy optimism, there is little doubt in my own mind that men by the tens of thousands will return to civilian life after the war with a new respect for synagogue and church. One private, lying wounded in a hospital in Sicily, spoke for many of his buddies when he wrote: "Chaplain Samuel Teitelbaum called yesterday, and cheered me so much that I felt immeasurably better. Before I was in the hospital, I attended the marvelous services conducted by Chaplains Teitelbaum and Stone. . . . Let me say before closing that I had not attended a synagogue back in the states for about 15 years."[7] His feelings were identical with those of the San Francisco man who, at his final service before leaving boot camp, held my hand firmly and said: "Chaplain, I'm

---

[7] Maj Daniel B. Jorgensen, USAF, *Air Force Chaplains: The Service of Chaplains to Army Air Units, 1917–1946*, vol. I (Washington, DC: Office of the Chief of Air Force Chaplains, 1961), 178.

sorry to say that, though I could easily have afforded it, I've never belonged to or supported a synagogue in my life. Maybe that's because I never knew before how much I really needed religion, or how much religion can do for me. Before I say goodbye, I want you to know that one of my first moves after I return to civilian life is going to be joining a synagogue."

So, there will be many men and boys—and the families of many men and boys—who will emerge from this catastrophe with a new and greater need for religion. But not just any kind of religion. If, as members of the military, they have developed a strange and sudden receptiveness to religion, that is because perhaps for the first time in their lives they have found a type of religion that meets their specific needs. They have discovered a religion of directness and crispness; they have found a faith that helps them meet practical problems; they have listened to sermons that are short, simple, and to the point. And they will respond in later years only to a similar kind of religion.

Not long ago, I exchanged opinions by mail on this very point with a highly intelligent sergeant. I knew him as a man of high integrity and firm convictions, but who had felt little attraction for organized religion before the war. In camp, he had attended our services faithfully. I was interested in knowing how, if at all, this new interest would affect or change him in the future. His answer was clear and unmistakable. In essence, what he said was this: "Yes, if I can find in civilian life the kind of religious help and inspiration that you've given me here, I most certainly will be ready and anxious to return, so to speak, to the fold. But if I am to be confronted again, as I once was, with a combination of gorgeous trappings, of austere aloofness, and of 'big business' in religion, I shall be less patient with it now and have less use for it in the future than ever before."

Aerial view of the Marine Corps beachhead, 12 days
after landing on Iwo Jima, 1945.
*Thayer Soule Collection (COLL/2266) at the Archives Branch,
Marine Corps History Division*

Anyone who reads such views with understanding intelligence will see in them not only the greatest promise, but equally the highest challenge that organized religion has faced in a long time. Men will not return from the wars willing to accept just any kind of religion. They will return ready to listen, ready to give civilian religion a chance. They will return ready to see if their minister, priest, or rabbi is a "good Joe," as their chaplain was, whether he speaks the same language and faces the same problems.[8] If he does, and if toward the solution of those prob-

[8] According to the Census Bureau, Joseph was among the top 10 names given to newborn American boys from the 1880s to the 1930s. The nickname "Joe" found many uses. For example, *Joe zilch* (someone of zero importance) was a 1920s term, *Joe blow* (average man) and *Joe college* (typical college student) are terms from the 1930s, and *a good Joe* or *an ordinary Joe* reached their peak popularity in the 1940s. See Stuart Berg Flexner, *I Hear America Talking: An Illustrated History of American Words and Phrases* (New York: Von Nostrand Reinhold, 1976).

lems he brings them religion's message of eternity clothed simply in the language and needs of today, men will turn to religion in civilian life just as eagerly and hopefully as many of them have done in uniform.

I like to think that what the men and boys who attend my services now will do for post-war religion can be symbolized by what one unit did for a Catholic Church on this island. One night, shortly after a large group of Marines had landed here, a nearby church was burned to the ground. Natives, among them many Japanese, were left without a place to pray. Now then, Marines at least by reputation are supposed to be a tough, calloused bunch. They are alleged to care but little for their own religion, let alone someone else's. But these particular Marines, hearing of the disaster that had befallen a native parish, "passed the hat." No one was pushed or even directly asked to give. Cigar boxes were conveniently distributed on first sergeants' desks, their purpose was explained, and a time limit was set. No one was allowed to give more than a dollar. But when the boxes were closed, and their contents counted, a grateful group of natives had $2,000 with which to build a new church. I daresay that house of worship is the only one in the world where the cornerstone is dedicated to a unit of the United States Marine Corps. Our fighting men, those who have come upon a new view of religion, may yet lay the cornerstone of a new kind of faith at home.[9]

---

[9] Historical documents for the period have yet to substantiate this event; however, it is likely to have occurred during operations in either Guam or Saipan. For more on these actions, see Cyril J. O'Brien, *Liberation: Marines in the Recapture of Guam* (Washington, DC: History and Museums Division, Headquarters Marine Corps, 1994); and Capt John C. Chapin, USMCR (Ret), *Breaching the Marianas: The Battle for Saipan* (Washington, DC: History and Museums Division, Headquarters Marine Corps, 1994).

Before we leave the subject of religion in the civilian future, there is one comment of a specifically Jewish nature, yet with profound overtones at the same time for Christianity, that ought to be made. In the experiences of some 500,000 American Jewish men and women now serving their nation in uniform, there lies, I think, the greatest hope in decades for unity in American Israel.[10] We Jews, like Protestants, have had our share of internal bickering and strife. The orthodox among us seek to practice our religion as nearly as possible to the manner of its original observance back in the days of the Bible and Talmud. Our reform wing is anxious to adjust Judaism, to modify it in keeping with modern times and modern views. Conservative Jews, finding it impossible alike to accept either view, lean more toward Alexander Pope's

> Be not the first by whom the new is tried,
> Nor yet the last to lay the old aside.[11]

And alas, in civilian life, too often there are those in all three groups who forget that we are still one people with one faith, who permit our minor differences of interpretation to obscure our major agreement on fundamentals. Today, in the Army, Navy, and Marine Corps there are no Orthodox, Conservative, or Reform Jews. There are just Jews. Some pray with their hats on, some with their heads uncovered. Some wear the tallit or prayer shawl, some do not. But all pray together. And all, if they have eyes to see, are recognizing that the whole of Jewish life and faith is more meaningful and important than

---

[10] The Jewish Welfare Board estimated that 550,000 Jews served in the armed forces of the United States between 1941 and 1945.
[11] Alexander Pope, "An Essay on Criticism," *Poems of Alexander Pope*, ed. E. Audra and Aubrey Williams, vol. 1, (New Haven, CT: Yale University Press, 1961), 276.

any of its parts. I, as a Reform rabbi, am wearing a tallit and cap at my services for the first time since my ordination.[12] My friend, the strictly Orthodox rabbi, is now praying meaningfully in English as well as Hebrew for the first time in his life. We are learning from each other and with each other. Unless we muff the greatest opportunity either of us has had in centuries, out of this war we shall together forge a new unity in the religious life of the Jew.[13]

There is another direction too in which Jews throughout the world are being bound closer together through this conflict. It was illustrated dramatically for me on the first Pacific island where I saw duty—Iwo Jima. There was one Jewish merchant on the entire island. I had been told of him in advance. He was a Turkish Jew of Spanish descent who had settled on these islands some 30 years ago. We had never seen each other before. He was of the East, I of the West. He worshiped according to the rites of Spanish Orthodoxy; I was a child of American Reform. But 40 minutes after first landing on the island, I held out my hand to Louis Amiel with a hearty "shalom aleichem." Ten minutes later, we were planning together for the religious welfare of Jewish men on the island. And since then, I have come to look on him as one of the most unusual friends and enthusiastic collaborators I have known.

Other Jewish chaplains, especially in the European theaters of conflict, have experienced the same thing on a much more magnified scale. Shortly after the liberation of Rome on 9 June 1944, a young American Jewish Army chaplain, Lieutenant Morris N. Kertzer, joined with the chief rabbi of Rome in reopening

---

[12] *Tallit* refers to the fringed prayer shawl.
[13] *Muff* refers to handling a situation poorly.

The Tiber River in Rome, showing Tiber Island on the left and the
Ponte Fabrizio (Pons Fabricius) at the center. The dome on the right
is the principal synagogue of Rome.
Courtesy of Nicholas Hartmann

the Great Synagogue of that city.[14] Their voices, linked together,
were carried by the magic of radio to every corner of the world.
Elsewhere in North Africa, in Sicily, in France, Jewish chaplains
from England and the United States have helped rebuild ruined
Jewish communities; have conducted services for Jews who had
been unable to worship for three years or more; have brought
them religious supplies, religious books; and more important by
far, religious inspiration and hope. Jewish unity has walked off
the pages of our textbooks and has become a literal, visible fact.

The implications for Christians are obvious. American

---

[14] See, Ari L. Goldman, "Rabbi Morris Kertzer Dies; Improved Interreligious
Ties," *New York Times*, 31 December 1983; and Ruth Ellen Gruber, "Happy
Birthday, Rome Synagogue," Jewish Telegraphic Agency, 20 June 2004.

Catholics who never dared dream of seeing the Vatican have stood with the pope and have by him been blessed. And American Protestants, who will well understand me when I speak of disunity among Jews, are perceiving an essential oneness among themselves that many of them did not see before. A regiment does not carry a Baptist, a Methodist, a Lutheran, and a congregational chaplain. It carries a *Protestant* chaplain—one Protestant chaplain for all.[15] Not that the rights of any particular Protestant sect are ignored; but one chaplain, within the limits of human endurance and strength, serves them all. As far as possible, according to the rites they have known at home; where that becomes impossible, in some way that will help all while offending none. My closest friend among the chaplains of my own division, a Congregationalist who does not believe in the necessity of taking Communion before death, nevertheless carries Communion gear with him into combat, because he knows that among the Protestant men of his regiment there are Lutherans and Episcopalians who do. Protestants, no less than Jews I am sure, can look forward, as a result of religion gone to war, to a new unity.

I feel very strongly that this chapter, as with the last, should end with the words of others, not my own. There is always a temptation for the chaplain, no matter how honest his intentions or how objective he sincerely strives to be, to read into the facts of experience before him the subconscious and perhaps even unexpressed desires of his own heart. I have tried to avoid that, and to read nothing *into* the facts that could not easily be read *out* of them.[16] Still, on the meaning of religion to men at

---

[15] Emphasis in original.
[16] Emphasis in original.

war—not to all men, but to considerable numbers—the testimony of the men themselves should be heard. Like that of a fine young boy in my own civilian congregation who, writing of his experiences in basic training, said:

> I've developed more than muscle down here though, and that is a faith in God. This may sound odd for you to hear and then again in your position you've heard it time and time again. I never prayed much at home. But since I joined the Army, I've prayed every night, and I believe that some have even been answered.

Another boy's letter surprised me even more. He had been far from an interested or cooperative student in our synagogue school. He had resisted every effort to give him religious instruction. He had even withdrawn from our program of religious training before time for confirmation. But from the California base where he had gone as an aviation cadet, of his own accord, he wrote me this:

> I think I've changed in many ways, that is, I've come to realize the wonderful things I've really had and I now know what my religion means to me. I attend regular services every Friday night. The chaplain at this base is a wonderful man, and we all like him. I know what a wonderful job you are doing, and I hope my letter brings some consolation that a former member of your congregation has done some repenting.

How about men who have finished their basic or boot training, who are closer to the dread imminence of combat? One young pharmacist's mate whom I met less than a year ago, but think of now as a lifelong friend, wrote me this from the ship that was carrying him farther and farther from his native land and closer and closer to combat:

> We have had Jewish sabbath services aboard. There is no Jewish chaplain, but one of the boys and yours truly have a little gathering every Friday and go through the ritual; we go through the same prayers you do. We have enlisted men and officers alike, and quite a nice attendance.
>
> Every Friday evening, the boatswain [petty officer] announces that Jewish services to be held in the mess hall. The mess hall is down in the hold, and the warmest place I have ever been in. As we go through the service and chant the traditional prayers, the perspiration literally drains off. It sort of reminded me of the descriptions I have read of how the old Talmudic students used to attend prayer in the hot, stuffy prayer houses in the poor sections of Europe.

A friend of whom I shall have more to say later, Lieutenant Martin H. Weinberg, wrote me from an island outpost how he missed his wife and friends, told me of his fears and doubts as he faced battle for the first time. Then he added that his greatest comfort and help had been the Jewish services conducted on his island: "The meetings we have been able to have are a great source of relaxation, release of tension, and enjoyment for the boys. There is nothing equal to a Jewish atmosphere, and thank God, wherever we Jews are, we are able to gather, to create that atmosphere, to be content beyond words."[17] Is there need to go on endlessly? To claim that all men feel this way, or even that most men do, would be patently dishonest and untrue. To me the important thing is that *some* men do, that considerable numbers do, surely much larger numbers than would have as civilians.[18] I for one rejoice in that fact, and face it humbly as a challenge I dare not treat too lightly. Let me now close this part of the story with the following poem found on the body of an American soldier killed in action. I offer it neither as excellent poetry nor as sound theology. Only all the warm, fervent, honest outpouring of a young boy's heart, touched for the first time by a new kind of experience.

WITH A FRIEND

Look God, I have never spoken to You
But now I want to say, "How do You do?"
You see, God, they told me You didn't exist
And like a fool, I believed all this

Last night from a shell hole I saw Your sky
And figured then they had told me a lie.
Had I taken time to see the things You made,
I'd have known they weren't calling a spade a spade.
I wonder, God, if You'd shake my hand.
Somehow I feel You will understand.
Funny I had to came to this hellish place

---

[17] 2dLt Weinberg served with 3d Battalion, 6th Marines, on Saipan. He was killed in action on 15 June 1944.
[18] Emphasis in original.

Before I had time to see Your face.

Well, I guess there isn't much more to say;
But I'm sure glad, God, that I met You today.
I guess the zero hour will soon be here
But I'm not afraid since I know You're near.

There's the signal—I've got to go . . .
I like You lots, I want you to know . . .
Look now, this will be a horrible fight.
Who knows? I may come to Your house tonight.

Though I wasn't friendly to You before,
I wonder, God, If You'd wait at Your door.
Look, I'm crying! Me! Shedding tears!
I wish I had known You these many years.

Well, I have to go now, God. Goodbye . . .
Strange, since I met You, I'm not afraid to die.
~ Private First Class J. J. W.[19]

---

[19] The poem, originally titled "Conversion," first published in a Catholic week-ly on 18 July 1943, was written by Frances Angermayer of Kansas City, KS. It was printed and recorded in multiple formats. See Frances Angermayer, "Con-version: Author of One of the World's Most Famous Poems," *Chicago Sunday Tribune Magazine*, 10 November 1957, 188; and Hazel Feldman, ed., *Poems that Live Forever* (New York: Doubleday, 1963), 334.

CHAPTER ELEVEN

Doggone It, Chaplain!

I owe my title for this chapter to one of the toughest, hardest, bluntest, but squarest-shooting line officers in the United States Marine Corps, Major (then Captain) Pete Owen, who so far as I know is still adjutant of the Training Command, San Diego Area, Fleet Marine Force. I was sitting one day in his office, urging him to do a special favor, to step just a bit beyond the strict limit of regulations for a boy in need of help. When I had finished what I thought was an effective and cogent plea, he thumped his open palm on the desk and said:

> Doggone it, Chaplain, you fellows have to remember that we aren't running a social service agency here. We've got a tough war to wage, and my job is to wage it, to get the right number of men in the right place at the right time, even if I have to step on a few toes to do it!

Pete Owen's "doggone it, Chaplain" helped me no little amount to see in fair perspective the work of the line officer vis-à-vis the chaplain. I dare to hope that I was at least of some small use in helping him to see the opposite. I know this: from that day on, I never once went to him with a fair request without having it granted. I never asked for reasonable help that was refused. It would be useless and foolish to deny that there are those in the armed forces who oppose and resent the presence of chaplains. There was a time even when the prevailing attitude of the Marine Corps was distinctly antichaplain. Men long in the naval chaplaincy tell me that the first few padres assigned to duty with the leathernecks were accepted with grudging reluctance. Even now, one occasionally comes across some old-time hard-bitten sergeant major who looks on the chaplains as a sign of soft decadence in what used to be a rough, tough outfit. Their stock reply to anyone who tries to appeal to their softer side is a derisive "tell it to the chaplain!"[1] And some of them carry in their desks so-called "sympathy chits," or as one of our Latin-minded instructors at Williamsburg used to call them, *chita sympathetica*.[2] Their practice, when men come with personal problems, is to hand out one of these chits, admitting the bearer to a mythical "order of the bleeding heart," and entitling him to 30 minutes of the nearest chaplain's time. The welcome extended by such men to the chaplain is only slightly less frigid than their reception of women in the Corps.[3]

It must be said in all fairness, however, that this attitude on both counts—chaplains as well as Women's Reserves—is far from typical and is rapidly disappearing. For one thing, too

---

[1] See, for example, Irwin Shaw, *The Young Lions* (London: Cape, 1949), chapter 17.
[2] See, for example, *Bureau of Naval Personnel Information Bulletin*, no. 329, August 1944, 61.
[3] Capt Linda L. Hewitt, *Women in the Marines in World War I* (Washington, DC: History and Museums Division, Headquarters Marine Corps, 1974); Col Mary V. Stremlow, *A History of Women Marines, 1946–1977* (Washington, DC: History and Museums Division, Headquarters Marine Corps, 1986); and Col Nancy P. Anderson, *The Very Few, the Proud: Women in the Marine Corps, 1977–2001* (Quantico, VA: Marine Corps History Division, 2018).

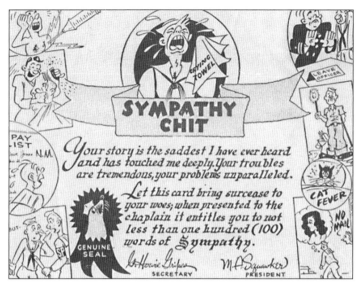

A 1943 sympathy chit.
U.S. Navy Seabee Museum in Point Hueneme, CA

many of those who "came to scoff, remained to pray."[4] Too many men who were free with *chita sympathetica* found the need at one point or another of seeking out a chaplain themselves. For another thing, the Marine Corps, such as the Army and Navy, is now made up for the most part of Reserves, of civilians in uniform. These men naturally and instinctively turn toward the chaplain in their moments of greatest need. And directly or otherwise, they influence even the oldest of the regulars.

Still another reason for the change is that more and more line officers and regulars are coming to realize that far from op-

---

[4] The origin of the expression "came to scoff, remained to pray" is a 1770 poem, "The Deserted Village," by Oliver Goldsmith.

posing each other, they and the chaplain are fighting the same fight, and they need each other. If a chain is only as strong as its weakest link, if a machine is only as enduring as its most fragile part, an army or navy is only as effective as its most inadequate human personality. Anything, therefore, that the chaplain may be able to do to strengthen such personalities if possible, otherwise to weed them out, is a direct aid to more efficient and victorious fighting. The reader who has come this far should need no lengthy urging. Turn back to any one of the individual stories these pages have already told. Ask yourself: How valuable a fighter was the weak, worried, frustrated Marine who first came into the chaplain's office? Then, also ask: What was his use to the Marine Corps when the chaplain had finished helping them?

A clear case in point—besides those that have already been described—was the 19-year-old boy who came in one day with a letter from his 17-year-old wife. Whether or not they should have been married in the first place, or whether their union had any real prospect of permanence, is right now beside the point. The undeniable fact is that they were married, and equally undeniable was the evidence that this most recent letter from his wife was not exactly increasing his usefulness to the Corps. They had been married a total of 15 months—7 of them lived together, 8 now spent in separation. Some silly little dispute had arisen between them. Distance and immaturity had conspired to magnify it into a major issue. And now the girl wrote, asking for a separation.

The military picture was such that a furlough to patch things up was out of the question. But to do nothing was equally impossible. The boy's record already showed one brig sentence, sustained some months before when worry over his wife's health had sent him over the hill. Even before reaching home, he had been picked up by the military police (MPs) and returned to camp. Notwithstanding that, if nothing were done to help him, I had little doubt that he would attempt the same thing again. The only thing possible seemed to be a letter from chaplain to wife. Such a letter was immediately written. It emphasized two things. First, marriage ought to have some more permanent basis than one that could be so easily shaken. Second, her husband was deeply in love with her; to break *from* him under such circumstances might well mean to break *him*.[5] How long the effect of my letter will last, or how permanently their quarrel was patched, I have no way of knowing. But I do know that the immediate effect was a profuse and loving apology to the boy, and I do know that no one interested in the sheer fighting efficiency of the Marine Corps could have found any reasonable disagreement with the time and effort spent trying to straighten this thing out.

Yes, the chaplain and line officer supplement rather than oppose each other. This is true in another and a negative sense too. No small part of the chaplain's function is to act as a screen, to run interference, so to speak, for the line officer in the backfield. If every boy with a real or imagined problem went directly to his commanding officer, the latter would have no time left for the direct business of waging war. The chaplain can sift cases out. Some he can immediately dismiss as inconsequential. Some he can recognize as problems of inner adjustment, which he can handle either alone or with the aid of competent medical personnel. Only the third group, those that require direct military action, need be brought to the attention of the commanding officer. I think this, more than anything else, was the secret of

_____

[5] Emphasis in original.

5th Marine Division command post, Iwo Jima, 1945. From left:
BGen Leo D. Hermle, MajGen Keller E. Rockey, (with phone), Col James F.
Shaw, and Col Ray Robinson.
*Thayer Soule Collection (COLL/2266) at the Archives Branch,
Marine Corps History Division*

my working partnership with Pete Owen. On that very first visit, as a postscript to his emphatic "doggone it," I made him this
promise:

> *Captain, I realize you've got more to do here than
> listen to men's troubles. I promise that you'll never
> even hear about nine-tenths of the boys who come
> to me with complaints they want me to bring top-
> side. I promise you two things more: that I shall
> carefully check my facts and be sure of them in ev-
> ery case that I do bring to you; and that when you
> see me walk through this door, you can be sure I've
> exhausted every possibility of helping the boy my-
> self, and can proceed only through you.*

I never violated that agreement, and Major Owen never declined to help.

I would not want to leave even the faintest suspicion that the Marine Corps is made up of mean, heartless ogres and that only the bravo, gallant chaplain is interested in human beings as such. To be sure, we have our due share of men without hearts, just as every factory, every business, every trade has. But these are not typical. The average officer *is* interested in the welfare of his men; if that were not so, the chaplain could not get to the plate, let alone reach first base.[6] It is not that they do not *want* to allow for individual differences and needs; it is just that they simply have not the time to.[7] War is an enormously complicated business, and the type of person best fit to carry on such a business is not apt also to be an expert or pedagogue. In short, the chaplain is very apt to be the only person who combines the time, the inclination, and the professional training to do these things. Many others share with him the desire or will.

And now, for Pete Owen's side of the picture. The chaplain has no fewer obligations toward the line officer than the latter has to him. Some of these have already been hinted at in my promise to Owen; the first of them has been specifically mentioned in an earlier chapter. Here, they ought to be stressed more emphatically. First, the chaplain must in every instance be sure of his facts. The most dangerous trap for him to be caught in is the reputation of being an easy mark. Requests for favors often come in epidemic-like waves. One man in an outfit secures a dependency discharge from the Service. Immediately, 40 others besiege the chaplain's office with stories that wring the heart,

---

[6] Emphasis in original.
[7] Emphasis in original.

especially if the mind is soft. One man in a replacement battalion goes to the hospital with appendicitis three days before the group shoves (deploys); within 12 hours, there are a dozen sudden cases of bellyache, all by some amazing coincidence of nature in the same outfit.

The first inclination of every chaplain, I think, is to accept as gospel truth every word that a suppliant tells him and to stride forth in immediate righteous wrath. He soon learns to check his facts and to walk slowly. A boy whom I visited in the brig gave me an excellent case for a furlough immediately upon completion of his sentence. I was convinced. I was ready for immediate action. Something—perhaps some inner instinct—made me check the facts first. I found that every word the boy had spoken was true. The trouble was not with what he had said, but rather with the things he left unsaid. He had (conveniently?) forgotten to mention that he had been convicted altogether of being AWOL (absent without leave) once and AUL (unauthorized leave) three times in addition to his present offense. The chaplain must check his facts.

Second, he must remember that primary purpose number one is to win the war. This is largely a matter of not confusing means with ends. Anything that helps to win the war is legitimate and proper. Anything that hinders winning the war is inexcusable and improper. It is as simple as all that.

Third, the chaplain, remembering that he is a military officer, must go through proper channels. From the moment he takes the oath, he is no longer the free agent he was as a civilian clergyman. He becomes subject to military rules and military procedures, and he must follow them.[8] That, as we have already

---

[8] See *Department of Defense Instruction No. 1304.28, Guidance for the Appointment of Chaplains for the Military Departments*, 20 March 2014.

seen, is one of the important reasons for establishing chaplains' training schools. Sometimes, incidentally, it is difficult to reconcile this third essential with the importance of checking facts. On one occasion, I was "read off" (chastised) severely by a battalion commanding officer for undertaking what he looked at as an unauthorized investigation of his outfit. A case of alleged injustice was reported to me. I felt I had no right to bother a busy commanding officer without first checking the facts. To do so, I had to talk to a dozen men familiar with the situation and secure their statements. When I had finally done that and, convinced that indeed there *was* a miscarriage of justice, I went to the commanding officer, he was peeved at my procedure.[9]

This brings us to the first of several obligations of a slightly different type that the chaplain has, obligations owed jointly to his men and their superiors. First, after checking facts and after honestly trying to proceed through proper channels, he must at all times be willing to "stick his neck out." No chaplain who is not willing to risk a stern rebuke for legitimate efforts on behalf of enlisted men is worth his weight in salt to those men. There are times when it is necessary either to compromise with one's soul or to say to a captain: "I'm sorry, but I'd much rather do this thing with you than against you. If you insist, I shall have to go to the colonel over your head." In my own experience, the need for this sort of approach is exceedingly rare. But now and then, it is needed, and the chaplain must be willing to risk it.

Second, the chaplain must help men—and their parents or wives—see that line officers have their worries and problems too. Shortly after my first conversation with Major Owen, I sat in his office one afternoon for about 45 minutes, just watch-

---

[9] Emphasis in original.

ing and listening. I learned a lot. I discovered that sometimes what seems to be heartlessness toward some individual is nothing more or less than the consequence of an inexorable order to have so many men on such and such a ship at a precise and exact hour. That is the way wars have to be fought; there is no other way. And the chaplain is in a unique position to help men see it.

Third, he is in a unique position also to show men themselves, not in a vacuum or alone, but as small parts of a much larger picture. Enough has been said about this on earlier pages to make more than a brief summary here unnecessary. A blunt "no" is never as effective an answer as a patient, sympathetic explanation of why it has to be "no." Part of the chaplain's job is precisely the business of patient, sympathetic explanations. He, better than anyone else, can give men perspective, can help them see the picture is nowhere near as simple as they think. As a matter of fact, right here, I think, is one of the highest and most difficult services a chaplain can perform. This is the opportunity of making the fine balance between the needs of an individual and the requirements of the military. Where the two can be reconciled or adjusted, fine. Where that is impossible, unfortunately but inevitably, it is the individual who must give way. Even the boy who wants a transfer or furlough or discharge more than anything else in the world must be made to see that there is one thing he really needs more, one thing without which the transfer, the furlough, the discharge will be worthless. That one thing is the speediest possible victory for ourselves and our allies.

I think that is what Pete Owen had in mind that day when he thumped the desk with a sincere, "Doggone it, Chaplain!"

CHAPTER TWELVE

Brothers All?

I wish that I could write here the kind of easy, pleasant chapter that most of my friends would like to read. In essence, it would run something like this: there are no group prejudices or antagonisms in the armed forces. The impact of Pearl Harbor and the process of living and fighting together have conspired to make us Americans all, brothers all. We have learned to know each other, hence to respect and like each other. The host of battle and the fire of suffering are forging a new, a united, a stronger America. Period.

I wish that I could write something like that without reservations, without violating either my conscience or the truth. It would make me at least as happy to say it as the reader would be to hear it. But it would not be true. Or shall we say, it would not be the whole truth. To be sure, the immediate effect of the blitz against Pearl Harbor was the melting of most difficulties and suspicions. Our more rabid hatelers went temporarily underground.[1] Welded together by the shock of attack and by a com-

---

[1] The term *hateler* describes someone who hates indiscriminately for no real reason.

mon and considerable danger, we faced the world as a united people. At least three things conspired, however, especially within the armed forces, to make our newfound unity and concord imperfect. To begin with, covering the outside of a man with a uniform does not change the deep-seated prejudices that may exist within him. Before the war, it would have been manifestly impossible to have gathered at random any thousand Americans without including among them a certain number who hated either Negroes or Catholics or Jews. Why, then should we have expected to take the same thousand Americans, and merely by clothing them alike, have them shed all such discriminations?

But the matter goes much deeper even than the antagonisms some of us harbored before the war and continued to carry within ourselves. There were a few of us who even during the bloom of American unity after Pearl Harbor risked unpopularity by daring to suggest that in the long run a war would increase rather than decrease the measure of prejudice in American life. True, it did not seem logical that men should quarrel and hate among themselves when they faced a strong and resolute enemy from without. But then we knew—some of us at least—that life has an annoying way of bypassing logic. We knew that it has always been precisely during the "times that try men's souls" that men's minds turn most against each other.[2] It is when men are frustrated and thwarted, when outer circumstance inhibits inner desire, that we cast about most bitterly for a scapegoat. It is not enough, it seems, to blame our misfortunes on God. After all, we cannot strike back at God. We need someone on whom to practice, so to speak, a vicarious atonement in reverse; someone on whom to blame our troubles, and then by striking that

[2] The phrase comes from Thomas Paine, "The American Crisis," *Common Sense*, December 1776.

someone down, act as if it were the trouble we had overcome. When the Russian peasants were held down by nobles and czar in the mire of misery, when the German masses or the American workers were deepest in the depths of depression, it was precisely then that they became most unreasonably bitter in their hatred of Jews or Negroes or whatever other helpless minority happened to be convenient. Because things had happened that way since the dawn of history, some of us were afraid they would happen that way again in the present war.

A third factor hastened the fruition of our fears. German propaganda: dirty, sneaking, lying, vicious, contemptible, but powerfully effective German propaganda. It may be decades yet before we know the full story of how effectively the bacteria of German propaganda have infected American life with decay. But let no man fool himself even for a fleeting moment that it has been without effect even within the American military! A Jewish pharmacist's mate who had served on a minesweeper in the Mediterranean once told me how, for want of radio fare better or other, the crew had listened daily to broadcasts from German stations on the continent. Entertainment was cleverly spiced with propaganda. Propaganda was largely anti-Jewish: "Look about you; see how few Jews there are in your company or crew! (Why not see how few there are in the population as a whole?) While you are here fighting for them, separated from your wives and families, the Jews are at home, profiting out of your misery!"[3] Ridiculous? Since when has the monstrosity of a lie prevented it from being believed? My Jewish friend ad-

---

[3] See, for example, Keith Somerville, "Nazi Radio Propaganda: Setting the Agenda for Hatred," in *Radio Propaganda and the Broadcasting of Hatred: Historical Development and Definitions* (London: Palgrave Macmillan, 2012), https://doi.org/10.1057/9781137284150_4.

mitted to me that after hearing the same kind of rubbish daily for months, had he not known the answering facts, he would have been ready to believe it himself. There are thousands who, because they do *not* know the facts, *do* believe.[4] Here, then, is the third reason why I cannot write this chapter as I should so much like to. There is an amount of undemocratic prejudice even among those who are allegedly fighting for the very life of democracy. And there will be such prejudice in considerable quantities even after victory shall have been won. The first step in combating this sort of thing is recognizing that it is clearly and unmistakably so.

Discrimination against minorities in the armed forces, as in American civilian life, directs itself primarily against two groups: the Negroes and the Jews. If I speak especially in this chapter of the latter, that is not because I would in any way minimize the heartaches and disappointments of the former. It is only because I am naturally more conversant with the group to which I belong. But first, a word about the Negro in our armed forces. That there is prejudice against them should surprise no one who is familiar with American history even as recently as one-quarter of a century ago. In World War I, colored Americans played a role of which they and we alike ought to be proud. When the wounded and hurt among them returned to the country they had helped defend, they found themselves excluded from the hospitals and rest homes that had been set up for white soldiers. To compensate at least in part for that fact, the federal government built a veterans' hospital exclusively for Negroes at the

---

[4] Emphasis in original.

Black U.S. servicemembers carry a Japanese prisoner on a litter from a stockade to be evacuated and treated for malnutrition on Iwo Jima, 23 February 1945. This image was taken by PFC Don Fox prior to his death in March 1945. Chaplain Gittelsohn was with him in his final hours.
Official Department of Defense photo

famed Tuskegee Institute in Alabama.[5] Finished, the problem of staffing it came up for discussion. The Negroes themselves quite naturally and reasonably felt that their own doctors and nurses, so largely rejected by other medical institutions, should at least be given preference here. Certain white groups in the

[5] The Tuskegee Institute was founded by Booker T. Washington in 1881 based on a charter from the Alabama state legislature to train teachers. The Tuskegee VA Hospital, opened in 1923, was the first and only medical facility staffed by black professionals.

South felt otherwise. So much so that one night—this, remember please, is after the World War, not the Civil War—several dozen hooded Ku Klux Klansmen rode out to the Tuskegee campus in protest.[6] No one will ever know what their original intention was or what they might have done. For on their arrival at the college, they were greeted by several hundred armed Negro veterans, men who wanted peace but who were silently, almost sullenly determined to keep and defend what was rightfully theirs.

I find that I cannot write even these brief paragraphs about Negroes without remembering the boy who wished I had never given him a ride. He was standing at the camp gate one evening as I drove out toward town. I picked him up, along with several others. It proved to be his misfortune that not only was he in my car, but he was seated immediately beside me in the front. Somehow—exactly how or why I don't recall—he made several remarks that showed prejudice against Negroes. I was just in the mood to be infuriated. Turning to him, I said:

> *It's too bad I didn't know you felt that way before I picked you up. If I had, I probably would have let you stand there, and would have looked for a Negro to occupy this seat instead! My advice to you, when you get into combat, is to make sure that if you're over in a tight spot you don't allow a Negro Marine to save your life. And by all means, make sure no Negro hand helped manufacture the carbine with which you may have to defend yourself. Otherwise, you haven't any right to the un-American prejudice you seem to enjoy!*

---

[6] "Negroes: K. K. K. at Tuskegee," *Time* 1, no. 20, 16 July 1923.

I am afraid that was the most uncomfortable 12-mile ride my prejudiced passenger ever had. In a sense, I suppose I was a bit unfair to him. I poured out toward him, as if he were a symbol, all the resentment I felt toward the millions who harbor such hatreds. I should not be surprised if from that day on, he stuck exclusively to the regular bus lines under the theory that bus drivers are not social crusaders.

Outside of incidents and conversations such as this, what form does discrimination against Negroes commonly take? There have of course been cases of flagrant injustice and even of violence. If I do not write of them here, it is because I want to limit this account to experiences that I have had myself, and fortunately, I have myself seen none of the uglier forms of discrimination. Within the scope of my own experience, I should say that discrimination against colored men shows itself primarily and especially in ever so much less opportunity to do the work they want or like. Do not get me wrong. Far from every white boy can do what he prefers in the Army or Navy. A military machine just cannot be run on a basis of elective courses. But the limits within which a boy can do anything at all are very much more narrowly circumscribed for a colored man than for his white parallel.

For example, one day my front seat passenger into town was more to my preference and liking—a Negro sailor from one of the air stations near San Diego. He had been married 13 years. Though he had no children of his own, he and his wife were father and mother to the five orphaned children of his sister. He had finished two years of college. Before joining the Navy, he had been a supervisor in the adult education program of a large southern state. His post in the Navy? A second class cook! And his case was unfortunately typical enough to be a fair example. In my own division, Negro Marines are used exclusively and only as either in the mess hall or as orderlies, nothing more.[7] Call that unfair, call it unreasonable, or call it a frightful waste of manpower. It is all that, and it is, over and above and beyond all that, undemocratic and un-American.

It would be unfair, however, to leave the story at that as it would be inaccurate to write it as a tale of troubled peace. With all there is to legitimately criticize—and I have scarcely scratched the surface—there is also much for which to be grateful and happy. No one can deny, and I think no Negro especially would want to deny that, since the last war, we have made encouraging progress. If it is true that opportunities for Negroes in the Marine Corps are limited, it is also true that this is the first time in 169 years of Marine Corps history that Negroes have been admitted on any terms. If it is apparent that things racial are not what they should be in the Navy, it is no less apparent that this war is the first in which Negroes have ever been commissioned as officers in our Navy, and in which Negro naval chaplains have been assigned for the religious welfare of Negro men. As I write, word has just come through that the first Negro women are about to be accepted by the Women Accepted for Volunteer Emergency Service (WAVES).[8] The picture is neither all black nor wholly white. At times, it is discouraging, disappointing, and depressing. But there has been improvement, there are signs of progress, there is good ground for hope.

Now, how about attitudes toward Jews as a barometer of democracy in our armed forces? Well, to begin with, there is one

---

[7] See, for example, Todd South, "First Black Marines Mark 75th Anniversary of the Segregated Boot Camp," *Marine Corps Times*, 26 August 2017.
[8] "First Black American Women Officers in the Navy Joined as WAVES," *CHIPS Magazine*, 23 March 2018.

thing to be said by way of preliminary preface. Let it be clearly established on the record, and by a Jewish chaplain, that not every case of apparent anti-Semitism is really that at all. I can remember how agitated and excited a particular Jewish boy was one Sunday morning at boot camp service that he could scarcely wait for the final "Amen" to rush forward with his complaint. He had been at the Army-Navy YMCA the night before. He happened to have been standing next to the desk when two large packages of literature were being unwrapped for distribution. He was shocked to observe that the title of the pamphlet being unwrapped was "I Am a Jew Hater." Immediately—and I suspect vehemently—he insisted that the contents of both packages be thrown out. The assistant director on duty, who was no more an anti-Semite than I, hastily complied. But the boy managed to salvage one copy of the thing to give me as proof of that had happened. It took me 30 seconds of quick reading to realize that the pamphlet, of which 2,000 copies had been destroyed, was a reprint from *Magazine Digest*, an eloquent and effective *answer* to anti-Semitism.[9] Granted, the choice of title was not the wisest or most discreet. One can hardly blame a Jewish boy for becoming initially agitated and concerned. But his imagination had betrayed him into destroying the very thing he wanted.

There have been other cases too in which reported prejudice proved to be imaginary. Men have on a very few occasions come to me with charges that their commanding officers had refused them permission to attend one or another type of important Jewish religious service. And I have found, after investigating, either that the commanding officer was not given all the facts, that some official directive had failed to reach him, or that the

---

[9] Emphasis in original.

Jewish boy had not applied through proper channels. I have personally seen only one instance in 18 months, where, with all the facts known and all the proper procedure followed, permission of this kind was still refused.

Sometimes also, boys will at first explain some failure or disappointment in terms of prejudice instead of searching for the real reason within themselves. There is such a man with whom I happen to be working right now. He came to me some weeks ago with a long tale of troubles. He did not feel at home in his outfit. The men did not seem to like him. He was left out of their little conspiracies and extra pleasures. And he was sure the fact of his being Jewish was the only reason. Extended inquiry had shown me that everything he had said was true except the reason he gave. The men of his platoon did dislike him, but they would have felt the same way no matter what his religious affiliation happened to be. The proof of the pudding was twofold. First, there were other Jewish men in the company, who were generally known to be Jewish but who had no such troubles. Second, these other Jews disliked the boy as much as anyone did. Clearly, this was a case in which the trouble lay not with prejudice from without, but with inadequacies of personality from within. One of the deepest satisfactions I have had in many months was the slow but sure process of turning that man's focus within himself and watching him make a brave effort to straighten himself out.

If I may be permitted here a paragraph in parentheses, it should be said that just as not every case of apparent prejudice is really that, so not everyone who seems to be a Jew is actually one. Shortly after reporting for my first Marine duty, I had occasion to seek information about a Jewish boy. Calling the first sergeant of the company by phone, I heard him answer, "Sergeant Goldberg speaking." Having finished my business with him, I asked his name again to be sure. Then I said, "I'm the new Jewish chaplain here. From your name, I assume you're a member of my congregation." "Oh no, sir," he quickly replied. "My name is spelled G-O-L-D-E-B-O-U-R-G; I'm Scandinavian." That was the last time I took any such thing as that for granted.

But after everything possible is said to eliminate imagination from the field, the unpleasant though unavoidable truth remains that there is prejudice that cannot be so easily explained away. As a matter of discouraging fact, there is prejudice even among those with whom we might reasonably expect never to find it; even among chaplains, who presume to be brotherly men of God! I have had a chaplain refuse to place on the shelves of his regimental library any books about or for Jews. I have heard a chaplain tell me there were too many Jews in governmental office! I have listened to a chaplain say there must be something wrong with Jews if so many people are prejudiced against them. And I have sat, saddened and stunned beyond belief, as a Catholic chaplain, forgetting the stand of his own church in the matter, said to me: "Father Coughlin is the greatest Catholic priest in the world. I would kiss the ground he walks on!"[10]

The most bitterly painful experience of this kind in my life as a chaplain occurred precisely at a time when it should least have been expected—in the midst of combat itself. We were about to dedicate the final resting place of our martyred dead, near the base of Mount Suribachi on the island of Iwo Jima. Our division

---

[10] Charles E. Coughlin was a Roman Catholic known as the "radio priest." In the 1930s, he developed one of the first loyal mass audiences in radio broadcast history, later expressing reactionary views that were increasingly anti-New Deal and loaded with anti-Semitic rhetoric. By 1942, his published works were banned and the Catholic Church ordered him to stop broadcasting. See, Albin Krebs, "Charles Coughlin, 30's 'Radio Priest'," *New York Times*, 28 October 1979.

chaplain, Commander Warren F. Cuthriell, had arranged a joint dedicatory and memorial service.[11] First, there would be a secular dedication at which, of course, the address would be given by Major General Keller E. Rockey.[12] Immediately following, all three faiths—Protestant, Catholic, and Jewish—were to unite in a joint religious memorial service, of which any group that so wished would be free to hold its own denominational service. As an eloquent expression of his own deep devotion alike to the noble teachings of Christianity and the high truths of democracy, Chaplain Cuthriell invited me, spokesman of the smallest religious minority in the division, to preach the memorial sermon. Unfortunately, his idealism was not matched by all our colleagues. One entire group of chaplains refused to participate on any terms in a joint memorial service. Two other individual chaplains protested vigorously against the very thought of a Jewish chaplain speaking over the graves of Christians as well as his own men. There was enough opposition—among chaplains—so that Commander Cuthriell was reluctantly forced to change the proposed plans. After a brief secular dedication, each denomination withdrew into its own specified corner to hold its own service of memorial. I do not remember anything in my life that has made me so painfully heartsick. We had just come

---

[11] Navy chaplain Cuthriell received a letter of commendation (with ribbon) for his work on Iwo Jima. See Capt Clifford Merrill Drury, *History of the Chaplain Corps*, vol. 2, *1939–1949* (Washington, DC: Bureau of Naval Personnel, 1948), 164; and Kenneth J. Brown, "Letters: Remembering Rabbi Gittelsohn as a 'Great Advocate of Peace'," *Spearhead News*, Fall/Winter 2015, 4–5.
[12] Rockey (1888–1970) was commissioned in the Marine Corps in 1913 and served through World War I and World War II, with additional service between the two wars in Nicaragua. He commanded the 5th Marine Division during the Battle of Iwo Jima. He retired as a lieutenant general in 1950.

Mass on the mount, 1945.
*John C. Scharfen Collection (COLL/272), in the Archives Branch,
Marine Corp History Division*

through nearly five weeks of miserable hell. Some of us at least had served men of all faiths and of no faith, without making denomination or affiliation a prerequisite for help. Protestants, Catholics, and Jews had lived together, fought together, died together, and now lay buried together. But we the living could not unite to pray together. My chief consolation was that another Jew besides myself would have been unacceptable as dedicator of the cemetery—even though these very men professed to teach in his name.[13]

These things are not easy to take. They are still harder to

---

[13] Donald M. Bishop, "Iwo Jima and 'the Purest Democracy'," *American Interest*, 23 December 2019.

tell. There are moments of deep discouragement when one cannot help but wonder what hope there is for laymen, if their religious leaders speak and act so. The answer, of course, is that these incidents are not universal. Were it not so, there would be little hope indeed. The average Christian chaplain is as scandalized by conduct of this sort as I could ever be. I dare to hope and believe that one of them, who was present when the library episode took place, spoke for more than himself when he came to my tent the next morning and said: "I just wanted you to understand clearly and directly that far from all of us feel the way . . . does. If there's anything I can do, now or ever, to cooperate, I want to be called on." After the distasteful episode of the cemetery dedication, three Protestant chaplains made a special point of attending our Jewish memorial service in a manifest gesture of understanding.

Things happen sometimes in the service that show how distressingly deep anti-Semitism is rooted in human behavior, and how long, therefore, the struggle against it will take. I was amazed to find anti-Semitism among the natives of a Pacific island for which only 3 or 4 of whose 350,000 inhabitants were Jewish. In a village where people had never knowingly even seen a Jew, one native was heard to say to another: "That shirt you bought is no good. Probably some Jew sold it to you." Strange, twisted perversion of the human mind! To hate any other folk, it is necessary to see, to know them. To hate Jews, one does not even need to have Jews! They told a story before the war about the Japanese who went to Germany to study the methods and techniques of the Nazis. After weeks of careful study, he expressed his surprise that nothing had been taught to him about anti-Semitism. "But you do not need anti-Semitism," his instructor insisted, "in Japan you have no Jews." "True," replied the Japanese, "true enough. But we want to be ready, we hear they are coming!"[14] Once, I thought that story funny. I no longer do.

Other discomfiting evidence that anti-Semitism is a deep and virulent infection; in our division, there is one particular lieutenant colonel who is known to drive his men mercilessly. He has no respect for religion of any kind. He is no more a Jew than Joseph Goebbels was. He is the one officer mentioned a moment ago who would not excuse his Jewish men back in the states to attend their Seder services on Passover. But when, in a certain phase of training, he insisted that his men go on Sunday problems, and would not excuse them for church, numbers of men in the outfit were heard to curse him as "that damn Jew who won't let us go to church!" It is not enough that we are made to pay for the imagined faults of real Jews; we must also be responsible for the real failings of imaginary Jews!

Another recent occurrence illustrated much the same sort of thing: the stubborn, lunatic deepness of anti-Semitism in mens' minds. A Marine sergeant came back to his tent at 2200 one night drunk. He walked in on a half-dozen men who were sitting there—one of them a Jew. Staggering over toward the latter, he berated him, "One good thing Adolf Hitler has done is to kill the Jews. The only trouble is that he didn't get all of them. I'd like to get back to the states in time to finish them off there too!" Fortunately, the Jewish boy had enough good sense, no matter how badly he was shocked, not to create an issue then and there. He walked out of the tent and reported the affair to me the next morning. Two things made the incident hurt even more than it otherwise might have. First, on the previous day,

---

[14] See, for example, Eri Hotta, *Pan-Asianism and Japan's War, 1931–1945* (London: Palgrave, 2007).

I had buried a Sergeant Aaron Levy, a Jewish Army boy who had known himself to have heart trouble, who had refused to turn in for medical examination because he was afraid he might be surveyed out of the Army before the war was over, and who had dropped dead in camp. Second, I had but recently left a good friend of mine, Corporal Heinz Gelles, whose father, once a lieutenant colonel in the Austrian Army, had been stripped of his decorations and killed in a concentration camp, and whose mother had been deported to Poland back in 1941.[15] Heinz had been in tears because, against his own preference, he was being returned to the states for V-12 Navy College Training and a probable commission.[16] "That isn't what I came into the Marine Corps for," he insisted. "I came in to help fight a war. When this job is finished, there'll be time enough for college." Was this, then, what Aaron Levy had died for, and what Heinz Gelles wanted to fight for—the right of a drunken sergeant to echo the fume and foam of fascist frenzy?

But the principal point of the story is yet to come. After discussing the incident with the sergeant's Protestant chaplain, the two of us decided to call him in and to speak to him together. We were considerably surprised to find him a freckle-faced, ruddy-headed typical farm boy from Iowa, and a hero at that.

---

[15] Robert A. Cohn, "Heinz Gelles, 87; Escaped Shoah and Started New Life Here," *STL Jewish Light*, 23 January 2013.

[16] The Navy V-12 program was created on 1 July 1943 to generate a large number of officers and to offset dropping enrollment at colleges. It paid tuition to participating institutions for courses taught to qualified candidates, including naval enlisted personnel who were recommended by their commanding officers and high school seniors who passed a qualifying exam.

He had been at Tarawa.[17] He was one of those who had pulled 75mm guns to within four or five dozen yards of murderous Japanese machine gun positions to blast them away. What made such a man tick? What made his tongue speak the lies of fascism after he had risked his life to kill the bearers of fascism? We found the answer in a bowed, dejected head that did not look up at us once in all the time we spoke. It still hung downward as he finally mumbled, "I've never been so ashamed of myself in my life. The worst part of it is that I don't really feel that way. Jews to me are like any other people, some good, some bad. I guess I just went crazy on too much beer, and said things that have made me uncomfortable ever since. I've wanted to apologize to Willie a dozen times, but didn't have the nerve." What an admission. What an indictment of human behavior. A man harbors no hate, presumably, against anyone. He succumbs to the influence of alcohol. And the first thing his unbridled mind does is to run amuck—against the Jew. How many centuries went into the making of that miserable moment? How many centuries more will it take to erase it?

If this sort of thing were a phenomenon isolated unto itself, perhaps it could be said with some measure of justice that a chaplain could afford to ignore it. Anyone with eyes and a mind knows, however, that anti-Semitism is the forerunner, the first symptom, and advance scout of fascism that, if left to grow, will be followed by the full fruits of the fascist seed. To fight anti-Semitism, therefore, to resist it with all the power at one's command, is at the same time to oppose fascism and to uphold

---

[17] Col Joseph H. Alexander (Ret), *Across the Reef: The Marine Assault of Tarawa* (Washington, DC: History and Museums Division, Headquarters Marine Corps, 1993).

democracy. The key to my own procedure in doing that is in the story just completed. I have never placed an enlisted man on report or pressed disciplinary charges against him for an offense of this kind. A talk like that with the sergeant, an attempt to help the man see that what he has done is undemocratic and un-American—up to the present, that is as far as I have gone. Usually such a conference is held jointly with the proper Catholic or Protestant chaplain; on some few occasions, it has to be done alone.

Here or there, however, where the offender happens to be a commissioned officer, the tactic differs. An enlisted farm kid from Iowa can be forgiven for a prejudice that is inexcusable in a college-graduated, commissioned officer who is in a position to translate purely personal prejudice into quasiofficial discrimination. Let it here be said for the record that in my own direct, immediate experience there have been only two such officers who exceeded the limits of propriety. One was a Navy doctor who made disparaging remarks and vehement accusations in the presence of a second physician whom he did not know to be Jewish. The other was a lieutenant colonel who evidently thought the proper way to refer to the Jewish chaplain was as "the Jew bastard," and who gave a captain and a lieutenant in his command a lecture on what he thought of Jews. And what he thought of Jews was a carbon copy of what Hitler thinks of Jews. In both cases, a simple, unemotional, straightforward report of the incident was followed by immediate and direct action from above. No matter what foolish prejudices there may be in the misguided minds of individuals here or there, be it said, to the everlasting credit of the United States and its armed forces, that those who are "topside" will not allow or excuse for a single moment any evidence or suspicion of discrimination if it is called to their attention. There, I think, is the most encouraging factor of all.

So far, the picture has not been too pleasant. If I have first sought to emphasize the relatively dark side of things, that has been with the deliberate intent of dismissing those wishful thinkers who indulge in paeans of praise for the wonderful new day—hallelujah—which will come if we but relax and await it. I would not want to leave the impression, however, that there is no hopeful, positive side to the picture. There most assuredly is. For every experience that depresses, there are two or three that uplift. There is a world of difference between saying that progress and understanding inevitably, automatically *must* come out of this conflict, and saying that they *can* result, if we understand both the issues and the dangers and play our hand wisely.[18] What, then, are the portents and signs that give one hope?

First, that Christians and Jews in the armed forces have an unparalleled opportunity to see each other, learn from and about each other. What I found to be true in this respect at chaplains' training school is, on a larger scale, true throughout the Army and Navy. Men who never before knew or saw a Jew are now living night and day with Jews. One of our Army chaplains has told that on a South Pacific island the natives, converted to Christianity by missionaries, were puzzled by the Magen Davids, or Stars of David, which mark Jewish graves in the Army cemeteries there. One of the native workers, who could contain his curiosity no longer, turned to a Christian chaplain and asked, "I know what the crosses stand for; but the six-pointed stars, are they for generals?"

South Sea islanders are learning about dead Jews. Of far

---

[18] Emphasis in original.

greater importance, American Christians are learning about living Jews. The fog of ignorance and superstition is at least partly being lifted. I have been invited more than once to groups, such as the Christian Service League, to spend a whole evening answering questions about Judaism and Jews. I have led a discussion group in which colored and whites together delved into the issues, while Christian and Jews combined to talk about anti-Semitism. Where ignorance is dispelled by knowledge, there is hope.

A second favorable factor is the official policy of the Army and Navy. To some extent, we have already seen what that official policy is in our discussion of the training that embryonic chaplains receive. At Williamsburg, we were constantly told: you are Navy chaplains first; denominational chaplains only second. Your job is to provide for the needs of *all* men, of *every* faith.[19] Rear Admiral Robert D. Workman, director of our chaplains' division, has issued a specific directive stating that every Navy chapel is to be provided with the paraphernalia and symbols of both Christianity and Judaism, but that neither are to be permanent, immovable fixtures of the building.[20]

But official policy, however liberal and intelligent, would be of small value were it not for the fact that by and large our individual chaplains follow it zealously. A substantial majority of the cases I have reported on these pages, for example, are not concerned with Jews at all. They deal with Gentiles who happened to come in when the Jewish chaplain was on duty. I am sure the opposite would be true of a good many Christian chaplains. As a matter of fact, unless a man comes with a prob-

---

[19] Emphasis in original.
[20] Drury, *The History of the Chaplain Corps*.

lem that is specifically theological in nature, we do not generally ask his faith or tell him ours. He is a human being, coming with a human problem, to a human chaplain. More than one man has called me "Father" as I tried to help him. One night when I had the duty in Norfolk, Virginia, a Catholic boy persisted in addressing me that way. The first few times, I passed it over. As he continued, I thought maybe he was under the impression that I was in actual fact a Catholic priest, so I decided to correct him. At his next pause, I said, "You don't have to call me 'Father.' I'm not a priest, but of course I would be glad to help you if I can." To which his immediate response was "Okay, Father."

This war has brought me enough pleasant and heartening experiences with my fellow chaplains to wipe out much of the taste of bitterness. On the night before Iwo Jima's D-day, the Protestant chaplain of our transport and I united to broadcast a joint preinvasion religious service over our ship's public address system. Weeks later, both Jewish and Christian men whom I greeted as they were carried into the division field hospital remembered that service and told me how very much it had meant to them in the critical moments or hours after they had been hit. I prayed—together with other chaplains—over the graves of more than a thousand Christian men as their bodies were committed to the earth. And whenever possible, at least one Christian chaplain was invited to join me in burying my Jewish men. One such service was unforgettable. It was the night before we boarded ship to leave the scene of combat. Since bodies were still being brought in for burial, we held off our final service of committal as long as possible to be sure that all would be included. Finally, as we descended into the last trench of maven, darkness had already fallen. Off to the west, the last suspicion of light was reluctant to leave the sky. Overhead, there were

Battle for Iwo Jima, ca. February–March 1945.
Chaplain E. Gage Hotaling committing a Marine's body to a grave.
U.S. Marine Corps photo

stars. All around there was peace—great, embracing quiet peace. And three chaplains—a Baptist, a Methodist, and a Jew—stood together before the last row of graves and held the flashlight for each other as they prayed.

Another experience that occurred just before our division left Iwo Jima was equally heartening. The Jewish Passover holiday was near at hand. It was obvious that our Seder service would be held on the ships carrying us back from combat to rest camp. But we had been able to carry with us into battle no Passover foods or supplies at all. Chaplain Newton C. Elder of the Army garrison forces on Iwo heard of our plight. Before we were even aware of his intentions, he had secured a plane, flew some 600 miles south to Saipan, and returned with nearly half a ton of gear for Passover. Because of him and his unsolicited co-operation, several hundred Jewish boys sat down onboard their respective ships to usher in the Passover festival of 1945. It is worth recording also that each Friday night while we remained together on Iwo, Chaplain Elder not only rounded up the Jewish men of his Army outfit for Sabbath services, but he also attended himself and worshiped with them.

An experience at the San Diego Marine Corps base will illustrate how most of our chaplains follow the policy set down by Chaplain Workman. It concerns Lieutenant Commander Walter A. Mahler, then senior chaplain at the base.[21] A Jewish boy came to him for counseling. It was apparent immediately that at least part of the man's trouble stemmed from the fact that he wore his Jewishness with uncomfortable awkwardness. He felt so pitifully exposed, as a member of a minority group, that he could not make a wholesome adjustment to his new surroundings and life. I suppose Walter Mahler could have slipped out easily from under that one if he had wanted to. He could have said it was none of his business as a Catholic chaplain to help a Jewish man adjust to his Jewishness. He might have told the lad to see the Jewish chaplain on his next visiting day at the base. He could have, and he might have, but he did not. For that

---

[21] Father Walter A. Mahler, a Catholic priest from the Diocese in Pittsburgh, PA, was ordained in 1933 and entered the Navy as a chaplain in 1939. He was the ship's chaplain for the USS *Astoria* (CA 34) and survived its sinking at Savo Island in 1942. He continued serving in the Navy during Korea and Vietnam, retiring as a captain. See "Resources," *Navy Chaplain* 3, no. 1 (1989).

would have been neither the "Navy way" nor Walter Mahler's way. Instead, Mahler patiently sat the young man down and said to him:

> Look here, my boy, don't you ever let me catch you walking around this base ashamed of the fact that you're a Jew. I, as a Catholic priest, get down on my knees every morning and pray to a Jew, Jesus! I hold a Jewish girl, Mary, to be one of the sacred personalities of my faith. You just walk out of this office and hold your head as high as you know how. Being a Jew is something to be proud of, not something to hide.

I had several occasions later to work with that Jewish boy. I doubt if anything I or another rabbi might have said could ever have awakened him in quite the way that Walter Mahler had. Suddenly, he had acquired a new and wholesome respect for himself, his people, and his faith. And he had also developed an abiding sense of gratitude to a Catholicism that was eager to acknowledge its origins in the faith of his own fathers. This is the Navy way.

What makes this way all the more potentially encouraging is the fact that where chaplains behave so, their men soon catch the spirit of the thing and do likewise. On Passover of 1944, a group of Marine Corps cooks and messmen—among them Greeks, Italians, Scotch-Irish, but not a single Jew—worked for weeks, laid in supplies, studied Jewish recipes, cooked gefilte fish and matzo-ball soup, borrowed sheets for tablecloths, and filled old ketchup bottles with flowers, so that 70 Jewish men and women could sit down to a traditional Seder feast. On the following Day of Atonement in an overseas camp, much the same sort of thing was repeated by a different group, by Christian men who gave up many hours of precious free time to prepare our dinner for the night of Yom Kippur, and who would not even allow our Jewish boys to show their gratitude by helping to clean up, because they said, "This is your holiday." And the same thing is true in reverse. Ever since the war began, at Army camps and naval stations throughout the world, Jewish soldiers and sailors have volunteered for extra duty on Christmas, have given up furloughs and leaves to which they were justly entitled, in order that their Christian buddies might have their most important religious holiday free. Truly, in the crucible of common suffering, at least *some* men are learning to live together.[22]

They are also learning to pray together. To pray together to the same God, without any one of them being asked to relinquish an ounce of this own distinctive faith. On one occasion, when a replacement battalion was about to shove off from Camp Elliott, the commanding officer phoned me. He wanted to have a joint service of worship for the Protestant and Jewish men in the battalion, a final occasion for all to pray together before they sailed. And though Protestants outnumbered Jews in that battalion by about 50 to 1, he asked me, a Jew to conduct the nonsectarian service. In a sense, I was anticipating my very good friend Chaplain Herbert Van Meter, a Congregationalist, who at a time when it was temporarily impossible for me to be with the Jewish men of one regiment conducted weekly Jewish

---

[22] Emphasis in original.

Sabbath services so proficiently that the boys began to call him *Rabbi* Van Meter.[23]

The most unusual experience I can remember of this kind was in the chapel of the base at San Diego. On Sunday mornings, that chapel was one of the busiest places in southern California. From 0730 until noon, a steady stream of worshipers could be seen flowing in both directions. Two Protestant services, alternating with two Catholic masses, were followed by my Jewish service at 1100. In three minutes, before I came in each week, the base chapel was converted from a Christian sanctuary into a Jewish synagogue. Almost before the echoes of the last Protestant hymn had died out, my congregation of Jewish Marines were singing in the service according to the faith of Israel. That in itself is worth commenting on, but what follows is, I think, even more remarkable.

One Sunday morning, a Marine walked in during our Jewish service. It was evident immediately that he was a Catholic, since he crossed himself as he entered and dropped at once to his knees in one of the rear rows. While we sang "Shema Yisrael," (Hear O Israel) the watchword of our Jewish faith, he, on branded knee and with bowed head, recited his own prayers. As we went on reading a Hebrew prayer together, he rose from

---

[23] Emphasis in original. Van Meter attended Oberlin Graduate School of Theology (1940–41) and completed his divinity studies at Yale University. Following his ordination, he was commissioned a Protestant naval chaplain. He served on Iwo Jima with the 26th Regiment, 5th Marine Division. The 26th Regiment went ashore on D-day and held the line until the Pacific island was secured. For his service, Van Meter received the Navy and Marine Corps Medal and the Bronze Star. For an account of Herbert Van Meter's war experiences, see Roland B. Gittelsohn, "Padre in Hell," *Leatherneck* 68, no. 12, December 1985, 44–47. Van Meter's personal papers can be viewed at Herbert and Josephine Van Meter Papers, 1923–1987, 1995–1996, Record Group 30/288, Oberlin College Archives, Oberlin, OH.

his knees, sat on the bench, took out his Catholic Missal, and continued his worship.[24] Very few members of my congregation even knew that he was there, but standing on the pulpit I could see him easily. When he had apparently completed his worship, he sat there for quite some time, listening to our prayers with obvious interest. Then he sank to his knees again, rose and crossed himself once more, and quietly left as our Jewish service continued. He returned to repeat the same performance three or four consecutive weeks. I assumed that his duties prevented his attendance at the earlier Catholic masses. So, he entered the chapel when he could, and without any embarrassment or self-consciousness on either his part or ours, while we worshiped God in our way, he, in the same sanctuary, worshiped the same God in his way.

What an inspiring example for civilian life in the world of tomorrow. Americans worshiping together because they have learned to live and suffer and rejoice together.[25] Americans all playing in harmony from the same score, but each preserving their own religious and cultural distinctions, as the members of a symphony orchestra preserve the qualities and tones of their

---

[24] A missal is a liturgical book containing the texts and prayers used by the priest and congregants during Catholic masses. Catholics attending mass now use seasonal "missalettes," but individual Catholics of that time had their own missals, perhaps given them when they were confirmed. Since Catholic masses were said in Latin at that time, the Marine's copy would have had Latin and English on opposite pages. The term *missal* comes from the Latin word *missa*, meaning mass.

[25] The celebrated Norman Rockwell painting, *Freedom to Worship* (1943), strikes the same theme—men and women together in prayer, "each according to the dictates of his own conscience." See Will Durant, "Freedom of Worship," *Saturday Evening Post*, 27 February 1943.

individual instruments.[26] That boy was not less Catholic, nor were we less Jewish, because we worshiped—each in his own way—the same God at the same time in the same room. But he knew and respected our faith more than he did before, even as we increased our knowledge and respect for his. Thus, do men at war learn to pray together.

What remains to be said, and what cuts perhaps deepest of all down into the marrow of things, is that they also learn to die together. Death knows no discrimination. Even Hitler's shells cut through Jewish and Gentile flesh exactly the same. And in that sameness is a cord that ought to bind men closer. If this fails, there is no hope indeed. To me, there are two symbols that embrace within themselves very nearly the whole meaning of this war. One is the picture of my friend and classmate, Rabbi Alexander D. Goode, standing on the icy deck of the USAT *Dorchester* troop transport that had been torpedoed in the dead

---

[26] In his 1963 "I Have a Dream" speech at the Lincoln Memorial, Dr. Martin Luther King said, "With this faith we will be able to transform the jangling discords of our nation into a beautiful harmony of brotherhood." The metaphor of the American nation as a symphony or orchestra has been much discussed, with Israel Zangwill's 1908 play, *The Melting Pot*, providing one starting point; see *Works of Israel Zangwill: The Melting Pot* (New York: American Jewish Book Co. 1921). John Rawls used the orchestra metaphor in his *Political Liberalism*, expanded ed. (New York: Columbia University Press, 2005), 204. See also David Biale, Michael Galchinsky, and Susannah Heschel, eds., *Insider/Outsider: American Jews and Multiculturalism* (Berkeley: University of California Press, 1998).

The U.S. Post Office issued a commemorative stamp honoring the four chaplains in 1948. Chaplain Goode is on the right.
Official U.S. Army photo

of a February night in 1943.[27] With him were three other chaplains. All four had given their lifejackets to seamen who were without them. The last that any mortal eye will ever see of them, they stood there near the rail—a Catholic, two Protestants, and a Jew—praying together the moment before they died together.[28]

The other symbol that has impressed itself indelibly on my mind is the life of Second Lieutenant Martin H. Weinberg. I

---

[27] Army Chaplain Alexander D. Goode (1911–43) was the rabbi among the four chaplains. He received his bachelor's degree from the University of Cincinnati in 1933, and he graduated from Hebrew Union College in 1937, a year after Gittelsohn. He earned a PhD from Johns Hopkins University in 1940 while serving at a synagogue in York, PA. Gittelsohn and Goode knew one another from campus life in a graduate school that enrolled only a few dozen students. For biographical material on Goode, see "A Finding Aid to the Alexander D. Goode Papers," American Jewish Archives, Cincinnati, OH.

[28] Sharon Otterman, "Remembering the Four Chaplains and Their Ultimate Sacrifice," *New York Times*, 4 February 2018.

said before that I would mention him again. Martin was the first Jewish Marine Corps officer I met after reporting for duty in San Diego. He was also the first at whose wedding I had the pleasure of officiating. In the fall of 1943, I married Weinberg to Miss Yetta Adler of San Diego. During the following two or three months, they, my wife, and I became close friends. Marty and his wife attended Friday services at Camp Elliott regularly. When he shipped out in a replacement battalion, his wife continued her attendance and we maintained our friendship with her. Marty wrote me several interesting letters from overseas. All of them indicated that he loved his work and that he was almost childishly proud of his commission in the Marine Corps. I was scarcely surprised at his enthusiasm, since I knew that he had pleaded for combat duty well before the time that he otherwise would have been sent across.

There was only one discordant note in his communications to me. He had been sent, as an officer replacement, to a Marine division. There, he met a small number of fellow officers who resented the fact that he was a Jew. By gestures and measures more obvious than subtle, they made it clear that they wanted no part of a Marine officer named Weinberg. Be it said at once, however, that their attitude, far from being typical, was more the exception than the rule. But it bothered my friend no little amount, and we exchanged our disturbed thoughts on the subject more than once.

Marty never wrote whether the passage of time mellowed any of those who had resented him. He never will. For during the campaign on Saipan, his wife received *the* telegram from General Alexander A. Vandegrift: "Regret . . . your husband . . . killed in action . . . service of his country . . . no details available

. . . deepest sympathy."[29] I think that telegram was the most final and irrevocable thing I have ever held in my hand or seen with my eye.

After I had left Yetta, and I had tried to utter whatever useless and futile words of comfort my lips could speak, the strangest thought kept racing through my mind. I wondered if the two or three who had resented him were there when it happened. Did they know that Martin Weinberg gave his life for a democracy they could not even understand? Had he—incomparable irony—stopped a bullet or piece of shrapnel that would otherwise have killed one of them? Did the life-bearing blood from his shattered veins mingle and merge with theirs as it trickled down some shell-pocked slope? I wondered . . .

I suggested all kinds of answers when Marty first wrote of his unpleasant experience overseas. He composed the most eloquent answer of all, the answer of his deeds. And the lines are but a pale reflection of the esteem in which I hold him. But there is something far more important here than a matter of personal friendship or affection. Whoever did not or would not welcome Martin Weinberg—no matter how high his rank, how numerous his medals—is an enemy of the United States, a faithless betrayer of our most cherished ideals. Whoever understands America—understands it and loves it—must also understand and love Marty Weinberg.

Well then, what does it all add up to? Is the picture bright or dark? Is the future clear or cloudy? The only honest answer is:

---

[29] Emphasis in original. Weinberg's name was listed in "Casualty Lists Released This Week Include More Names from Saipan," *Marine Corps Chevron*, 29 July 1944.

"We do not know." No one knows. There is, in the total picture, much to give encouragement and much to sadden and depress. My own feeling is that war, with its fears and frustrations, has its way of magnifying and emphasizing both extremes. Those who came into the Service with their hatreds, big and little, probably feel them more bitterly now than ever. And those who came with sparks of decent goodness, with faith in men of every creed, are stronger and firmer now than they ever hoped to be.

Perhaps the future belongs to the great majority who are at neither extreme. They can join the men of bitter violence. Or they can remain indifferent and lose the fight by default. Or they can rise up in righteous wrath, and give democratic understanding a new birth in the hearts and minds of men.

CHAPTER THIRTEEN

Black Sand–Red Blood

Someone has said with devastating accuracy that war consists of being bored to death 90 percent of the time and excited to death the other 10 percent.[1] For us of the 5th Marine Division, all that occurred during a year at Camp Pendleton, San Diego, California, and at our overseas base was pointed at the 35 days we spent with the 3d and 4th Marine Divisions in the conquest of Iwo Jima. It would manifestly be an injustice to the reader, and even more so to the officers and men of our division, to close this account without commenting on what all correspondents agree was the bloodiest battle of the Pacific up to February of 1945. I have neither desire nor right, however, to speak as a military expert or to interpret the progress of military events. Others have done that and will continue to do so. My only hope here is to speak soberly of how combat looks to the chaplain's eye. From the moment that our first assault wave sank into the coarse, ugly, black gravel of Iwo's eastern "beaches," everything

---

[1] While not a direct quote, the sentiment is expressed in "The Baptism of Fire," *London Times*, 4 November 1914.

we had planned and thought was under severe test. How did we make out? What did we learn?

First, and perhaps foremost, we learned that ordinary American kids are capable of courage that is incredible even to one who has seen it! Combat is not pleasant. One young officer I know turned almost completely gray haired in five weeks of it. Even now, many restful weeks later, none of us has completely recovered from the shocking, shattering effect that combat had on our emotions and nerves. But the courage of ordinary boys from Main Street is such that more than once I wanted to bow humbly and say with Jacob of old: "Indeed, the Lord is in this place, and I knew it not."[2]

I saw that courage even before leaving our transport. For the first 48 hours of the operation, my assigned duty was to remain on the ship to render whatever service I could to wounded men being brought back aboard. Some of them had lain in the open evening cold for hours before they could be evacuated. Some had been soaked to the skin with salt spray on the trip back to the transport area. Many were painfully hurt, very painful-ly. But none of them—literally, truthfully, *none*—whimpered or cried.[3] I held one young sailor's hand while a surgeon dug out large pieces of shrapnel from a hole in the back of his knee big enough for two fists. I was to let the doctor know when and if the pain became too great. So, every moment or so, I would lean over and ask the boy if he was being hurt. His face was pale with pain; his teeth had punctuated his lips with blood; his fingernails dug into the palm of my hand with marks that were still visible hours later. But his answer, each and every time I asked whether the doctor's probing was painful, was NO! And

---

[2] Genesis 28:16.
[3] Emphasis in original.

believe me, he was no exception. In five weeks of intensive combat, through many hundreds of contacts with men who were badly hurt, the only men I ever heard cry were those who were telling of a buddy who had been killed before their eyes, or those who themselves had cracked mentally under a strain too great to bear. Quentin Reynolds expressed more than the title of a book in his sentence: "The Wounded Don't Cry."[4]

There were so very many instances of incredible courage just within the scope of my own knowledge and experience on Iwo that the problem now in prospect is one of limiting ourselves to a few typical examples rather than searching for enough. On D-day, in a rain of murderous mortar fire, Joshua Rosenfield picked up a buddy who had just lost three fingers, gave him first aid, and carried him several hundred yards to the beach—with men dropping all along the way but a few feet from him—delivered him to an aid station, walked back the same death-dealing way, and carried on his duties as though nothing exceptional had occurred. Later when I complimented him on his heroism, he looked at me as though I spoke a language he did not understand and said, "Heroism? What else *could* I have done?"[5]

Second Lieutenant Dewey A. Erickson was on the front lines with our Reconnaissance Company, 28th Marines, one night in the third or fourth week of action. He and his men had to cross an open ridge, exposed to enemy machine gun cross fire. Erickson bounded across in a moving parenthesis of bullets and reached cover safely. His first glance backward showed him that his runner, who had followed by a few steps, had been less lucky; he lay on the ground wounded. Erickson knew what the chances were of getting safely through that fire a second time,

---

[4] Quentin J. Reynolds, *The Wounded Don't Cry* (New York: E. P. Dutton, 1941).
[5] Emphasis in original.

but he also knew that a kid who was hurt lay out there in plain view of the enemy. Without pausing even long enough to regain his breath, out he went again. It was after he had picked up his runner and carried him to within a few precious steps of safety that Dewey Erickson's great heart was pierced by the bullet that ended his life.[6]

Pharmacist's Mate Third Class Aaron Cohen was one of my best friends in the division—a young boy of about 19 or 20 years, who had been with me for more than a year in three different camps. On several occasions, Cohen sat in my tent far into the night telling me of fears he would have been ashamed to confess to others. As a hospital corpsman, he knew what it meant to be a company aid man, to go in with the first assault waves and to have the lives of frontline troops depend on his courage and skill. When he expressed to me his very real doubts about his ability to measure up, I could only comfort him with the assurance that when the time came, he would be stronger than he suspected. And indeed, he was. It was on D-day, after he had already administered aid to half a dozen men, that he left the relative safety of his own foxhole to attend another boy who held been hit. That boy's mother still has her living son, because it was not until his wounds had been bandaged that Aaron Cohen was killed.[7]

Pharmacist's Mate First Class Jacob S. Fishke is a few months one side or the other of 50 years old. He was born in one of the ghettoes of Poland, came to the United States as a young man, served in our Army during the First World War.

_____

[6] Erickson received the Silver Star (posthumously) as a result of this action on 14 March 1945. See "Dewey A. Erickson," Valor.MilitaryTimes.com.

[7] PhM3c Aaron Cohen was mortally wounded during the Battle of Iwo Jima on 19 February 1945.

No one could have blamed him if in this war he had chosen to remain at home with his wife and three daughters. Instead, he enlisted as a corpsman in the Navy, became a pharmacist's mate, and *requested* combat duty with the Marine Corps.[8] On the front lines on Iwo with the 26th Marines, he undertook more than one dangerous mission that made younger men hesitate. Almost as important as the medical aid he gave was the morale-building influence in his regiment of "Pop" Fishke's gray hair in the front lines.[9]

One night, a Japanese shell landed in one of our ammunition dumps far behind the lines. The result was a combination of the most fantastic fireworks and the most astounding terror most of us had over experienced. The shock of the initial explosion was great enough to feel as if some giant had lifted our foxhole several times and had dropped it from a height of some dozen feet. For long, frightful hours after the shell struck, explosions big and little rocked our end of the Motoyama Airfield Number 1. But for the men who were living immediately adjacent to the dump, there was no time even to notice the explosions for there were other dumps nearby. And minute by minute with increasing fury, burning pieces of flares and grenades or red-hot hunks of shrapnel kept falling in places where just a few minutes' start would have sufficed to set off another dump. That the fire was limited, and kept from catastrophic proportions, was due to the cool, calm courage of several hundred white boys and Negroes who kept dashing out of their foxholes to stamp out burning

---

[8] Emphasis in original.
[9] PhM1c Jacob S. Fishke received the Bronze Star for his efforts on Iwo Jima between 19 February and 25 March 1945. *The History of the Medical Department of the United States Navy in World War II: A Compilation of the Killed, Wounded and Decorated Personnel in the Medical Department* (Washington, DC: Bureau of Medicine and Surgery, Navy Department, 1951), 163.

Having pushed the Japanese back from Motoyama Airfield Number 1,
the U.S. Marines commence immediate construction work on the Iwo Jima
bomber strip. In the background, Mount Suribachi is visible.
Thayer Soule Collection (COLL/2266) at the Archives Branch,
Marine Corps History Division

fragments, while other pieces continued to fall all around them.
Not all the heroes of Iwo Jima are even known by name.

And so, it went for day after incredible day. We knew these
boys of ours were "tops." We had lived with them and trained
with them for months. We had been out with them on problems
and maneuvers. We knew in our hearts long before D-day that
no one would have to apologize for the 5th Marine Division in
action. But we neither knew nor could we in advance have suspected, that plain, simple American boys could rise to the kind
of courage we saw on Iwo. Major General Julian C. Smith did
not exaggerate in the least when he said: "I can never again see
a United States Marine without experiencing a feeling of rever-
ence."[10]

---

[10] Richard F. Newcomb, *Iwo Jima* (New York: Henry Holt, 1965), 74. Smith
commanded the 2d Marine Division on Tarawa. See Col Joseph H. Alexander
(Ret), *Across the Reef: The Marine Assault of Tarawa* (Washington, DC: History
and Museums Division, Headquarters Marine Corps, 1993).

Not all the courage was front line. One morning just after breakfast my clerk, Sergeant Julius L. Abramson of Des Moines, Iowa, came back to our foxhole pale as a ghost. It took a moment before he could tell me that he had just walked by one of the hospital operating rooms in time to see two feet, cut off above the ankles—still clad in socks and shoes—thrown by a corpsman into a GI can. It took plenty of courage—tough, stubborn, and resolute courage—for boys who worked at the aid stations and hospitals to see that kind of thing day after heartsick day. I keep thinking reverently of the young boy whom I watched for three hours one afternoon at a corps evacuation hospital on the beach. I was waiting for one of my boys who had been badly wounded to regain consciousness. The hospital corpsman on duty could not have been a day older than 17. He had the face of a high school sophomore, without a trace of either beard or of hair under his arms and on his chest. He was a child moving among men—men who were hurt. But for three hours, he was the nearest thing I have ever seen to an angel of mercy, hurrying with steady self-assurance from patient to patient, carefully taking one man's pulse, tenderly lifting another's head to give him a drink, and unflinchingly cleaning up the mess a third man had just vomited onto the deck. Where did this boy, who should have been bent over school books instead of broken bodies, secure such courage and strength? Where?

From where did the strength come that enabled 50 Negroes and 25 white boys to work at our division cemetery every day for nearly a month? No task from tip to tip of Iwo Jima called for greater or nobler courage. I would not even try—quite as much out of consideration for my own feelings as for those of the reader—to describe the sort of thing we had to face there repeatedly. Like trying to identify a hand, part of a foot, and 12

Iwo Jima Cemetery, 1945.
Ralph J. Vaccaro Collection (COLL/5245) at the Marine Corps Archives,
History Division

or so inches of torso brought in one day for burial. I found as a
chaplain that my two or three hours a day in the cemetery taxed
more than the last ounce of my endurance and strength. These
boys who worked there had not two or three hours but a whole
day every day like that. Digging graves and filling them—collect-
ing and carrying bodies—taking prints of fingers so long dead
that they had to be blown up first, trying to identify the un-
identifiable, going through blood-soaked uniforms and pockets,
coming across the body of a friend, seeing the burned maimed,
crushed, and broken stumps of human beings. Courage? I bow
before it humbly. It would have been far easier to go forward
into the lines, to die there once rather than a thousand times
where they were.

It is not easy, after you have lived and watched that sort of thing for day after harrowing day, to remain calm and rational when you find "Carnegie Steel" stamped on the metal of which Japanese field pieces were made, or when you see Japanese rifle ammunition marked WRA (Winchester Repeating Arms) 42.[11] Some of us found it easier to control our sorrow on Iwo than it will be to harness our anger if ever again American corporations seek profit at the expense of American boys. We will not soon forget the kind of courage we bowed before in combat.

What is it that enables men to reach such heights of courage, to live through the unlivable? I am afraid the answer, based on actual experience, will be very much less spectacular than some might expect. At least part of the answer is what I would call the effect of "combat anesthesia."[12] Most of us never even realized at the immediate moment the full extent of the dangers we faced. I have compared notes with scores of others to make sure that my experience was theirs too in this respect. It was. We

---

[11] In 1892, the industrialist Andrew Carnegie (1835-1919) and other partners consolidated a number of Pennsylvania steel works to form the Carnegie Steel Company. In 1901, it became a subsidiary of the U.S. Steel Corporation. The Winchester Model 42 was an American pump-action shotgun produced by the Winchester Repeating Arms Company from 1933 to 1963. Japan was a regular purchaser of scrap metal from the United States in the 1930s, and some American firms continued to sell scrap metal to the Japanese until President Roosevelt's embargo in 1940. See "Japan, China, the United States and the Road to Pearl Harbor, 1937–41," Office of the Historian, Department of State, accessed 31 December 2019.

[12] Most uses of the term *combat anesthesia* refer to medical anesthesia that blocks pain from wounds received in combat. Gittelsohn's use of this term seems more related to "psychic numbing" or other psychological responses to traumatic events. The "2,000-yard stare" observed among Marines after battles on the Pacific Islands would be one manifestation. See, for example, Gregory W. Rutecki, "Peleliu as a Paradigm for PTSD: The Two Thousand Yard Stare," *Hektoen International* 9, no. 4 (Fall 2017); and Laura Brandon, "Making the Invisible Visible: Post-Traumatic Stress Disorder in Military Art in the 20th & 21st Centuries," *Canadian Military History* 18, no. 3 (2018).

felt at the time almost as if we were doped, as if we had not fully emerged from an anesthetic. As if we were figures moving not so much by the compulsion of our own will as by the manipulation of strings that controlled us. As if we were passively watching someone else go through motions on a screen rather than acting ourselves. Weeks later, in fact, to this very moment, thinking back to some of the episodes we had experienced made us more violently upset in retrospect than we had been at the time.

Example number one: on the night of D+2, Japanese artillery was firing on a landing ship, tank (LST) that was unloading vital supplies. Their forward observers were operating from a half-submerged Japanese barge beached not far away. It was their instruction, radioed back after each round, which directed enemy fire. No more than about 50 yards beyond the LST were a hundred or more drums of high-octane gas and ammunition. The crew of the LST and the shore party men unloading it knew exactly what the consequences would be if only one shell landed a mere 50 yards beyond the target. There was enough dynamite there to blow the entire left flank of the beach sky high. That was one occasion when the accuracy of Japanese artillery paid dividends for us. No less than 11 shells landed *precisely* on target. Not one reached the dump of explosives![13] Later, I asked several men who had been unloading the ship how they felt on that nerve-racking night. Felt? They had not had time to feel. They paid little or no attention to the terrifying possibilities. Did not even think of them. There was a ship to be unloaded, and they were assigned the task of unloading it. In their crowded, benumbed consciousness at that moment, there was room for nothing else. Later, when we marveled at the closeness of their

---

[13] Emphasis in original.

call, one could see their faces perceptibly pale as they realized the full measure of what they had been through almost unwittingly. Combat anesthesia!

Example number two: something very similar happened to those of us who had to face the sights and smells of the division cemetery. Without any conscious thought on our part, we found ourselves barricaded behind a kind of emotional insulation. We built up a wall of impersonality. We went through fairly thoughtless motions, as though we were committing to the earth only these rows of pale-green shrouds, nothing in them. We looked on the dried and drying blood of human beings as we might have accepted the blood of cattle in a slaughter house. It was only later, in your foxhole at night or on the ship returning to rest camp, that a sudden wave of nausea came over you with the dread realization: "My God! These were not empty shrouds or quarters of beef. Yesterday, these were the sons of mothers and husbands of wives!" But by the next day, somehow mercifully, the anesthetic had taken hold again, the wall of impersonality had been restored, and we were once more able to continue. I shudder to think what the permanent consequences might be—how very many more of us might have cracked mentally—were it not for the blessing of combat anesthesia.

Our second source of strength was America's great gift to the human race: an unquenchable, irrepressible sense of humor. We Americans have had many assets and advantages in this war: an industry that produced literal miracles; an organized labor that kept its no-strike pledge to the thrilling extent of 99.9 percent; and an Army, Navy, and Marine Corps that performed the impossible. But greater than all these, I suspect, and in some measure at least responsible for all these, is a type of human being who can laugh even when life approaches the intolerable.

Not one of our 35 days of combat, from first to last, went without at least one good belly laugh. Any people who can laugh on Iwo Jima are unconquerable!

We first saw this American sense of humor as a saving grace during our seven weeks of boredom and insufferable tension on board ship, headed toward combat. There were nicknames, for example. From nowhere they sprang. One morning, a captain came to breakfast in the wardroom with a colossal precoffee grouch. Immediately, someone dubbed him "Laughing Boy," a name he has not entirely lost yet. A major who has not relaxed his poker face twice in the last year was baptized "Smiley." A certain chaplain—shall we keep this strictly impersonal?—whose cranial vegetation has known lusher days, was affectionately labeled by some of his intimates as "Curly." And so it went.

There was the entertainment, as another example. With movies only on the few nights we were in port, with room for less than half of us to play cards at any given moment, we still managed to keep ourselves entertained. Sometimes by seeing who could count the greatest number of flying fish in a given number of minutes. Sometimes by resorting to games like casino (card game) and 20 questions, which most of us had not played since junior high school days. One day in particular hit a positive high in entertainment. Forty or 50 of us were lined up at the port rail. From somewhere topside, a sailor was lowering a bucket on a line to scoop up a pail of sea water. We all followed the bucket, bouncing along the waves, with rapt attention. Each time it filled, spontaneously we let loose with a war cry of triumph. When the momentum of the ship bounced the water out before it could be raised to the deck, a groan of feigned dismay swept from stem to stern. Once the full bucket reached a point some 20 feet above the water, we cheered madly. Then a gust of wind caught the line, dumped the bucket, and the whole business started over again, accompanied by heartrending moans of sympathy and sorrow. Fifty Marines helping one little sailor get a pail of water. It was wonderful!

And the same kind of humor carried us through more than one bad moment on Iwo. One day at noon, about a dozen of us were squatted around a regimental observation post enjoying our lunch of K-rations and sardines.[14] Suddenly, we heard a sinister sputter like that of a grenade. Knives, crackers, mess gear, and Marines all flew into instant and scattered confusion. We all hit the deck and waited tensely for the inevitable explosion. But there was none. Finally, we lifted our heads cautiously. A hysterically laughing chaplain's clerk explained what had happened. Determined to introduce a bit of culinary variety into the drabness of our K-rations, he had hit on the brilliant idea of grilled cheese. After putting a can of cheese on the fire to melt, he had forgotten one thing: to open a few holes in advance. But the laws of physics operate inflexibly even in the command post of the 26th Marines. When the heated can was finally opened, there were three immediate results: the helpless "chef" was generously sprayed with a coating of thick, gooey cheese; a dozen

---

[14] A K-ration was an individual daily combat food ration that was introduced by the U.S. Army during World War II. It was originally intended for issue to airborne troops, tank crews, motorcycle couriers, and other mobile forces for short durations, when the more complete A- and B-rations were not available. The letter "K" was used because it was phonetically distinct from other letter-name rations. A-ration: garrison ration of fresh, refrigerated, or frozen food from dining halls or field kitchens. B-ration: field ration of canned, packaged, or preserved foods from field kitchens without refrigeration. C-ration: individual ration of a complete precooked and ready-to-eat canned meal. D-ration: emergency ration with bars of concentrated chocolate and other ingredients to provide high calorie content. The K-ration was declared obsolete in 1948. The current military forces consume meals, ready-to-eat (MRE).

men ranging in rank from private to lieutenant colonel moved faster than they had thought possible; and to our American arsenal of secret weapons was added a new one we have not stopped laughing about yet—the "cheese grenade!"

Not even our grimmest experience was untouched by flashes of humor. Chaplain Van Meter was in charge of the burial detail for his regiment. His was the disagreeable and dangerous task each morning of leading a working party into the front lines to locate and retrieve the bodies of dead Marines. One morning, his men got the shock of their lives. They had moved one body no more than a few yards when suddenly the "corpse" sat bolt upright on the stretcher and demanded: "Hey, where the hell do you guys think you're taking me?" A Marine still very much alive had "crapped out" for a badly needed nap, and had spread a poncho over himself to keep out the noise and light.[15] To a weary burial detail, any human lying prone under a poncho with only two feet showing meant a "customer." It would be hard to tell who was more rudely shocked: the astonished stretcher-bearers or the corpse who sat up and talked. But both laughed heartily more than a few times in retelling the story afterward.

On another occasion our boys captured several items of Japanese military equipment as they advanced. Among them was an enemy bugle. The platoon was still under fire, with the enemy still on three sides of them. Carbines—ours and theirs—were still cracking out their staccato syllables. Suddenly from one of the foxholes, with death threatening on every hand, a Marine picked up the Japanese bugle and sounded, of all things, a movie and

---

[15] For our purposes, the term *crapped out* refers to going to sleep. This usage, ca. 1920s to 1940s, was military slang for sleeping during work hours or during a crap game. Christine Ammer, *The American Heritage Dictionary of Idioms* (New York: Houghton Mifflin Harcourt, 2003).

liberty call. Surely, there is something refreshingly wonderful about a people whose sense of humor is as irrepressible as that.

Sometimes, the relationship between our sense of humor and our courage is more immediately apparent. A very painfully wounded boy was brought one day into a battalion aid station. Both legs had been pretty badly shot up. The medical officer immediately prepared the boy's left arm for an injection of whole blood. As he picked up the needle, the patient, who up to that moment had seemed more dead than alive, looked up and said, "Doc, I'll bet you a nickel you can't hit a vein on your first try." The doctor laughed, tried, and succeeded. Without a word, the boy reached with his free right arm into his pocket, took out a nickel, and handed it to the winning marksman. There is more than one kind of courage and far more than one explanation of it. Somewhere way up near the top of the list, I submit, belongs a sense of humor that can even laugh death in the face.

Next to their colossal courage, the thing that strikes one most about young America in combat is that for these kids of ours nothing is impossible. In training, we had done our full share of griping about military inefficiency and red tape. We said there were three ways to do a thing: the right way, the wrong way, and the Marine Corps way. Back at Camp Pendleton, one of our regimental executives had a sign over his desk that read: "Wait! There May Be a Harder Way!" One night, an unidentified wag corrected the sign to read: "Proceed! There Is No Harder Way!"[16]

Yes, indeed, we joked, as every military outfit does, about the impossibility of getting things done. But brother, when the chips were down, when it was a case of hanging on by sheer

---

[16] The term *wag* refers to a habitual joker, ca. 1553.

guts or getting pushed back into the sea, our boys accomplished the impossible and then some. They say the motto of the Navy Seabees is reputed to be: "The difficult we can do immediately. The impossible takes a little longer."[17] I have not heard a better motto yet to cover the kids who took Iwo Jima.

Let anyone who doubts that stand, as three of us did after Mount Suribachi had been secured, on top of Iwo's southern tip volcano, and look down on the sea lanes through which we approached and the ugly black beaches where we made our landings. From there, believe me, the wonder is not that we suffered such grievous losses, but that we succeeded in taking the island at all. In the face of what American Marines and sailors accomplished against the impossible odds of Iwo, the cheap prattle of a William Randolph Hearst about unnecessary losses is nothing less than blasphemy.[18] The answer is that we took beaches every inch of which were under observation and fire from heights that were overwhelming. We took caves and systems of caves that staggered the imagination even after one had seen them. We took one huge block house that a tank had to fire on at point blank range for three days before breaking a small hole. No one will ever again be able to use the terms *American* and *impossible* in the same sentence to me. For 40 years, the Japanese painfully hauled their supplies to the top of Suribachi by rope and rugged mountain trail. A few days after Associated Press photographer Joseph Rosenthal snapped his famous shot of Mount Suribachi crowned by Old Glory, our Seabees were building a two-lane highway up the mountain. Three tired chaplains, having climbed

---

[17] Dale Eng, "The Impossible Takes a Little Longer," *Sextant*, 9 July 2018.
[18] George Seldes, "Farewell: Lord of San Simeon," in *Lords of the Press* (New York: Blue Ribbon Books, 1938).

Flag raised on Mount Suribachi.
*James T. Dockery Collection (COLL/4445) in the Archives Branch,
Marine Corps History Division*

to the very summit, sat down on a log to rest. A Seabee, his cap cocked jauntily on his head, shuffled over and drawled: "Hey you guys, you'll have to move. I gotta push a road through here." As though bulldozing a road to the top of a rocky volcano were just an ordinary day's work.

Along with a humble respect for the average American's courage, I carried back with me from Iwo an admittedly ego-tistical pride in the fact that for him, nothing is impossible. I also carried a deep-rooted conviction that at heart, he is just a good, sweet, decent, sentimental kid after all. William H. "Bill" Mauldin has done his best to portray our fighting men as rough, tough, bedraggled-looking specimens who shave, if at all, with

This rare Bill Mauldin cartoon is one of the last ones he drew for the *45th Division News*, 8 January 1944. The cartoon features Willie (of Willie and Joe fame) talking to an Army Air Forces corporal: "Wot's your job—steady K.P.?", referring to the corporal's weight. The high rank of Army Air Forces enlisted men, symbolized by the many chevrons worn by the wrench turners, was often remarked on by soldiers in ground combat units.

Courtesy of *45th Division News*

blow torches.[19] Storybook Marines confirm that impression, doubled in spades. But in this respect at least, there is little in common between storybook Marines and real Marines. I found

---

[19] William H. "Bill" Mauldin (1921–2003) began his career as a cartoonist in the Army, first assigned to the 45th Infantry Division, which fought in Sicily, Italy, France, and Germany, and then to the *Stars and Stripes* military newspaper. The famous characters in his war cartoons were "Willie and Joe," two infantrymen who endured life "up front" with stoic humor. After the war, he drew cartoons for major newspapers, twice receiving a Pulitzer Prize. See "Mauldin at War, 1943–1945," Library of Congress, 7 August 2003.

the latter, especially in combat, to exhibit a warm, soft, almost gentle human kindness.

Our long, tense, boring cruise from rest camp to the beaches of Iwo Jima was an example. We lived more closely and annoyingly crowded together than words can describe. Eighty of us officers lived in the space of about a five-room apartment. The average bunk had less than the headroom of a Pullman lower.[20] It was almost impossible to stretch without tickling the fellow next to you. Lack of space to stow our personal gear reduced any notion of private property to the realm of pure speculative theory. Most of the time, all of us were hot, sweaty, nervous, agitated, and lonely. In short, here were all the raw materials for quickness of temper and shortness of patience. But in all our time aboard, not once did I hear any quarrel that could be considered even remotely serious. There was an unconscious consideration and kindness on the part of men who knew that in all literal truth they were in the same boat. It was not that the thing was actually planned or reasoned out so; most of the fellows would doubtless have been embarrassed to have it recognized. But the fact remains that men facing the most uncomfortable present and the most frightening future of their lives were wonderfully human toward each other.

That was perhaps even more noticeably and remarkably so on the island itself, and nowhere more than in the division cemetery. One of the most pathetic and touching sights imaginable was that of men just relieved from the front lines, coming to the cemetery even before washing or eating, dragging one weary

---

[20] Passenger trains in the twentieth century often included sleeping cars; most were manufactured by the Pullman Company of Chicago, IL. Passengers could buy tickets for upper or lower berths; Pullman lowers had more headroom and were more expensive than uppers.

The 5th Marine Division, enroute to Iwo Jima, make themselves as comfortable as possible in their cramped quarters aboard the transport.
Thayer Soule Collection (COLL/2266) at the Archives Branch, Marine Corps History Division

foot after the other as they passed down the long rows of crosses and stars looking for the name of a missing buddy. Marines who never cried over their own hurts and wounds were not ashamed to shed open floods of tears over the graves of friends. One of the most beautifully human pictures snapped during our entire operation was taken when Corporal Joseph Schwartz happened by coincidence to see two boys—a Catholic and a Protestant—kneeling in prayer by the grave of a Jewish buddy. I remember clearly one morning when two Christian boys asked me to pray with them over a Jewish grave. That same afternoon, I entered the cemetery to find one of our Jewish hospital corpsmen weeping freely and bitterly over the grave of a Catholic who had died next to him in the lines.

Just a few days before we left Iwo, a most remarkable thing happened. Officially, each grave was marked with either a cross or a Jewish star, nothing more. But someone discovered that the peculiar sandstone that caused us so much trouble at the north end of the island could be smoothed and carved. That began a veritable epidemic of utterly exhausted boys, kids whose last ounce of strength had been sapped long since, bending for hours over stones they wanted to leave on the graves of friends. The night before we left, I strolled alone one last time through the cemetery and paused for one final look at each grave. I do not know when any single experience in my life has touched me so deeply. There must have been easily three or four hundred stones set over an equal number of graves. Some of them looked almost professional. But all of them had something that no professionally carved stone will ever have—love! They were fashioned with infinite love. The love of those who had fought but a few feet away when these men were killed, who had bound and dressed their wounds, who had carried them through fire to medical aid, and who now could not bear the thought of leaving them forever without at least this small token of how they felt. One of these stones will remain with me forever. Its eloquent

Marine kneels at a cemetery cross during dedication ceremonies
on Iwo Jima, 15 March 1945.
Official U.S. Marine Corps photo

inscription read: "To Zeke . . . God keep you! . . . Your childhood
buddy." Marines, tough? Do not let them ever kid you. They
are tough only when they face a bitter, ruthless enemy. But in
their inmost heart of hearts, they are soft. And decent. And pro-
foundly, everlastingly good!

CHAPTER FOURTEEN

Earth to Earth

Something of the chaplain's work in actual combat has of course become evident "by indirection" in the previous chapter. I would not close, however, without a more direct word on the subject. Though the padre's chief aim under fire is very much the same as before, the circumstances controlling them and the techniques he must use are apt to be considerably different. It would be foolish to pretend for an instant that such a thing as a well-ordered schedule or typical day is even remotely possible during an action. Still, it is possible, looking back on the combat experience as a whole, to distinguish different types of activity experienced by every chaplain in greater or lesser numbers. No more need be said about the division cemetery, except that it has become an indelible, inerasable memory of nightmare. For the rest of my life, I doubt if I shall ever be able to officiate at a civilian funeral, surrounded by the sweet softness of flowers, without catching in the nostrils of memory some fleeting re-membrance of what it is like to stand in a trench of 20 graves to commit 20 bodies to the ground and 20 souls to their Maker. In many respects, the regimental chaplains, who were at or near the front lines with their troops, had a harder time of it than those of us who spent a part of each day in the rear. But one thing they need never regret missing is the devastating experience of duty hours at the cemetery.

Beyond that, what can chaplains under fire do for the living? Pretty much what you would expect them to do. Most of us spent an hour or two each day either in a battalion or regimental aid station or at the division field hospital. Lighting a cigarette or giving a drink of water or just a smile of reassurance can be a mighty big thing in the life of a kid who has just been carried in on a stretcher. Or writing a letter by dictation for a boy whose missing right arm or sucking chest wound makes it impossible for him to get off the message he is so desperately anxious to have his mother or wife receive. There is no gratitude on Earth quite like that of the wounded man for whom the chaplain has done some such favor as this.

Any chaplain worth his weight in black volcanic sand spends some amount of time "up front" also. I for one have never known a welcome quite as fervent as the handshake of a boy whose chaplain slips into his foxhole up at the battalion command post to shoot the breeze for a moment. Men will scold their chaplain severely for taking chances, and then talk about them favorably for weeks precisely because he did take chances. They want to know that he shares as much of their combat experience as military regulations and his own duties will permit.

And of course, there are religious services. In combat, they are held at any time, in any kind of place, for any available number of men, large or small. The church or synagogue might be a shell crater, a foxhole, a revetment, a hillside, or an abandoned bombproof shelter. And any time that two or more can be relieved from combat, can meet together to give thanks that they have survived and to renew their faith and courage, is the Sabbath. There was something deeply, intensely personal about our religious services on Iwo, something I have never felt elsewhere in public worship. I remember the first two Jewish services ever conducted on Iwo, both held in the booming cacophony of 150mm howitzers nearby. I remember a service held one afternoon for an infantry battalion that had just been relieved from the lines. I passed the word from mouth to ear that a Jewish service would be held near the command post in an hour. When the time came, of eight Jewish men in the battalion, eight were there for worship. But whether attendance was 8 or 3 or 65, there was something desperately urgent about religion in uniform that we would do well to capture for our more comfortable but less deeply personal religious life at home.

Unfortunately, not all the chaplain's work under fire is as directly gratifying or rewarding. There are times when a deeper desire than he has ever felt before to help some unfortunate human being, combined with his complete and utter inability to do anything at all, produces an explosive sense of frustration. Like the afternoon I spent with Private First Class Don Fox. Fox was a good friend of mine in the division—a nice, decent kid who was one of our photographers. On a Saturday afternoon, word came over the field phone that Don had been hit in the head by a sniper and was in a battalion aid station. I grabbed a jeep and in quick succession just missed him at each of several aid stations along the way, finally catching up to him at a beach evacuation hospital, where he had been taken so that a competent brain surgeon might attend him. I spent the next three hours with Don, though he never regained consciousness to know that or anything else. His face will haunt me for the rest of my life—the face of a good, sweet boy—his eyes so horribly blackened, his throat so gasping for breath, his life's blood

In memory of Don Fox; gravestone at 5th Division Cemetery, February 1945.
Photo by Pfc. E. D. Drdek, official U.S. Marine Corps photo

so freely flowing on the deck. The surgeon told me at once there
was no hope. Nothing could be done except to sit there and
watch a fine young friend die; nothing then for him, nothing
then or later for his grieving parents. It is not good, at one and
the same time, to want to do so much, yet be able to do less than

little. A chaplain suffers that feeling of futility not infrequently.

I did again the morning I searched for Herman Podzoba. Just before blackout the night before, I received a joyous letter from his wife, begging me to tell him that she had just given birth to a baby girl, their first child. Because we were in combat, the American Red Cross could not clear a cable to him, and she thought contacting me would be the quickest and surest way of reaching her husband. I felt happy to have such a mission. It was good, in the midst of carnage and death, to bear the blessed tidings of new life. Directly after breakfast in the morning, I set out in search of Herman. Because he had been recently transferred, it took some time to locate him. But I finally succeeded. Just before noon, I found Herman Podzoba—a corpse awaiting burial in our cemetery. This too is part of the chaplain's work in combat.

Out of the same pattern, it is the task that filled most of our waking hours after we returned to rest camp. Even before our arrival, the flood had begun of tearful, pathetic letters from next of kin. Each day's mail still brings its painful quota of broken hearts in search of hope. A stranger hears the chaplain's name mentioned in the radio, or reads some word of him in the press, and writes in the urgent, desperate hope that here may be an untapped source of new information. Drowning souls, like drowning bodies, will seize on any straw. *How did my boy die? Was he killed instantly, or did he suffer pain? What were my husband's last words, his final thoughts? Did he leave me any message? Where and how and by what was he hit? Who was there to tell me now every detailed shred of what took place? Who? Where? How? Why? Above all, why?*[1]

---

[1] Emphasis in original.

How is the chaplain to answer, when all those who were there and saw now are themselves sleeping in the ground? What is he to say when the horrible, harrowing truth would only add to an already unbearable burden of grief? More than one chaplain has found this aftermath of hell to be even more shattering to his emotions and nerves than combat itself.

Probably as good a way as any to close this, one chaplain's story of combat, will be in his parting words to friends who still remain on Iwo, serving there now in the garrison eternal. On 21 March 1945, we of the Jewish faith stood solemnly at the south end of our 5th Marine Division Cemetery, almost in the shadow of Mount Suribachi. Lovingly, we thought of our comrades who would not return with us. Reverently, we intoned Israel's ancient dirge of lamentation. Hopefully, we pronounced the Kaddish, our age-old affirmation in the presence of death of God's greatness and goodness. And I tried thus, however haltingly and hesitatingly, to say the things all of us felt deeply in our hearts:

> This is perhaps the grimmest, and surely the holiest
> task we have faced since D-day. Here before us lie
> the bodies of comrades and friends. Men who un-
> til yesterday or last week laughed with us, joked
> with us, trained with us. Men who were on the same
> ships with us, and who went over the sides with us
> as we prepared to hit the beaches of this island. Men
> who fought with us and feared with us. Somewhere
> in this plot of ground may lie the man who could
> have discovered the cure for cancer. Under each of
> these Christian crosses, or beneath a Jewish Star of
> David, there may rest now a man who was des-
> tined to be a great prophet, to find the way, perhaps,

Entrance to the 5th Marine Division Cemetery, ca. February–March 1945.
Official U.S. Marine Corps photo

for all to live in plenty, with poverty and hardship for none. Now, they lie here silently in this sacred soil, and we gather to consecrate this earth in their memory.

It is not easy to do so. Some of us have buried our closest friends here. We saw these men killed before our very eyes. Any of us might have died in their places. Indeed, some of us are alive and breathing at this very moment only because men who lie here beneath us had the courage and strength to give their lives for ours. To speak in memory of such men as those is not easy. Of them too can it be said with utter truth: "The world will little note nor long remember what we say here. It can never forget what they did here."[2]

No, our poor power of speech can add nothing to what those men and the other dead of our division who are not here have already done. All that we can even hope to do is follow their example. To show the same selfless courage in peace that they did in war. To swear that, by the grace of God and the stubborn strength and power of human will, their sons and ours shall never suffer those pains again. Those men have done their job well. They have paid the ghastly price of freedom. If that freedom be once again lost, as it was after the last war, the unforgivable blame will be ours, not theirs. So, it is we the living who are here to be dedicated and consecrated.

We dedicate ourselves, first, to live together in peace the way they fought and are buried in war. Here lie men who loved America because their ancestors generations ago helped in her founding, and other men who loved her with equal passion because they themselves or their own fathers escaped from oppression to her blessed shores. Here lie officers and men, negroes and whites, rich men and poor—together. Here are Protestants, Catholics, and Jews—together. Here, no man prefers another because of his faith or despises him because of his color. Here, there are no quotas of how many from each group

---

[2] Abraham Lincoln, "The Gettysburg Address" (speech, Gettysburg, PA, 19 November 1863).

Chaplain Gittelsohn reading his famous sermon at the dedication
of the 5th Marine Division Cemetery on 21 March 1945.
*Ralph J. Vaccaro Collection (COLL/5245) in the Archives Branch,
Marine Corps History Division*

*are admitted or allowed. Among these men, there is
no discrimination. No prejudices. No hatred. Theirs
is the highest and purest democracy.*

*Any man among us the living who fails to un-
derstand that will thereby betray those who lie here
dead. Whoever of us lifts his hand in hate against a
brother, or thinks himself too superior to those who
happen to be in the minority, makes this ceremony
and the bloody sacrifice it commemorates, an empty,
hollow mockery. To this, then, as our solemn, sacred
duty, do we the living now dedicate ourselves—to
the right of Protestants, Catholics, and Jews, of
white men and negroes alike, to enjoy the democracy for which all of them have here paid the price.*

To one thing more do we consecrate ourselves

in memory of those who sleep beneath these crosses and stars. We shall not foolishly suppose, as did the last generation of America's fighting men, that victory on the battlefield will automatically guarantee the triumph of democracy at home. This war, with all its frightful heartache and suffering, is but the beginning of our generation's struggle for democracy. When the last battle has been won, there will be those at home, as there were last time, who will want us to turn our backs in selfish isolation on the rest of organized humanity, and thus to sabotage the very peace for which we fight. We promise you who lie here: we will not do that! We will join hands with Britain, China, Russia in peace, even as we have in war, to build the kind of world for which you died.

When the last shot has been fired, there will still be those whose eyes are turned backward, not forward, who will be satisfied with those wide extremes of poverty and wealth in which the seeds of another war can breed. We promise you, our departed comrades: this too we will not permit. This war has been fought by the common man; its fruits of peace must be enjoyed by the common man![3] We promise, by all that is sacred and holy, that your sons, the sons of miners and millers, the sons of farmers and workers, will inherit from your death the right to a living that is decent and secure.

When the final cross or star has been placed in

---

[3] Emphasis in original.

the last cemetery, once again, there will be those to whom profit is more important than peace, who will insist with the voice of sweet reasonableness and appeasement that it is better to trade with the enemies of mankind than, by crushing them, to lose their profit. To you who sleep here silently, we give our promise: we will not listen! We will not forget that some of you were burnt with oil that came from American wells, that many of you were killed by shells fashioned from American steel. We promise that when once again men seek profit at your expense, we shall remember how you looked when we placed you reverently, lovingly, in the ground.

Thus, do we memorialize those who, having ceased living with us, now live within us. Thus, do we consecrate ourselves the living to carry on the struggle they began. Too much blood has gone into this soil for us to let it lie barren. Too much pain and heartache have fertilized the earth on which we stand. We here solemnly swear: this shall not be in vain! Out of this, and from the suffering and sorrow of those who mourn this, will come—we promise—the birth of a new freedom for the sons of men everywhere.

Amen.

POSTSCRIPT

Now I Believe It!

I suppose the story could have ended with the previous chapter. That, however, would have left at least the author with a strange feeling of unfinished business. Sometimes, as I look backward and inward on myself, I wonder whether I am the same "I" who found it so hard to believe on that fateful Sunday afternoon when, for an electric instant, the universe shook and God stopped breathing. I do not know what surprises me more: the stubborn pacifist of 1940 or the military chaplain of 1944. Perhaps the trouble is that I cannot entirely forget the one, and I am not yet altogether adjusted to the other. But whatever the real cause, there are moments when, thinking of myself then and myself now, I wonder if I have not suffered from a sort of spiritual schizophrenia.

What happened to the pacifism that was once so vital a part of my very credo? Where has it gone? Why did it fail? The experiences recounted on these pages, and the many hours of painful thinking that these experiences have stimulated have, I think, given me at least fragments of an answer.

Surely, one cause of pacifism's failure is that it was compromised and cornered from the beginning. It never had a chance.

It was whittled away, piece by piece, until not enough to live was left. Like a person who is never attacked directly, but from whom, one by one, the foods he needs to live are slyly withdrawn. Until one day, he finds himself without the strength even to search for food, and so he dies. Exactly thus did pacifism perish. We allowed the nourishment it needed to be withdrawn from the world up to the point where we had on our hands an ideal that was no longer relevant in the new circumstances of international life.

Do I make myself clear? Let me put it, then, this way: at intervals far too frequent, the chaplain comes in contact with husbands or wives who are faced with ruined lives because one has been unfaithful to the other. Seldom was there an original intent to do wrong. More often, one thing just led to another. A date that seemed harmless, a drink that appeared innocent, led to another date or an additional drink, and behold, before the thing had finished, a man or a woman had done something that was never intended and would forever after be regretted. What was it our ancient rabbis said? "One sin begets another; one good deed leads to another."[1] The time to avoid trouble in one's personal life is in advance of the first date, before the initial drink.

So with pacifism. It could have been saved. It could have worked. If, at any one of a hundred points along the way, we had put down our foot stubbornly and said, "No! We will not yield another inch! Inches add up to feet, and feet make yards. When yards are reached, it will be too late."

Or let me say it this way: a man has a building that he is anx-

---

[1] The Hebrew phrase *mitzvah goreret mitzvah, averah goreret averah* or "one good deed will bring another good deed, one transgression will bring another transgression," is found in Pirkei Avot 4:2.

ious to protect from fire. In the beginning, he has an extinguisher that is provided in due proportion to the size of the building. But in the course of time, they add to the structure—a few feet here, a yard or so there. No one addition is by itself enough to make much difference. But through the course of years, the changes mount. Soon, the building is two times, three times, four times its former size. But the extinguisher is the same. One day, the structure catches fire. The extinguisher is hopelessly too small. And so, the building burns. Who or what is to blame?

Surely the simile needs no further pointing. By 1939, our pacifism had been forced into a corner where it could not work. The cards were stacked against it. The cards were callous indifference in Manchuria, a winking of the eye in Ethiopia, outright deceit in Spain, and shameful appeasement of Berlin. Against such odds as these, what chance did pacifism or pacifists stand? In a world where two and two made four, we could have succeeded. But not in the world of Munich, Germany.

Of all possible choices, perhaps pacifism is still the best. But by the days of Dunkirk, France, we no longer had all possible choices. By then, every choice but two had been eliminated, in part for the very reason that pacifism had been bypassed. It was then either slavery or war. What use, at such a time, to lament what might have been? Too late!

In a sense, this was the most unjust hoax of all. For 20 years, men of prophetic vision and faith had cried out their warnings, "If this and this and this is done, the sum total will unavoidably be war!" Their words went unheeded. Their warnings were ignored. And so, the sum total did come. And with it, the most difficult dilemma of all for the very men who had foreseen it. What to do now? If only they could stand somehow off on a detached platform—they and their loved ones—separated from all this, untouched by the fury before them. What high historic justice there might have been in saying: "We told you so. We warned; you would not listen. Now go to your doom. Now fight this war that your deafness made unavoidable!"

But they were not detached, and could not be, these people of vision and understanding. They were in this world and part of it. And so—grim irony of fate—they who more than once had tried to stop this thing, they to whom the others would not listen, became colonels and corporals and chaplains. They said, with Gideon Jackson in *Freedom Road*, "there comes a time when a man does what he must!"[2]

In a larger and deeper sense, our failure was religious. Professing the beliefs of Christians and Jews, we pacifists had acted as though we were Romans and Greeks. These ancients had believed that each human virtue could be deified by itself and followed for its own sake. So, they had a goddess of love, a separate goddess of beauty, another god of truth. And each became, if an end at all, purely an end by itself without regard for the others.

The great virtue of Israel's belief in one God, which became the belief also of Mohammedans and Christians, was that it saw life whole. Truth is not truth apart and aside from mercy. There are times when to be wholly truthful is to be cruelly unmerciful; one must choose between the two. There are occasions when either love or justice must prevail, not both. Our God is a God of all these virtues, not of any one or two or three. He is a God who combines and expresses all our human ideals in one great

---

[2] See either the original book or the later film, Howard Fast, *Freedom Road* (New York: Duell, Sloan & Pearce, 1944); and *Freedom Road*, directed by Jan Kadar, starring Muhammad Ali and Kris Kristofferson (Beverly Hills, CA: Braun Entertainment Group, 1979), 186 min.

pattern of perfection. God is truth and peace and justice and love; God is mercy and kindness and charity and order. All together. All parts of one whole. All related to and tempered by each other.

Our mistake as pacifists was that we held peace up as our God and forgot that peace can come only along with the rest. Peace among nations, such as happiness in the lives of individuals, is something of a byproduct, not a goal to be sought directly for itself. Our rabbis knew that, "on three things does the world stand," they said. "On truth, on justice, and on peace."[3] So! First, on truth! Second, on justice! And only then on peace! Establish a world in which truth prevails, in which justice is triumphant, and you shall have peace. Without truth and justice, your leagues will be empty shells, your pledges hollow mockeries, your pacifism will be a ghastly joke.

Pearl Buck has put it eloquently:

> Peace cannot be made as one makes a machine or as one makes a business or even as a war is made. Peace comes only as the result of other accomplishments. There will be peace in the world only when there are equality and security everywhere for all human beings. These peace plans on which men consume their days and brains are useless. We must first think and plan how to remove oppressions and hunger and ignorance. When people are content, there will be peace. While people are oppressed by bad governments and by ignorance and by hunger there can be no content and therefore no peace. To work for peace, as though it were a thing in itself,

---

[3] Pirkei Avot 1.

with no relation to causes, is the crowning folly of
our foolish age.[4]

The war will end, and peace—of a sort—will come again. Then our task will only have begun. Then we shall have to face the anguished challenge of Martin Weinberg's widow:

> *My only thought and prayer now is that Marty's death was not in vain. He held his ideals very high, and was willing to die for them. Should they ever be destroyed, I would lose all faith and trust in humanity!*

This is indeed a heavy responsibility. Let no man who ever wants to sleep again take it lightly.

---

[4] Pearl S. Buck, *Tell the People: Talks with James Yen about the Mass Education Movement* (New York: John Day, 1945), 1.

APPENDIX A

Padre in Hell

by Roland B. Gittelsohn,
Leatherneck, December 1985[1]

He was my closest friend in the 5th Marine Division. From the
end of World War II until his death on 2 April 1982, we remained in touch, and saw each other whenever circumstances
allowed.

In the beginning, our relationship was based on a series of
coincidences. We happened to be classmates in the summer of
1943 at the Naval Training School for Chaplains in Williamsburg,
Virginia. Herbert Van Meter came there directly after graduating from Yale Divinity School; I had completed seven years of
civilian pulpit experience after ordination at the Hebrew Union
College. We studied Navy Regulations, ran obstacle courses, did
calisthenics, and practiced abandoning ship together.

Next set of coincidences: after two months of training at
the College of William and Mary, we were both assigned to Fleet
Marine Force, Pacific, at Camp Elliott in San Diego, California. A few months later, we were transferred to the 5th Marine
Division, then in its early training stages at Camp Pendleton,

---

[1] Published by permission of *Leatherneck*. Minor revisions were made to the
text based on current standards for style, grammar, punctuation, and spelling.

California. He became the Protestant chaplain of the 26th Regiment; I was the Jewish chaplain and assistant division chaplain attached to headquarters battalion.

During our year in the San Diego area, we and our families spent a lot of time together. He and his wife were Uncle Herb and Aunt Jo to my young son and daughter.

A key to Herb's character was revealed during the weeks our division was being shipped to Hawaii for advanced training. It was late summer and early fall of 1944. Because I was the sole Jew among 17 chaplains, it was decided that I should remain stateside until more than half our troops had arrived at Camp Kamuela (Waimea) on the big island. At that point, I was flown over to be with a majority of the men I served.

Herb, in the advance echelon, reached Hawaii six weeks before I did. On my arrival, I discovered that without any conversation or consultation on the matter between us, he had organized and led Jewish Sabbath services. Some of my Jewish Marines had started calling him "Rabbi Van Meter."

I attended several of his religious services and Bible classes; he came quite regularly to mine. On Christmas Eve 1944, I worshiped with him and his men at their outdoor midnight service. It was an unforgettably beautiful night. Stars shone brilliantly overhead. Marines, knowing that in a week they would be sailing for combat, that some of them would never again participate in a Christmas Eve service, probably prayed more fervently than ever before.

At about 0100, we walked together from the amphitheater to Herb's tent. Passing the Quonset hut, which served as the officers' club for the 26th Marines and hearing the raucous singing and shouting from within, Herb turned to me and with his dry, droll sense of humor said: "You know, Roland, from the sounds in there one might think this is the birthday of Lord Calvert, not Jesus."[2]

On the occasion of the 40th anniversary of our attack on Iwo Jima, Herb's widow invited me to go through his accumulated military papers and files. Memories that I thought had been mercifully repressed into my subconscious were acutely revived. Along with them, my estimate of a remarkable chaplain—a wonderfully decent, noble human being—was enhanced. What he was and did can be best appreciated against a background of the Iwo Jima campaign at large and the role played in it by the 26th Marines.

Herb Van Meter was one of 3,256 officers and men of the 26th Marines who landed on D-day. In our first two weeks of combat, 1,644 had been killed or wounded.

And the horror was not even near its end. It would require three more weeks of the bloodiest, most brutal fighting earth had ever known before the final pockets of Japanese resistance could be silenced. In Herb's own words, written two months later to the bereaved mother of Private Robert C. Chalmers:

> *Robert was killed on the 21st of March near the end of the operation. By that time our forces had driven the Japanese into a narrow pocket on the north*

---

[2] George Calvert, first Lord Baltimore, visited Virginia in 1628 and was granted the land that would become the state of Maryland. Chaplain Van Meter's lighthearted comment may refer to Lord Calvert Whiskey. In 1934, Seagram's acquired Maryland Distillers of Relay, MD, which produced an unaged "low-quality Prohibition-era whiskey," and upgraded the spirit to become "a premium American blend." See "Lord Calvert," TheLiquorCollection.com, accessed 27 January 2021.

end of the island. But the battle was not over. They resisted desperately. The rough and broken terrain favored the defense, for it provided excellent concealment.... Ours was the difficult and heartbreaking task of, one by one, blasting their caves and destroying their positions. We used tanks as much as we could but there were places where only riflemen could do the job. Robert was struck down by machine gun fire while with his squad in the attack. There was nothing our corpsmen could do for him.

What could one chaplain named Van Meter accomplish under such circumstances? He would crawl between attacks from one foxhole to another, trying to reassure and encourage his weary, frightened Marines. He would grasp the hand of one, squeeze the shoulder of another, and hold firmly the uncontrollably trembling body of a third. He prayed with them, read psalms to them, helped them feel unashamed of their fear by confessing that he was terrified himself. Van Meter collected their hastily scribbled letters for later dispatch homeward. And when he had received emergency messages from their loved ones, he would deliver the messages.

He helped the corpsmen stop the bleeding and bind wounds. He carried the broken fragments of their bodies back to our division cemetery, returning them reverently to mother Earth and reciting over them words of faith strong enough to survive even the horrors of hell. And, thank God, he was where he was needed most, praying that his own conduct would set the right example for those who depended on him.

Little enough. Yet, more than any man or woman should ever be expected to do.

Then, on the long, slow, emotionally tumultuous journey back to Hawaii—and for so many weary, heartbreaking weeks thereafter—he answered the letters of mothers and fathers, of sweethearts and wives. I found and read scores of such letters in Herb's files, each punctuated with anguish and pain.

Did you know my boy? . . . Are you sure there was no mistake? . . . Isn't it possible that he is really a prisoner of war or missing in action? . . . Can you tell me where and how and by what kind of weapon he was killed? . . . Was he conscious at the end? . . . Did he suffer? . . . Leave any last messages for us? . . . Was he buried properly or just thrown into a trench with others? . . . Can you send us his watch, his ring, his dog tag, his pen? . . . So it went—on and on and on—page after aching page—the dried tears of 1945 mingling now with mine as I read.

Herb answered every single letter. He was still answering six months after the Iwo action had ended. Wherever there was specific information about an individual, he included it in his reply. He went to incredible lengths to obtain such information. He sought out men who had been in the same outfit, looking especially for any who might have witnessed the death itself. Pinned to many of his letters were the actual field notes he wrote, describing the circumstances he had discovered.

When he could, Herb told the families whether their loved one had been killed by rifle shot, mortar, artillery, or grenade; whether he had been evacuated to a battalion aid station, then a field hospital, and then a ship. He told them all he could, which cemetery their boy was buried in, even his grave number if Herb knew, and if Herb had personally helped carry the body to its resting place. He told the family if their son or husband or sweetheart had given his own life while trying to save another's. He told one bereaved father that his son's final act, just before being killed, was to offer a wounded man the last sip of water from his canteen. To another father, who had apparently been recently remarried, he wrote how much his deceased boy had enjoyed the letters sent by his new stepmother and how eagerly he anticipated meeting her. To another set of parents, he disclosed that their son, a sergeant, had gone back for rations and water himself instead of sending someone of lower rank for them. He had succeeded in obtaining rations, but was killed while returning for water. No effort was spared by Herb—indeed, superhuman effort was expended to discover and report details that might bring a measure of solace and balm to hearts that were anguished with grief.

Every letter of consolation contained a variant of the following paragraphs:

> *The cemetery is a beautiful spot high on the western shore of the island between the mountain and the first airstrip. It is in the shape of a huge cross and is surrounded by a white picket fence. It will be well-tended by the garrison forces now on Iwo. . . .*
>
> *A touching witness was our departure from the island. Picture, if you can, a transport loaded with troops weary from their month of combat, glad to be away from the scene of so much suffering, standing, as the ship cleared its anchorage, silently, reverently at attention in memory of the comrades they were leaving behind. All eyes were fixed on the flag in the 5th Division Cemetery, flying at half-mast over the graves of those they had known and loved.*
>
> *It was a holy moment. Words cannot express the feelings that rise in a man's heart at such a time.*

> There were men thinking of Charles as there were
> men whose thoughts were with those who lie beside
> him. . . .
>
> There were prayers and there were tears. We
> will not forget.

Chaplain Herb Van Meter's pervasive sense of responsibility extended beyond the men he served and their families to encompass seminary students who might have to face similar duties in the future. While still in combat, he received Yale's *Divinity School News*, reporting on the number of young men preparing for chaplaincy positions in the Navy's V-12 program. Back on Hawaii, three weeks to the day after leaving Iwo, he wrote to a friend on the Yale Divinity School faculty. Here are excerpts from his letter.

> One long night in a foxhole it occurred to me that
> the experience I was having might help them see the
> job they want to do a little more clearly. . . .
>
> I don't have suggestions to make. I want only
> to ask some questions. They are questions I've been
> asking myself. I'm not at all sure I've discovered adequate
> answers. But if the fellows in training can
> ask themselves questions like these and anticipate
> the answers, they are going to be ready for the job
> when their outfit storms ashore. . . .
>
> What am I going to say and do for the lad who
> creeps over to my foxhole at night, terrified by the
> mortar fire that is falling all around and trembling
> anew each time the artillery opens up? His fright
> has made him almost incoherent. Tears stream down
> his face. . . .

What am I going to say to the lads who have broken under the strain of three weeks unrelieved on the line? They come wandering into the battalion aid station, or are brought back by friends, with a conviction of failure. Grown men cry like babies, mumble incoherently over and over: Shorty, Whitey, O my God, they're gone! The best pals a guy ever had... Shorty, Whitey, where are you? Shorty, keep your head down ...

Here they come, you take the one on the right ... Shorty, keep your head down—Look out!

What can I say to a man when, after an afternoon searching the battlefield, we find the broken, bloated body of his brother? ...

What can I say to a man who, on the tenth day of battle, gets a letter, not from the wife to whom he's been happily married for four years, but from her lawyer, saying she wants a divorce? ...

What am I going to say to the man on a stretcher who is struggling to keep from crying out in pain while the doctor splints his broken leg? Or to a man who has lost the back of his head and can't possibly live the night, though he is conscious now and looking to me, waiting for me to speak? Or to the boy who regains consciousness and asks how badly hurt he is? He's lost both legs. ...

What will I say to the men who help me pick the bodies of our dead from off the battlefield? Death is sudden and violent. There is nothing dignified about it. There are few clean wounds. Heads are blown open and brains spilled out. Arms are shattered, legs twisted and bent. Flame bakes the flesh so that it falls apart like a well-done roast. . . .

What shall I say to the man who has just had two other fellows in the foxhole with him killed by a grenade and he himself has escaped unharmed? . . .

Where will I get the strength day after day to go down into the trenches dug to receive the dead and read the committal service—not for one man or two, but for a dozen or twenty or forty at a time— day after day—as the toll rises, not to hundreds but to thousands? . . .

If the fellows are wondering just what a chaplain does, tell them he wishes he could be in a dozen places at once. There are no dull moments.

Tell them, too, that these are the greatest kids in the world to be working with. They are tough; they are hard; they are careless and heedless. You despair at times. But you learn to love them and you wouldn't be anywhere else but with them. The chaplaincy is a grand ministry.

It was a grand minister named Herbert Van Meter who helped make the chaplaincy a grand ministry. Very, very few of us, among his colleagues, could equal him. No one will ever be able to count the numbers of men and women—Marines and those who mourned them—whose spirits were strengthened, sadness assuaged, faith restored by this extraordinary human being.

APPENDIX B

Brothers All?

by Roland B. Gittelsohn
The Reconstructionist[1]

According to the apocrypha of the Hebrew Union College, when the late Mrs. Neumark, wife of the distinguished [German] philosopher, first came to Cincinnati, a group of faculty wives took her under their maternal wing to teach her the English language.[2] Since she was immediately absorbed by the city's social life, it is said that her very first lesson in English consisted of the following statement: "No thank you, I have had an ample sufficiency; any more would be a superfluity."[3]

---

[1] Published by permission of *The Reconstructionist*. Minor revisions were made to the text based on current standards for style, grammar, punctuation, and spelling. Footnotes have been inserted to provide background or context to the author's narrative.

[2] The Hebrew Union College is the oldest extant Jewish seminary in America, with three locations in the United States—Cincinnati, OH; New York City; Los Angeles, CA—and one location in Jerusalem for training rabbis, cantors, educators, and communal workers in Reform Judaism.

[3] While the exact origination of this phrase is not known other than an approximate date of the 1800s, see Frederic G. Cassidy, "Among the Old Words," *American Speech* 55, no. 4 (Winter, 1980), 295-97.

THE DANGER OF CHERISHING
ILLUSIONS ABOUT BROTHERHOOD

True or not in its original context, this conclusion can certainly be applied without exaggeration to chaplains and their observations since the end of the recent war. If, then, I risk adding superfluity to sufficiency, it is only because I believe it is time for someone to protest against the Pollyanna optimism which has been far too current since the war's end. One chaplain returned from service overseas to make the statement in public lectures that, in his three years of military experience, he had *never once* seen a case of anti-Semitism. An official Jewish Welfare Board came back from a survey of foreign fronts with the amazing assurance that, when men face combat together, there is no such thing as discrimination. That particular bit of optimism hit me via the mails just a day or two after I had myself endured the most discouraging, sickening instance of anti-Semitism in my entire career as a chaplain.

If this kind of nonsense represented nothing more than the foolish projection of wishes, perhaps it would not be so important to answer and deny it. Actually, however, it is far more serious and dangerous than mere wishful thinking. It is the artificial confidence which precedes total disillusionment. Far too many American Jews have already lived through the successive stages of (1) being sold a bill of goods that after the war all would be sweetness and light; then (2) discovering for themselves that prejudice and discrimination have survived the crisis of war; and finally (3) suffering a complete collapse of morale in the conviction that the war accomplished nothing. This kind of cynicism can be avoided only my being realistic in the first place. And realism in the first place requires that we recognize the existence of prejudice in the very midst of a war which was presumably fought to destroy it.

Indeed, why not? Why should anyone have been so naïve as to suppose that covering the outside of a man with a uniform would in any way change the deep-seated prejudices which existed within him? Before the war it would have been manifestly impossible to have gathered at random any thousand Americans without including among them a certain number who hated Jews. Why, then, should we have expected to take the same thousand Americans, and merely by clothing them alike, have them purified from all such blemishes? And why, in particular, should we have supposed that as a time of greatest frustration and insecurity, men would have less rather than more need for scapegoats?

The logic and pattern of history regarding such prejudice as anti-Semitism is so undeniably clear that even if one had no actual experiences to the contrary, there would be a strong temptation to say the rosy pictures of perfect concord brought back by some of our chaplains simply *cannot* be true. But we need not rely only on logic. Some of us have had experience to the contrary, and it is time now for such experience to be shared.

INCIDENTS OF ANTI-SEMITISM IN THE SERVICE

It is not my purpose or intention to give here a catalog of all the anti-Semitic incidents in 31 months of experience as a chaplain. Two such incidents might well be repeated, however, because they show how distressingly deep are the roots of anti-Semitism in Gentile behavior, and how long, therefore, the struggle against it will take.

The first concerns a lieutenant colonel in our Marine division, a man who was known to drive his men mercilessly. He had no respect for religion of any kind. He was no more a Jew than Goebbels was. He was the only commanding officer I had met while we were still in our stateside training who would not even excuse his Jewish men to attend their Seder on Passover. But when, in a certain phase of overseas training, he insisted that his battalion go out on Sunday maneuvers, and would not excuse them for church, considerable numbers of men in his outfit were heard to curse him as "that damn Jew who won't let us Christians go to church!" And no amount of persuasion could have convinced most of them that their commanding officer was not a Jew. It was not enough that we were made to pay for the imaginary faults of real Jews; we also had to be accountable for the real failings of imaginary Jews!

The second incident illustrating the stubborn, lunatic depth of anti-Semitism in men's minds concerned a Marine sergeant who entered his tent at 2200 one night drunk. He walked in on a half-dozen men who were sitting there—one of them a Jew. Staggering over toward the latter, he berated him as follows: "One good thing Hitler has done is to kill the Jews. The only trouble is that he didn't get all of them. I'd like to get back to the states in time to finish them off there too!" Fortunately, the Jewish boy had enough good sense, no matter how badly he was shocked, not to join the issue there. He walked out of the tent and reported the incident to me the next morning.

After discussing the case with the sergeant's Protestant chaplain, the two of us decided to speak to him together. We were considerably surprised to find him a freckle-faced, ruddy-headed, typical farm boy from Iowa, and a hero at that. He had been at Tarawa. He was one of those who had pulled 75mm guns to within four or five dozen yards of murderous Japanese machine gun positions to blast them away. What made such a boy speak as he had? We found the answer in a bowed, dejected head that did not look up even once in all the time we spoke. It still hung downward as he finally mumbled: "I've never been so ashamed of myself in my life. The worst of it is that I don't really feel that way. Jews to me are like any other people—some good, some bad. I guess I just lost myself in too much beer, and said things that have made me uncomfortable ever since. I've wanted to apologize to Willie a dozen different times but didn't have the nerve." What an admission! A man claims to harbor no hate against anyone. He succumbs to the influence of alcohol. And the very first thing his unbridled mind does, *by instinct*, is to run amuck against the nearest Jew. How many centuries went into the making of that miserable moment? How many centuries more will it take to erase it?

ANTI-SEMITISM AMONG CHAPLAINS

Incidents of this kind are discouragingly revealing, but anyone with the least bit of realism might have expected them. What was not to be expected, and was therefore the more shocking when it occurred, was prejudice of no minor kind even among chaplains who are presumed to be brotherly men of God! Try as I do to be dispassionate and objective, I cannot escape the grim conclusion that, as a matter of actual fact, the very worst prejudice I met was on the part of my fellow chaplains. I think back, for example, to the time when I made available for our regimental libraries copies of two volumes—the Anti-Defamation League (ADL) collection called "Questions and Answers about the Jews," and the first edition of the Jewish Welfare Board

(JWB) pamphlet, "Fighting for America."[4] At a staff meeting of chaplains, I announced that these books were available and requested the Protestant chaplains, who served in our division as regimental librarians, each take whatever number he wished for placement on his shelves. At the end of the meeting, one Protestant chaplain voiced his vigorous objection to both books. He had previously read them. The JWB collection he refused to take because it "made Jews out to be perfect patriots." The ADL questions he rejected because one page stated that the Romans had crucified Jesus, while "anyone who knows anything at all knows that is was the Jews who were guilty." His final conclusion was: "If you want your Jewish boys to read this trash, give it to them yourself. I refuse to put it on the shelf for Christians to read!"

I think back with no less pain to the morning when I somehow found myself on the receiving end of a barrage from three of my colleagues—two Catholics and the same Protestant described above. What I learned from them about Jews was an illiberal education! I was told that the trouble with our government in Washington was that too many Jews had a part in running it. I was assured that the entire Lincoln Brigade in Spain consisted of Jews, which was to be expected since all the Jews were godless Communists.[5] I was charged with being a poor chaplain

---

[4] The first document may well represent something close to the ADL's current curriculum, "Understanding Judaism and the Jewish Community," ADL.org, Summer 2006. The JWB pamphlet is discussed in *The Jewish News* 5, no. 6, 28 April 1944, 19.
[5] During the Spanish Civil War (1936–39), almost 40,000 men and women from 52 countries, including 2,800 Americans, traveled to Spain and voluntarily joined the international brigades fighting with Spanish Republican forces. The U.S. volunteers were collectively known as the Abraham Lincoln Brigade.

because I spent too much time trying to fight anti-Semitism in the division instead of teaching Judaism! I was told there obviously must be something wrong with Jews if people are not born prejudiced, yet so many of them acquire anti-Jewish inclinations somewhere along the line. By chaplains, by men at whose side I had lived and worked nearly a year! The climax of that particular session came when one of the Catholics—incidentally the most popular priest in our division—said to me as I sat there, saddened and stunned beyond belief: "Father Coughlin is the greatest Catholic priest in the world. I would kiss the ground he walks on!" The reader will not be blamed if they read of these experiences incredulously. I myself find it hard to believe them now, nearly two years after they occurred.

THE TRUTH ABOUT
THE DEDICATION
OF THE IWO JIMA CEMETERY

The most bitterly painful experience of this kind, however, took place later—precisely at a time when it should least have been expected: in the midst of combat itself. It is commonly supposed throughout the country that the sermon I delivered at the dedication of the 5th Marine Division Cemetery on Iwo Jima was preached at a common, interdenominational service of dedication. It was not. And therein lies my saddest experience of brotherhood in arms.

Our division chaplain, Warren F. Cuthriell, had indeed originally planned such a joint service. First there was to be a secular dedication, at which, of course, the address would be given by our commanding general. Immediately thereafter, all three faiths were to unite in a combined religious memorial service, after which any group that so wished would be free to hold its own denominational service. As an eloquent expression of his own devotion to the teachings of Christianity and the high truths of democracy, Chaplain Cuthriell invited me, as a spokesman for the smallest religious minority in the division, to preach the memorial sermon. I learned later that, immediately after the announcement of his plans, two of our Protestant chaplains visited Cuthriell to express their vigorous objection to the Jewish chaplain preaching over graves that were predominantly those of Christians. His answer was that the right of the Jewish chaplain to preach such as sermon was precisely one of the things for which we were fighting the war. When that approach failed, the six Catholic padres with us on Iwo sent their senior representative to the division chaplain to speak for all of them. They were opposed in general to any joint service of memorial, and they were opposed in particular to a sermon preached by the Jewish chaplain! Furthermore, if he insisted on carrying out his original intention, they would refuse to participate or attend!

All this I discovered only later. Ten days had passed between the invitation to preach at the cemetery and the day when Chaplain Cuthriell called me in to explain his dilemma. The objection of two Protestants he could withstand. The objection of an entire church, which would surely have made a *cause celebre* out of the incident, was another matter. I had no right to expose my senior to that kind of embarrassment. I withdrew. After a brief secular dedication, each faith went to its own specified corner to hold its own service of memorial. The sermon I had written for the combined service was actually delivered at our own little Jewish service. Perhaps it should be added here that not one word of the original manuscript was changed as a result of this incident. Whatever in the sermon may seem to reflect the background of its delivery had been written before any of the foregoing was even known to me.

I do not remember anything in my life that made me so painfully heartsick. We had just come through nearly five weeks of miserable hell. Some of us had tried to serve men of all faiths and of no faith, without making denomination or affiliation a prerequisite for help. Protestants, Catholics, and Jews had lived together, fought together, died together, and now lay buried together. But we the living could not unite to pray together! My chief consolation at the moment was that another Jew besides myself would have been unacceptable as dedicator of the cemetery—even though these very men professed to teach in his name!

SOME HEARTENING EXPERIENCES

So, the picture of wartime understanding is not nearly as lovely and unblemished as our professional backpatters would like to pretend. At the same time, however, it would be just as dangerous to assume that the kind of experiences described above constitute the whole picture as it would be to accept the other extreme of wishful thinking. Along with the heartache of open discrimination by fellow chaplains, I found also much that was enheartening. Paradoxically enough, the wide publicity given my Iwo sermon was a direct result of the prejudice that prevented its being preached as originally intended. When the inside story of the cemetery dedication plans became known to the other chaplains in our division, three of the Protestant ministers were so incensed that they boycotted their own religious service to attend mine as members of the congregation! It was one of these three men, following our Yizkor service, who borrowed the only copy of my sermon and, unknown to me, mimeographed several thousand copies that he distributed all over the island.[6]

There were other encouraging experiences too. Had it not been for these, one could scarcely have stood the strain of prejudice. During a period of about two months, when I was unavoidably separated from the men of one regiment, the Protestant chaplain of that outfit himself conducted weekly Jewish services so inspiringly that I rejoined the men later to discover they were calling him *Rabbi* Van Meter!

Another true friend was Army Chaplain Newton C. Elder, whom I met on Iwo. The three Jewish Marine chaplains who were involved in that campaign had all planned, on the basis of our preliminary briefing, to be back in rehabilitation camps in time for Passover. None of us, therefore, had arranged for Seder provisions. The campaign, however, dragged out to the point where it became obvious that our Seder services would be held either on Iwo or on ships that would be carrying us back. When Carl Elder heard of our plight, he unassumingly secured a cargo plane and pilot, flew some 600 miles south of Saipan, and returned with nearly half a ton of matzos, gefilte fish, Haggadahs, and wine to be divided among the three of us.[7] It is worth recording that each Friday night, while we remained together on Iwo, Elder not only rounded up the Jewish men of his outfit and provided them with transportation for Shabbat services—he also attended himself and worshiped with them!

One other inspiring experience remains with me indelibly. It was our last night on Iwo before sailing away. Three chaplains

---

[6] Yizkor (Hebrew for "may he remember") is the memorial prayer said during Holy Day services to remember the dead.
[7] Haggadahs are the Jewish texts used during the Passover Seder.

were still on duty in the division cemetery. Since bodies were still being brought in for burial, we held off our final service of committal as long as possible to be sure all would be included. Finally, as we descended into the last grim trench of graves, darkness has already fallen. Off to the west, the last suspicion of light was reluctant to leave the sky. Overhead there were stars. It was the first night since our arrival that no sounds of firing could be heard from the cemetery. All around there was peace—great, embracing, quiet peace. And three chaplains—a Baptist, a Methodist, and a Jew—wearier than they had ever been before, climbed into the trench, stood there together before the last row of graves, and held the flashlight for each other as they prayed. It is just as impossible to forget the brotherhood and love of men like these as it would be to erase the jealous hatred of the others.

WHAT OF THE FUTURE?

What does it all add up to? Is the picture bright or dark? Is the future clear or cloudy? The only honest answer is: no one knows. Though my present purpose is to report, not to evaluate and weigh, I am not sure I could add all this up to the correct total even if I tried. There is, in the total picture, much to give encouragement and much to sadden and depress. My own feeling is that war, with its fears and frustrations, has had its way of magnifying and emphasizing both extremes. Those who came into the Service with their hatreds, big and little, probably came out feeling them more bitterly than ever. And those who came with an initial stock of decent goodness, with faith in people of every creed, are stronger and firmer for the experience of war. The one positive conclusion that is inescapable is this: the record constitutes a damning indictment of the Christian church. No organization can rightly call itself either Christian or a church so long as it harbors among its leaders and spokes-people those who act as too many of my own colleagues did.

I found chaplains, divided in almost equal numbers, at both extremes. Perhaps the future belongs to the vast majority of ordinary people who are at neither. In time, they can join the people of bitter violence. Or they can remain indifferent and lose the fight by default. Or they can rise up in righteous wrath and give democratic understanding a new birth in the hearts and minds of all.

APPENDIX C

Biographical Sketch
of Rabbi Roland Gittelsohn

Roland B. Gittelsohn was born on 13 May 1910 in Cleveland, Ohio.[1] Graduating Phi Beta Kappa, he received a bachelor of arts degree in 1931 from Western Reserve University in Cleveland and a bachelor of Hebrew letters from Hebrew Union College in Cincinnati in 1934. He was ordained at Hebrew Union College in 1936. He also studied at the Teachers' College, Columbia University and New School in New York. He received two honorary degrees in 1961, the first being a doctor of divinity degree from Hebrew Union College, Jewish Institute of Religion, and the other a doctor of science degree from Lowell Technological Institute (now Lowell University) in Massachusetts.

Gittelsohn led an active life, both as a rabbi and in his political life. He hardly distinguished between the two, arguing that the role of a rabbi, and all religious leaders for that matter, is to lead by positive example, especially when political issues affect

---

[1] Biographical sketch based on information from the Roland Bertram Gittelsohn Papers, Jacob Rader Marcus Center of the American Jewish Archives, Cincinnati, OH; and Biographical Files, Archives Branch, Marine Corps History Division, Quantico, VA.

the poor, homeless, marginalized, or otherwise unlucky of society. His early sermons, prior to World War II, made his pacifism quite evident. One early student sermon, "More Human Bondage," so impressed the Reform movement that its leadership commissioned him to write the movement's study guide on war and peace. As related in this volume, the attack on Pearl Harbor led him to reconsider his pacifist convictions, and in 1943 he became a chaplain in the Navy. Gittelsohn then attended the school for chaplains at the College of William and Mary from 21 June to 15 August. During World War II, Rabbi Gittelsohn was assigned to the Marine Corps' 5th Marine Division and ministered to servicemembers of all faiths on Iwo Jima, about 1,500 Jewish Marines among them. He received three service medals— the American Campaign Medal, the Asiatic-Pacific Campaign Medal, and the World War II Victory Medal. For his efforts to comfort the wounded on Iwo Jima, he received the Navy Commendation Medal. His sermon at the dedication of the 5th Marine Division cemetery on Iwo Jima was widely publicized.

By the end of the war, Americans needed to understand— intellectually and emotionally—why they had fought and why so many had died. Rabbi Gittelsohn's sermon provided the answer. "The Purest Democracy" so resonated with the public from the 1940s to the 1960s that it was published in many nationwide newspapers and in *Time* magazine. During the era of Senator Joseph McCarthy and House Un-American Activities Committee (HUAC), Gittelsohn publicly denounced the attack on civil liberties in America in a time of overinflated fears.

While clearly a contradiction—a pacifist going to war—Gittelsohn's participation in World War II solidified his determination that war must be a last resort for the good of humanity. Gittelsohn was particularly outspoken in his condemnation of the Vietnam War, a controversial position in the 1960s. He was labeled a traitor by some, but an upholder of democracy by many others whether they agreed with his position or not.

Beyond his public political life, Gittelsohn was devoted to his congregations. He served at the Central Synagogue of Nassau County in Rockville Center, Long Island, New York from 1936 to 1953 before moving on to Temple Israel in Boston, Massachusetts, where he remained for the rest of his career. Gittelsohn also was active in many organizations such as the Social Action Commission of Reform Judaism, of which he was a founding member in 1951 and continued to serve until his death in 1995; the Massachusetts Board of Rabbis, where he was president from 1958 to 1960; the Jewish Community Council of Metropolitan Boston, where he was president from 1961 to 1963; the Central Conference of American Rabbis (CCAR), where he was president from 1969 to 1971; the Association of Reform Zionists of America (ARZA), where he was the founding president from 1977 to 1984; and the World Zionist Executive & Jewish Agency Board of Governors, where he served as president from 1978 to 1984. He was also extremely active in the Union of American Hebrew Congregations (UAHC, now the Union for Reform Judaism), serving on its board of trustees and as the vice chairman from 1973 to 1977. He was an honorary life member and the chairman of the Commission on Jewish Education from 1959 to 1968. Gittelsohn received two awards from the UAHC, the Maurice N. Eisendrath Bearer of Light Award in 1983 for service and the Jay Kaufman Award in 1984.

Gittelsohn's focus on political causes went beyond religion. He was asked by Harry S. Truman to serve on the President's Committee on Civil Rights in 1947, which produced an extensive report—*To Secure These Rights: The Report of the President's*

Committee on Civil Rights—that proposed to establish a permanent Civil Rights Commission, a Joint Congressional Committee on Civil Rights, a Civil Rights Division in the Department of Justice, and recommended other federal protections. He sat on the State Advisory Council of the Governor's Commission to Survey Massachusetts Courts in 1955. He served on a subcommittee of the Massachusetts Commission to Investigate the Advisability of Abolishing Capital Punishment from 1957 to 1958. From 1960 to 1962, he served on the Governor's Committee on Migratory Labor, and later the Governor's Committee to Survey Operation of Massachusetts Prisons from 1961 to 1962.

Gittelsohn was equally committed to writing, publishing numerous articles and books, such as *Little Lower than the Angels* (1951); *Modern Jewish Problems: A Textbook for High School Classes and Jewish Youth Groups* (1955); *Man's Best Hope* (1961); *Consecrated Unto Me: A Jewish View of Love and Marriage* (1965); *My Beloved Is Mine: Judaism and Marriage* (1969); *Wings of the Morning* (1969); *Fire in My Bones: Essays on Judaism in a Time of Crisis* (1969); *Love, Sex, and Marriage: A Jewish View* (1976); *The Meaning of Modern Judaism* (1978); *The Extra Dimension: A Jewish View of Marriage* (1983); *Here Am I: Harnessed to Hope* (1988); *How Do I Decide?: A Contemporary Jewish Approach to What's Right and What's Wrong* (1989); *Love in Your Life: A Jewish View of Teenage Sexuality* (1991).

Rabbi Roland Gittelsohn died on 13 December 1995 in Boston. His first wife was Ruth Freyer with whom he had a son, David B. Gittelsohn, and a daughter, Judith Fales. His second wife was Hulda Tishler. He had two stepsons, Gerald Tishler and Douglas Tishler, four grandchildren and three step-grandchildren.

APPENDIX D

Selected Chronology

13 May 1910	Roland B. Gittelsohn is born in Cleveland, OH.
1931	Gittelsohn receives a bachelor of arts degree from Western Reserve University in Cleveland.
1934	Gittelsohn receives a bachelor of humanities degree from Hebrew Union College in Cincinnati.
1936	Gittelsohn is ordained as a rabbi at Hebrew Union College.
	Gittelsohn serves at the Central Synagogue of Nassau County, NY.
7 July 1937	A clash between Chinese and Japanese forces near the Marco Polo (Lugou) Bridge outside Beijing opens World War II in Asia.
1 September 1939	Germany invades Poland, opening World War II in Europe.
3 September 1939	France and the United Kingdom declare war on Germany.

1940

9 May	Germany invades Luxembourg, Belgium, and the Netherlands.
14 May	German forces enter France.
26 May–4 June	The evacuation of British, French, and Indian Army troops from the port of Dunkirk makes a strong impression on Rabbi Gittelsohn.
30 June	U.S. Marine Corps strength at 28,345.
16 September	The Selective Training and Service Act of 1940 takes effect, providing for men between the ages of 18 and 35 to register for potential military service. Those between the ages of 21 and 35 who are conscripted will serve for 12 months. Drawing the first numbers takes place on 29 October, and the first draftees begin their service in the Army on 18 November. Ministers of religion and divinity students are exempt under classification IV-D.
27 September	Japan joins with Germany and Italy in the Tripartite Pact, forming the Axis alliance.

1941

22 June	Hitler's German Army invades the Soviet Union.
30 June	U.S. Marine Corps strength at 54,359.
26 July	United States Armed Forces, Far East, commanded by Gen Douglas MacAr-

	thur, is activated to defend American interests in the Philippines.
18 August	President Roosevelt signs the Service Extension Act of 1941. It extends the service of drafted soldiers to 30 months. No change is made to the exemption for ministers of religion and divinity students.
7 December	The Japanese attack Pearl Harbor and Midway.
8 December	United States declares war on Japan. The Japanese attack American bases that include Marines in their garrisons at Wake Island, Guam, and the Philippines.
10 December	The Japanese land on and capture Guam, including Marine barracks defenders.
20 December	The Selective Training and Service Act of 1941 requires all men between the ages of 18 and 64 to register, and makes all men between the ages of 20 and 44 eligible for military service for the duration of the war plus six months. Ministers of religion and divinity students continue to be exempt.
23 December	The Japanese land on and capture Wake Island, including a 1st Marine Defense Battalion detachment and Marine Fighter Squadron 211 (VMF-211).

24 December	2d Marine Brigade is activated at Camp Elliott, CA, for duty in Samoan Islands.

1942

7 January	U.S. forces in the Philippines are forced to withdraw to the Bataan Peninsula.
February	U.S. Naval Chaplains School is established in Norfolk, VA.
9 April	American troops are forced to surrender to Japanese forces on Bataan.
5–6 May	The Japanese land on Corregidor in the Philippines and the garrison, including the 4th Marines (Reinforced), become prisoners of war.
1 June	Black Marine recruitment begins. These black Marines train at Montford Point, NC.
4 June	The Japanese attack Midway, whose defenders include Marine Aircraft Group 22 (MAG-22) and the 6th Marine Defense Battalion (Reinforced).
30 June	The active duty strength of the Marine Corps is 142,613 (7,138 officers and 135,475 enlisted).
7 August	1st Marine Division lands in assault against Japanese forces on Guadalcanal and Tulagi, Solomon Islands.
17–18 August	2d Marine Raider Battalion lands

	from submarines on Makin Island in the Gilbert Islands and destroys the Japanese garrison.
20 August	The forward echelon of MAG-23 arrives on Guadalcanal.
3 September	The command echelon of the 1st Marine Aircraft Wing (1st MAW) arrives at Guadalcanal.
16 September	3d Marine Division is activated at Camp Elliott.
1 October	I Marine Amphibious Corps is activated at San Diego.
7 November	U.S. Marine Corps Women's Reserve is authorized by the U.S. Congress and signed into law by President Franklin D. Roosevelt.
13 November	An amendment to the Selective Service Training and Service Act makes registered 18- and 19-year old men eligible for military service. The exemption for ministers of religion and divinity students remains unchanged.
5 December	All volunteer enlistments in the armed forces between the ages of 18 and 37 stop. All men in this age bracket, starting in January 1943, are drafted through the Selective Service System. The Marine Corps continues to enlist 17-year-old volunteers and to encourage Selective Service volunteers.
9 December	1st Marine Division is relieved at Gua-

dalcanal and departs for Australia. 2d Marine Division remains.

1943

25 January	Composite Army-Marine Division (25th Infantry Division and 2d Marine Division units) is established to defeat the Japanese on Guadalcanal.
29 January	The commandant of the naval base at Norfolk, VA, moves the Chaplains' School to the College of William and Mary in Williamsburg, VA
9 February	Guadalcanal is declared secure.
13 February	Organization and recruitment of Marine Corps Women's Reserve is officially announced.
21 February	Marines of the 3d Raider Battalion and the Army's 43d Infantry Division occupy the Russell Islands, an archipelago of the Solomon Islands, to use as a staging point for subsequent operations in New Georgia, the Solomon Islands, and the Bismarck Islands.
12 May	Roland Gittelsohn is commissioned a lieutenant (junior grade, Chaplain Corps) in the U.S. Navy.
21 June	Gittelsohn begins training at the Naval Chaplains School, now located at the College of William and Mary in Williamsburg, VA.
21–22 June	4th Marine Raider Battalion, followed

	by companies of the Army's 103d Infantry Regiment, lands at Segi Point in the New Georgia group, beginning the New Georgia campaign.
30 June	The active duty strength of the Marine Corps is 308,523 (21,384 officers and 287,139 enlisted).
15 August	Gittelsohn completes training at chaplains school.
16 August	4th Marine Division is activated at Camp Pendleton, CA.
25 August	Bairoko Harbor is captured on New Georgia, ending Japanese resistance on the island.
	V Amphibious Corps is activated at Camp Elliott.
28 October	2d Marine Parachute Battalion lands on Choiseul Island, Solomon Islands, in a diversionary raid prior to the Bougainville operation.
1 November	3d Marine Division (Reinforced) lands in assault on Bougainville, Papua New Guinea, at Cape Torokina as part of I Marine Amphibious Corps.
20 November	2d Marine Division (Reinforced) lands in assault on Betio Island, Tarawa Atoll, as part of V Amphibious Corps.
23 November	All organized Japanese resistance on Betio ceases.
28 November	Last organized Japanese resistance on Tarawa Atoll ceases.

15 December	Army XIV Corps assumes control of Bougainville operation from I Marine Amphibious Corps.
26 December	1st Marine Division lands in assault on Cape Gloucester, New Britain.

1944

1 January	LtGen Alexander A. Vandegrift becomes the 18th Commandant of the Marine Corps, relieving LtGen Thomas Holcomb, who had served as Commandant since 1937.
16 January	The withdrawal of the 3d Marine Division from Bougainville is completed.
21 January	5th Marine Division is activated at Camp Pendleton as part of V Amphibious Corps.
31 January	Troops of the 4th Marine Division, as part of V Amphibious Corps, land on and capture adjoining islands to Roi-Namur, Kwajalein Atoll. The Army's 7th Infantry Division, also under V Amphibious Corps, similarly captures islands off Kwajalein Island.
1 February	4th Marine Division assault troops land on Roi-Namur. The 7th Infantry Division troops assault Kwajalein.
2 February	All organized Japanese resistance on Roi-Namur ceases.
8 February	Kwajalein Atoll is declared secure.
10 February	Operations in the Cape Gloucester

	area of New Britain are declared ended.
17 February	Units of the 22d Marines begin landing on islands of the Eniwetok Atoll under the command of Tactical Group 1, V Amphibious Corps.
22 February	The capture of Parry Island by 22d Marines completes the successful seizure of Eniwetok Atoll by Marine and Army assault forces.
20 March	4th Marines (Reinforced) land on and secure Emirau, St. Matthias Islands, completing the isolation of the Japanese stronghold at Rabaul, New Britain.
4 May	The last elements of the 1st Marine Division withdraw from New Britain.
5 June	Commander in chief, U.S. Fleet, is issued a dispatch naming the commanding general, V Amphibious Corps, as commanding general of all Marine units in the Pacific Ocean area and establishes the Fleet Marine Force, Pacific, under his command.
15 June	The assault troops of V Amphibious Corps (2d and 4th Marine Divisions) land on Saipan, Mariana Islands.
22–24 June	As Soviet forces approach Lublin, Poland, they liberate the Majdanek concentration camp before the Germans can fully destroy the crematoria. That summer, the Soviets overrun the sites

of the Belzec, Sobibor, and Treblinka extermination centers.

30 June	The active duty strength of the Marine Corps is 475,604 (32,788 officers and 442,816 enlisted).
9 July	Saipan is declared secure.
21 July	The assault troops of III Amphibious Corps (3d Marine Division and 1st Provisional Marine Brigade) land on Guam, Mariana Islands.
24 July	The assault troops of the 4th Marine Division, followed by those of the 2d Marine Division, land on Tinian in a shore-to-shore amphibious attack mounted from Saipan.
1 August	Tinian is declared secure.
10 August	All organized resistance on Guam ceases.
7 September	1st Provisional Marine Brigade is re-designated 6th Marine Division on Guadalcanal.
15 September	1st Marine Division (Reinforced), as part of III Amphibious Corps, lands in assault on Peleliu, Palau Islands.
17 September	Headquarters, Fleet Marine Force, Pacific, activates and takes control of all Fleet Marine Force commands.
12 October	The assault phase of the Peleliu operation is declared over.
16 October	The last combat elements of the 1st Marine Division on Peleliu are re-

lieved by troops of the Army's 81st Infantry Division.

25 December–14 January	5th Marine Division embarks in Hawaii for operations in the Pacific. Chaplain Gittelsohn is assistant division chaplain.

1945

27 January	Soviet troops enter Auschwitz, freeing some survivors.
19 February	Assault troops of V Amphibious Corps (4th and 5th Marine Division with 3d Marine Division in reserve) begin landing on the southeastern beaches of Iwo Jima, Bonin Islands, with 5th Marine Division on the left.
23 February	A combat patrol from 28th Marines raises the American flag on Mount Suribachi, Iwo Jima.
4 March	The first U.S. Boeing B-29 Superfortress bomber, which has too little fuel to return to the Mariana Islands after a mission to Japan, lands on Iwo Jima. Thirty-five more land on the island before the close of hostilities, and many more will land on Iwo's airfield before the end of the war.
16 March	Iwo Jima is declared secured.
16–26 March	5th Marine Division performs mopping-up duties on northwestern Iwo Jima.

Strength of 5th Marine Division during Iwo Jima operations: 1,200 officers and 22,050 enlisted. Casualties during the operations (8,749): 95 officers and 2,148 enlisted killed in action; 257 officers and 6,082 enlisted wounded in action; 3 officers and 139 enlisted missing in action.

21 March	At the dedication of the 5th Marine Division cemetery on Iwo Jima, Rabbi Gittelsohn gives "The Purest Democracy" sermon.
1 April	Tenth Army, including XXIV Corps and III Amphibious Corps (1st and 6th Marine Divisions with the 2d Marine Division in reserve) and Tactical Air Force, Tenth Army (primarily 2d MAW) land in assault on Okinawa.
4 April	Units of the U.S. Third Army liberate the Nazi concentration camp at Ohrdruf, Germany, a subcamp of Buchenwald. This is the first Nazi camp liberated by American troops. The full extent of atrocities is revealed when Buchenwald is liberated on 11 April.
7 April	North American P-51 Mustangs of the U.S. Army Air Forces' VII Fighter Command first launch missions from Iwo Jima, allowing fighters to escort B-29 bombers to and from Japan.
12 April	President Franklin D. Roosevelt dies

	at Warm Springs, GA. Vice President Harry S. Truman is sworn into office as president.
29 April	Troops of the U.S. 45th Infantry Division and the 42d Infantry Division liberate Dachau concentration camp in Germany.
21 June	Okinawa is declared secured.
30 June	The active duty strength of the Marine Corps is 474,680 (37,067 officers and 437,613 enlisted).
5 July	The Philippines campaign, in which Marine air and artillery units participated, is declared ended.
6 August	A B-29 of the 509th Composite Group of the Twentieth Air Force, flying from Tinian in the Northern Mariana Islands, drops the first atomic bomb on the Japanese city of Hiroshima. An estimated 70,000 Japanese die from the attack.
9 August	The Twentieth Air Force drops the second atomic bomb on Nagasaki. Japanese deaths number approximately 40,000 people.
10 August	Fleet Landing Force (4th Marines and Marine and sailor landing forces of Task Force 31) are authorized for the occupation of the Yokosuka area of Japan.
14 August	President Truman announces that a

	cease-fire with Japan is in effect and the war is over.
30 August	4th Marines, as part of Fleet Landing Force, land at Yokosuka Naval Base on Tokyo Bay, Japan.
2 September	Formal signing of surrender terms takes place on board the battleship USS *Missouri* (BB 63) in Tokyo Bay.
7 September	First echelon of MAG-31 flies into Yokosuka Airfield, the first Marine aviation unit to operate in Japan.
22 September	5th Marine Division, V Amphibious Corps, lands at Sasebo, Kyushu, Japan, as part of the occupation force.
23 September	2d Marine Division, V Amphibious Corps, lands at Nagasaki, Kyushu, Japan, as part of the occupation force.
30 September	The leading elements of III Amphibious Corps (1st Marine Division and 1st MAW) lands at Tanggu, Hebei Province, China, to disarm and repatriate Japanese troops.
11 October	6th Marine Division, III Amphibious Corps, lands at Qingdao, Shandong Province, China, to disarm and repatriate Japanese troops.
15 November	Naval Chaplains School, now located at the College of William and Mary in Williamsburg, VA, is decommissioned.

| 28 November | 4th Marine Division is deactivated at Camp Pendleton. |
| 28 December | 3d Marine Division is deactivated on Guam. |

1946

27 January	Rabbi Gittelsohn is released from service in the U.S. Navy.
28 January	1st Special Marine Brigade is activated in Quantico, VA, and Camp Lejeune, NC, as a ready force for expeditionary service.
5 February	5th Marine Division is deactivated at Camp Pendleton.
15 February	V Amphibious Corps is deactivated in Japan.
1 April	6th Marine Division is redesignated 3d Marine Brigade at Tsingtao, North China.
10 June	III Amphibious Corps is deactivated at Tianjin and Qingdao, China, and 3d Marine Brigade at Tsingtao, North China. All remaining Marine units are reorganized as Marine Forces, China, primarily 1st Marine Division, 4th Marines attached, and 1st MAW.
30 June	The active duty strength of the Marine Corps is 155,679 (14,208 officers and 141,471 enlisted).
1 August	Marine garrison at Qingdao is reduced

| | to reinforced battalion strength, 3d Battalion, 4th Marines. |
| 1 October | All reservists and draftees are eligible for discharge regardless of length of service. |

SELECTED
BIBLIOGRAPHY[1]

GENERAL WORKS

Abercrombie, Clarence L., III. *The Military Chaplain.* Beverly Hills, CA: Sage, 1977.

Barish, Louis, ed. *Rabbis in Uniform: The Story of the American Jewish Military Chaplain.* New York: Jonathan David Publishers, 1962.

Bergen, Doris L. *The Sword of the Lord: Military Chaplains from the First to the Twenty-first Century.* Notre Dame, IN: University of Notre Dame Press, 2004.

Bergsma, Cdr H. L. (CHC, USN). *The Pioneers: A Monograph on the First Two Black Chaplains in the Chaplain Corps of the United States Navy.* Washington, DC: Government Printing Office, 1981.

Brown, William Young. *The Army Chaplain: His Office, Duties, and Responsibilities, and the Means of Aiding Him.* Tyler, TX: Sparklight Press, 2012.

The Chaplain as Counselor. Washington, DC: Department of the Army, 1958.

---

[1] This bibliography was constructed based on topics covered in the text and with the coordination of the editors and Cdr James L. Dance, who has been on active duty for 18 years as Navy chaplain and is currently serving as the director of Professional Development and Training at the Naval Chaplaincy School and Center in Newport, RI.

The Chaplain and Military Morale, ST 16-155. Carlisle Barracks, PA: Army Chaplain School, 1950.

Connelley, Carroll J., and Paolo Tripodi, ed. *Aspects of Leadership: Ethics, Law, and Spirituality*. Quantico, VA: MCU Press, 2012.

Craugwell, Thomas J. *Heroic Catholic Chaplains: Stories of the Brave and Holy Men Who Dodged Bullets While Saving Souls*. Gastonia, NC: TAN Books, 2018.

Drazin, Israel, and Cecil B. Currey. *For God and Country: The History of a Constitutional Challenge to the Army Chaplaincy*. Hoboken, NJ: KTAV Publishing House, 1995.

Drury, Capt Clifford Merrill (USNR). *The History of the Chaplain Corps, United States Navy*, vol. 1, *1778-1939*. Washington, DC: U.S. Navy Chaplain Corps, 1948.

———. *The History of the Chaplain Corps, United States Navy*, vol. 2, *1939-1949*. Washington, DC: U.S. Navy Chaplain Corps, 1949.

———. *United States Navy Chaplains, 1957-1972: Biographical and Service-record Sketches of USN and USNR Chaplains—Volume II of the Series on the History of the Chaplain Corps, United States Navy*. Washington, DC: Government Printing Office, 1974.

———. *United States Navy Chaplains, 1953-1957: Biographical and Service-record Sketches of 2,800 USN and USNR Chaplains Including Corrections and Additions to 2,227 Sketches Which Appeared in Volumes III and IV of This Series*. Washington, DC: Government Printing Office, 1957.

Elkins, Dov Peretz. *God's Warriors: Dramatic Adventures of Rabbis in Uniform*. Middle Village, NY: Jonathan David Publishers, 1974.

Frazier, John B. (CHC, USN). *The Navy Chaplain's Manual*. Washington, DC: Secretary of the Navy, 1918.

Gilroy, William F. R., and Timothy J. Demy. *A Brief Chronology of the Chaplain Corps of the United States Navy*. Washington, DC: Chaplain Corps, Department of the Navy, 1983.

Hansen, Kim P. *Military Chaplains and Religious Diversity*. New York: Palgrave Macmillan, 2012. https://doi.org/10.1057/9781137025166.

Honeywell, Col Roy J. (USA) *Chaplains of the United States Army*. Washington, DC: Office of the Chief of Chaplains, Department of the Army, 1958.

Hutcheson, Richard G., Jr. *The Churches and the Chaplaincy*. Atlanta, GA: John Knox Press, 1975.

Ingle, Clifford. *The Military Chaplain as a Counselor*. Kansas City, KS: Central Seminary Press, 1953.

Keller, W. Phillip. *Bold under God*. Chicago, IL: Moody Press, 1973.

Kennedy, Nancy B. *Miracles and Moments of Grace: Inspiring Stories from Military Chaplains*. Abilene, TX: Leafwood Publishers, 2011.

Kibben, Margaret Grun. "Religious Freedom in the Armed Forces." *Military Chaplain* 89, no. 2 (Summer 2016): 7–9.

Korn, Bertam W. *Centennial of the Jewish Chaplaincy in the United States, 1862–1962*. New York: n.p., 1963.

Kroll, Lt C. Douglas (CHC, USNR). *A History of Navy Chaplains Serving with the U.S. Coast Guard*. Washington, DC: Chaplain Corps, Department of the Navy, 1983.

Lewis, T. L. *From Bootcamp to the Battlefield: Training Church Workers for Service*. Nashville, TN: Boyd Publications, 1997.

Loveland, Anne C. *Change and Conflict in the U.S. Army Chaplain Corps since 1945*. Knoxville: University of Tennessee Press, 2014.

Ludwig, Dean C., and Clinton O. Longenecker. "The Bathsheba Syndrome: The Ethical Failure of Successful Leaders." *Journal of Business Ethics* 12, no. 4 (1993): 265–73, https://doi.org/10.1007/bf01666530.

Lunze, Stefan. *The Protection of Religious Personnel in Armed Conflict*. Frankfurt am Main: Peter Lang, 2004.

Martin, Cdr H. Lawrence (CHC, USN), and Lt Timothy J. Demy (CHC, USNR). *Sea Padres: Some Chaplains of "the Old Navy."* Washington, DC: Chaplains Division, Bureau of Naval Personnel, Department of the Navy, 1984.

Martin, Cdr H. Lawrence (CHC, USN), and Lt William F. R. Gilroy (CHC, USNR). *The Uniforms of the Chaplain Corps, United States Navy*. Washington, DC: Chaplain Corps, U.S. Navy, 1985.

Navy Chaplains Bulletin. Washington, DC: Chaplains Division, Bureau of Naval Personnel, Department of the Navy, 1954-.

O'Brien, Thomas R., ed. *Blessings from the Battlefield*. Huntington, IN: Our Sunday Visitor Publishing Division, 2002.

Patterson, Eric, ed. *Military Chaplains in Afghanistan, Iraq, and Beyond: Advisement and Leader Engagement in Highly Religious Environments*. Lanham, MD: Rowman & Littlefield, 2014.

Proctor, Pam, and William Proctor. *Women in the Pulpit: Is God an Equal Opportunity Employer?* New York: Doubleday, 1976.

Ramsay, Nancy J., and Carrie Doehring. *Military Moral Injury and Spiritual Care: A Resource for Religious Leaders and Professional Caregivers*. Saint Louis, MO: Chalice Press, an Imprint of Christian Board of Publication, 2019.

Reagan, Ronald. "Remarks at the Baptist Fundamentalism Annual Convention." Speech at the District of Columbia Convention Center, Washington, DC, 13 April 1984.

Resnicoff, Arnold E. "Prayers that Hurt: Public Prayer in Interfaith Settings." Open Siddur Project, 17 February 2019.

Riddle, John, and Bonnie J. Ceban. *For God and Country: Four Stories of Courageous Military Chaplains*. Uhrichsville, OH: Barbour, 2003.

Robinson, Harold L. "Free Exercise Meets the Establishment Clause in Military Service." *Military Chaplain* 89, no. 2 (Summer 2016): 16–18.

———. "A Solemn Duty: Citizens' Responsibilities for the Nation's Wars and Warriors." In *Jewish Choices, Jewish Voices: War and National Security*. Edited by Elliott N. Dorff and Danya Ruttenberg. Philadelphia, PA: Jewish Publication Society, 2010.

Stahl, Ronit Y. *Enlisting Faith: How the Military Chaplaincy Shaped Religion and State in Modern America*. Cambridge, MA: Harvard University Press, 2017.

Staudacher, Rosemarian V. *Chaplains in Action*. New York: Farrar, Straus & Cudahy, 1962.

Todd, Andrew, ed. *Military Chaplaincy in Contention: Chaplains, Churches and the Morality of Conflict*. Farnham, UK: Ashgate, 2013.

Waring, George J. *Chaplain's Duties and How Best to Accomplish His Work*. Washington, DC: Government Printing Office, 1912.

Washburn, Henry Bradford. "The Army Chaplain." *Papers of the American Society of Church History* 7 (1895).

Wildhack, William A. "Navy Chaplains at the Crossroads: Navigating the Intersection of Free Speech, Free Exercise, Establishment, and Equal Protection." *Naval Law Review* 51 (2005).

Woodbery, Jerry Maddox. "Prophets and Warriors: Military Chaplains, the Advisement of National Strategic Military Leaders, and the Revision of Joint Publication 1-05, 'Religious Affairs in Joint Operations'." Dissertation thesis, Wesley Theological Seminary, 2012.

Zumwalt, Adm E. R., Jr. (USN). "Z-gram #116: Equal Rights and Opportunities for Women." Naval History and Heritage Command, 7 August 1972.

AMERICAN REVOLUTION–1812

Black, Jeanette D., and William Greene Roelker, eds. *A Rhode Island Chaplain in the Revolution: Letters of Ebenezer David to Nicholas Brown, 1775–1778*. Providence: Rhode Island Society of the Cincinnati, 1949.

Brace, F. R. *Brief Sketches of the New Jersey Chaplains in the Continental Army, and in the State Militia, during the War of Independence*. Paterson, NJ: Press Printing and Publishing, 1909.

Crowder, Jack Darrell. *Chaplains of the Revolutionary War: Black Robed American Warriors*. Jefferson, NC: McFarland, 2017.

Dickens Jr., William E. *Answering the Call: The Story of the U.S. Military Chaplaincy from the Revolution Through the Civil War*. Privately published, 1999.

Headley, J. T. *The Chaplains and Clergy of the Revolution*. New York: Charles Scribner, 1864.

———. *The Forgotten Heroes of Liberty: The Chaplains and Clergy of the American Revolution*. Birmingham, AL: Solid Ground Christian Books, 2005.

McLane, Curren R., ed. *American Chaplains of the Revolution*. Louisville, KY: National Society Sons of the American Revolution, 1991.

1812–61

Lawson, Kenneth E. *Reliable and Religious: U.S. Army Chaplains and the War of 1812*. Washington, DC; Department of the Army, 2002.

———. *Religion and the U.S. Army Chaplaincy in the Florida Seminole Wars, 1817–1858*. Columbia, SC: Eastside Printing, 2006.

CIVIL WAR

Armstrong, Warren B. *For Courageous Fighting and Confident Dying: Union Chaplains in the Civil War*. Lawrence: University Press of Kansas, 1998.

Betts, Alexander Davis. *The Experience of a Confederate Chaplain, 1861–1864*. LaVergne, TN: Kessinger, 2012.

Bineham, Maj Michael L. (USA) "Role of Southern Baptist Chaplains and Missionaries in the Civil War." Master's diss., U.S. Army Command and General Staff College, 2003.

Bradford, J. H. *The Chaplains in the Volunteer Army*. Aurora, CO: Biographical Center for Research, 2009.

Brinsfield, John Wesley, comp. and ed,. *The Spirit Divided: Memoirs of Civil War Chaplains—The Confederacy*. Macon, GA: Mercer University Press, 2006.

———. *Summon Only the Brave!: Commanders, Soldiers, and Chaplains at Gettysburg*. Macon, GA: Mercer University Press, 2016.

Brinsfield, John W., William C. Davis, Benedict Maryniak, and James

I. Robertson Jr., ed. *Faith in the Fight: Civil War Chaplains.* Mechanicsburg, PA: Stackpole Books, 2003.

Budd, Richard M. *Serving Two Masters: The Development of American Military Chaplaincy, 1860–1920.* Lincoln: University of Nebraska Press, 2002.

Cathey, M. Todd. *Combat Chaplain: The Life and Civil War Experiences of Rev. James H. McNeilly, Army of Tennessee.* Macon, GA: Mercer University Press, 2017.

Conyngham, David Power. *Soldiers of the Cross, the Authoritative Text: The Heroism of Catholic Chaplains and Sisters in the American Civil War.* Notre Dame, IN: University of Notre Dame Press, 2019.

Corby, William. *Memoirs of Chaplain Life: Three Years with the Irish Brigade in the Army of the Potomac.* Edited by Lawrence Frederick Kohl. New York: Fordham University Press, 1992.

Furry, William, ed. *The Preacher's Tale: The Civil War Journal of Rev. Francis Springer, Chaplain, U.S. Army of the Frontier.* Fayetteville: University of Arkansas Press, 2001.

Hayes, Patrick J., ed. *The Civil War Diary of Rev. James Sheeran, C.Ss.R.: Confederate, Chaplain, and Redemptorist.* Washington, DC: Catholic University of America Press, 2016.

Heagney, Harold J. *Chaplain in Gray, Abram Ryan: Poet-Priest of the Confederacy.* New York: P. J. Kenedy & Sons, 1958.

Humphreys, Charles A. *Field, Camp, Hospital and Prison in the Civil War, 1863–1865.* Boston, MA: Press of Geo. H. Ellis, 1918.

Jones, J. William. *Christ in the Camp or Religion in the Confederate Army.* Harrisburg, VA: Sprinkle Publications, 1986.

Miller, Benjamin L. *In God's Presence: Chaplains, Missionaries, and Religious Space during the American Civil War.* Lawrence: University Press of Kansas, 2019.

Pitts, Charles F. *Chaplains in Gray: The Confederate Chaplains' Story.* Nashville, TN: Broadman Press, 1957.

Quintard, C. T. *Balm for the Weary and the Wounded*. Columbia, SC: Evans & Cogswell Printers, 1864.

Twichell, Joseph Hopkins. *The Civil War Letters of Joseph Hopkins Twichell: A Chaplain's Story*. Edited by Peter Messent and Steve Courtney. Athens: University of Georgia Press, 2006.

Woodworth, Steven E. *While God Is Marching On: The Religious World of Civil War Soldiers*. Lawrence: University Press of Kansas, 2001.

1865–1917

Budd, Richard M. *Serving Two Masters: The Development of American Military Chaplaincy, 1860–1920*. Lincoln: University of Nebraska Press, 2002.

Stover, Earl F. *Up from Handymen: The United States Army Chaplaincy, 1865–1920*. Forest Grove, OR: University Press of the Pacific, 2004.

WORLD WAR I

Appelbaum, Peter C. *Loyalty Betrayed: Jewish Chaplains in the German Army During the First World War*. Chicago, IL: Vallentine Mitchell, 2014.

Duffy, Francis P. *Father Duffy's Story: A Tale of Humor and Heroism, of Life and Death with the Fighting Sixty-Ninth*. New York: George H. Doran, 1919.

Fiennes, Peter. *To War with God: The Army Chaplain Who Lost His Faith*. New York: Random House, 2011.

Hogan, Martin J. *The Shamrock Battalion in the Great War*. Edited by James J. Cooke. Columbia: University of Missouri Press, 2007.

Levinger, Lee J. *A Jewish Chaplain in France*. New York: Macmillan, 1922.

Shay, Michael E. *Sky Pilots: The Yankee Division Chaplains in World War I*. Columbia: University of Missouri Press, 2014.

Schweitzer, Richard. *The Cross and the Trenches: Religious Faith and*

Doubt among British and American Great War Soldiers. Westport, CT: Praeger, 2003.

Talbot, Neville S. *Religion Behind the Front and After the War*. London: Macmillan, 1918.

Waring, George J. *United States Catholic Chaplains in the World War: Ordinariate Army and Navy Chaplains*. Westminster, MD: Willow Bend Books, 2003.

WORLD WAR II

Bernstein, Philip S. *Rabbis at War: The CANRA Story*. Waltham, MA: American Jewish Historical Society, 1971.

Carpenter, Alton E., and A. Anne Eiland. *Chappie: World War II Diary of a Combat Chaplain*. Fountain Hills, AZ: Mead Publishing, 2007.

Cavanaugh, Paul W. "Pro Deo et Patria (For God and Country): The Personal Narrative of an American Catholic Chaplain as a Prisoner of War in Germany." Unpublished manuscript, Woodstock Theological Library, Georgetown University, 2004.

Crosby, Donald F. *Battlefield Chaplains: Catholic Priests in World War II*. Lawrence: University Press of Kansas, 1994.

Dorsett, Lyle W. *Serving God and Country: U.S. Military Chaplains in World War II*. New York: Dutton Caliber, a Penguin Books imprint, 2013.

Fighting for America: A Record of the Participation of Jewish Men and Women in the Armed Forces during 1944, 1944 ed. New York: National Jewish Welfare Board, 1944.

Gregg, John A. *Of Men and Arms: Chronological Travel Record of Bishop John A. Gregg with Messages of Cheer and Good Will to Negro Soldiers on All War Fronts*. Nashville, TN: A. M. E. Sunday School Union Press, 1945.

Grobman, Alex. *Rekindling the Flame: American Jewish Chaplains and the*

> *Survivors of European Jewry, 1944-1948.* Detroit, MI: Wayne State University Press, 1992.

Guerra, Peter J., and Suzanne Doré Guerra. *But He Dies Not: The Life, Faith, and Sacrifice of Father Joseph Verbis Lafleur, Priest, Military Chaplain.* Opelousas, LA: Andrepont Printing, 2010.

Hotaling, Kerry. *Go Forward into the Storm: An Iwo Jima Journal.* Gleneden Beach, OR: Christopher Matthews Publishing, 2016.

Jones Jr., Capt Wilbur D. (USNR). *Gyrene: The World War II United States Marine.* Shippensburg, PA: White Mane Books, 1998.

Keith, Bill. *Days of Anguish, Days of Hope: Chaplain Robert Preston Taylor's Ordeal and Triumph as a POW in World War II.* Fort Worth, TX: Scripta Publishing, 1972.

Kirkpatrick, Thomas I. *The Love that Endures: Remembering My Mother and My Father, U.S.S. Arizona's Chaplain at Pearl Harbor.* Half Moon Bay, CA: Greenbrier Publications, 2011.

Knapp, George W., and Gayle E. Knapp. *A Chaplain's Duty: Letters Home from a WWII Chaplain.* Athens, GA: Deeds Publishing, 2011.

Kurzman, Dan. *No Greater Glory: The Four Immortal Chaplains and the Sinking of the Dorchester in World War II.* New York: Random House, 2005.

Mandel, Lee. *Unlikely Warrior: A Pacifist Rabbi's Journey from the Pulpit to Iwo Jima.* Gretna, LA: Pelican Publishing, 2014.

McWilliams, Tennant. *The Chaplain's Conflict: Good and Evil in a War Hospital, 1943-1945.* College Station: Texas A&M University Press, 2012.

Moore, Deborah Dash. *GI Jews: How World War II Changed a Generation.* Cambridge, MA: Belknap Press of Harvard University Press, 2004.

———. *Worshipping Together in Uniform: Christians and Jews in World War II.* San Francisco, CA: Swig Judaic Studies Program at the University of San Francisco, 2001.

O'Callahan, Joseph T. *I Was Chaplain on the Franklin.* Annapolis, MD: Naval Institute Press, 2019.

Rabey, Steve. *Faith under Fire: Stories of Hope and Courage from World War II*. Nashville, TN: Thomas Nelson Publishers, 2002.

Rogers, Capt Edward K. *Doughboy Chaplain*. Ponca City, OK: Meador Press, 1946.

Roper, Richard S. *Brothers of Paul: Activities of Prisoner of War Chaplains in the Philippines during WWII*. Odenton, MD: Revere Printing, 2003.

Slomovitz, Albert I. *The Fighting Rabbis: Jewish Military Chaplains and American History*. New York: New York University Press, 2001.

Stroop, Russell Cartwright, and Richard Cartwright Austin. *Letters from the Pacific: A Combat Chaplain in World War II*. Columbia: University of Missouri Press, 2000.

Szymczak, Chester J. *When Time Stood Still: The Sinking of the S.S. Dorchester*. Philadelphia, PA: Dorrance, 1956.

Thornton, Francis Beauchesne. *Sea of Glory: The Magnificent Story of the Four Chaplains*. New York: Prentice-Hall, 1953.

Walker, Conrad N. *The Leapin' Deacon: The Soldier's Chaplain*. Austin, TX: Langmarc Publishing, 2004.

Walstad, Clarence E. *Pages from a World War II Chaplain's Diary*. CreateSpace, 2015.

Wickersham II, George W. *Marine Chaplain, 1943–1946*. 7th ed. Bennington, VT: Merriam Press, 2017.

Wukovits, John F. *Soldiers of a Different Cloth: Notre Dame Chaplains in World War II*. Notre Dame, IN: University of Notre Dame Press, 2018.

Yost, Israel A. S. *Combat Chaplain: The Personal Story of the WWII Chaplain of the Japanese American 100th Battalion*. Honolulu: University of Hawai'i Press, 2006.

Zimmerman, Leslie F. *Chaplain Prisoners of War in the Pacific, 1941–1945*. Maxwell Air Force Base, AL: USAF Chaplain Service Institute, 1993.

COLD WAR

Tarr, Herbert. *The Conversion of Chaplain Cohen: A Novel.* New York: Bernard Geis Associates, 1963.

KOREAN WAR

Beecher, Earl S. *An Army Chaplain from the Church of Jesus Christ of Latter-Day Saints (in Korea).* Las Vegas, NV: TopLink Publishing, 2019.

Caruso, John, and Aaron Elson. *Semper Fi, Padre: The Mathew Caruso Story.* New Britain, CT: Chi Chi Press, 2015.

Dowe, Ray M. *Father Kapaun: The Ordeal of Chaplain Kapaun.* Notre Dame, IN: Ave Maria Press, 1954.

Griepp, Frank. *The Circuit-riding Combat Chaplain: The Chaplain of the Seventh Cavalry in the Korean War.* Self-published, 2000.

Maher, William L. *A Shepherd in Combat Boots: Chaplain Emil Kapaun of the 1st Cavalry Division.* Shippensburg, PA: Burd Street Press, 2002.

Rosen, Milton J. *An American Rabbi in Korea: A Chaplain's Journey in the Forgotten War.* Edited by Stanley R. Rosen. Tuscaloosa: University of Alabama Press, 2004.

Schumacher, John W. *A Soldier of God Remembers: Memoir Highlights of a Career Army Chaplain.* Souderton, PA: Grace Brethren North American Missions, 2000.

Tonne, Arthur. *The Story of Chaplain Kapaun: Patriot Priest of the Korean Conflict.* Emporia, KS: Didde, 1954.

Wenzl, Roy, and Travis Heying. *The Miracle of Father Kapaun: Priest, Soldier and Korean War Hero.* San Francisco, CA: Ignatius Press, 2015.

Wick, Pat, ed. *A Saint Among Us: Remembering Father Emil J. Kapaun.* Wichita, KS: Father Kapaun Guild, 2005.

VIETNAM WAR

Autry, Jerry. *Gun-Totin' Chaplain: A True Memoir.* San Francisco, CA: Airborne Press, 2007.

Bergsma, Cdr Herbert L. (CHC, USN). *Chaplains with Marines in Vietnam, 1962–1971*. Washington, DC: History and Museums Division, Headquarters Marine Corps, 1985.

Bowers, Curt. *Forward Edge of the Battle Area: A Chaplain's Story*. Kansas City, MO: Beacon Hill Press, 1987.

Caldwell, J. T. *The Chaplain's Assistant: God, Country, and Vietnam—A Novel*. Mount Pleasant, MI: Glenn Street Press, 2010.

Davis, Elvernice "Sonny." *Reflections of an Army Chaplain: From Sonny to Reverend Davis to Chaplain Davis to Dr. Davis to Sonny—Just Tell the Truth*. Bloomington, IN: WestBow Press, 2020.

Dulany, Joseph P. *Once a Soldier: A Chaplain's Story*. Self-published, 2001.

Gribble, Richard. *Navy Priest: The Life of Captain Jake Laboon, SJ*. Washington, DC: Catholic University of America Press, 2015.

Hopkins, Samuel W., Jr. *A Chaplain Remembers Vietnam*. Jacksonville, TX: Sampat Publisher, 2007.

Johnson, James D. *Combat Chaplain: A 30-Year Vietnam Battle*. Denton: University of North Texas Press, 2001.

Litecky, Charles J. *Renunciation: My Pilgrimage from Catholic Military Chaplain, Vietnam Hawk, and Medal of Honor Recipient to Civilian Warrior for Peace*. San Francisco, CA: Charles J. Litecky and Judith Balch Litecky Trust, 2017.

Mode, Daniel L. *The Grunt Padre: The Service and Sacrifice of Father Vincent Robert Capodanno, Vietnam, 1966–1967*. Oak Lawn, IL: CMJ Marian Publishers, 2001.

Moore, Cdr Withers M. (CHC, USN). *Navy Chaplains in Vietnam, 1954–1964*. Washington, DC: Chief of Chaplains, Bureau of Naval Personnel, Department of the Navy, 1968.

Moore, Adm Withers M. (CHC, USN), Capt Herbert L. Bergsma (CHC, USN), and Lt Timothy J. Demy (CHC, USNR). *Chaplains with U.S. Naval Units in Vietnam, 1954–1975: Selected Experiences at Sea and Ashore*, vol. IX. Washington, DC: History Branch, Office of the Chief of Chaplains, Department of the Navy, 1985.

Newby, Claude D. *It Took Heroes: Continuing the Story and Tribute to Those Who Endured the Darkest Days of Vietnam*, vol. II. Orem, UT: Bonneville Books, 2000.

O'Connor, John J. *A Chaplain Looks at Vietnam*. Cleveland, OH: World Publishing, 1969.

Scott, Quincy, Jr. *The Battle Is Not Mine: The Life of a Black Army Chaplain during the 1960s and Early '70s*. Dikaisian Books, 2014.

Whitt, Jacqueline E. *Bringing God to Men: American Military Chaplains and the Vietnam War*. Chapel Hill: University of North Carolina Press, 2014.

GULF WAR

Ammerman, E. H. Jim, Charlene Ammerman, and Andrew Collins, *After the Storm*, 1st ed. Nashville, TN: Star Song Communications, 1991.

1991–PRESENT

Adams, Cdr George (CHC, USN). *Chaplains as Liaisons with Religious Leaders: Lessons from Iraq and Afghanistan*, Peaceworks No. 56. Washington, DC: U.S. Institute of Peace, 2006.

Blair, LtCol John R. (USAF), and LtCol H. Bryan Highfill (USAF). *Servants in the Storm*. Maxwell Air Force Base, AL: Air War College, Air University, 1992.

Brown, David Reid. *Spirit Soundings: A Chaplain's Journal of Life at Sea*, vol. I, *Sailing into a Hazardous World*, vol. II, *The Patriot's Call*, vol. III, *Returning to America*. Maitland, FL: Xulon Press, 2016.

Cash, Carey H. *A Table in the Presence: The Dramatic Account of How a U.S. Marine Battalion Experienced God's Presence Amidst the Chaos of the War in Iraq*. Nashville, TN: Thomas Nelson, 2006.

Gordon, Lt Terry C. (CHC, USN). *The Chaplain as Religious Liaison in the Global War on Terror (GWOT)*. Newport, RI: Joint Military Operations Department, Naval War College, 2006.

Lawson, LtCol Kenneth E. (CHC, USA). *Faith and Hope in a War-torn Land: The US Army Chaplaincy in the Balkans, 1995–2005*. Fort Leavenworth, KS: Combat Studies Institute Press, 2006.

Lindsey, Guy L. *Peace in the Desert Storm*. Cleveland, TN: White Wing Publishing, 1991.

Lloyd, Scottie R. *Chaplain Contact with Local Religious Leaders: A Strategic Support*. Carlisle Barracks, PA: U.S. Army War College, 2005.

Lounello, Mark. *Eternity Matters: A Journey of a Chaplain Assistant Post 9-11*. Meadville, PA: Christian Faith Publishing, 2016.

McLaughlin, Capt Paul. *The Chaplain's Evolving Role in Peace and Humanitarian Relief Operations*. Washington, DC: U.S. Institute of Peace, 2002.

Ortiz, Mike. *Green Beret Chaplain*. Bloomington, IN: Xlibris, 2013.

Scordo, Joseph A. *Postcards from a Navy Chaplain*. Washington, DC: Self-published, 2016.

Waite, Douglas J. *By the Grace of God: The Autobiography of a Navy Chaplain*. CreateSpace, 2016.

Yee, James. *For God and Country: Faith and Patriotism Under Fire*. New York: Public Affairs, 2005.

IRAQ

Basu, Moni. *Chaplain Turner's War*. Evanston, IL: Agate Digital, 2012.

Benimoff, Roger. *Faith Under Fire: An Army Chaplain's Memoir*. New York: Three Rivers Press, an imprint of Crown Publishing, 2009.

Bryan, Jeff. *Memoirs from Babylon: A Combat Chaplain's Life in Iraq's Triangle of Death*. La Vergne, TN: Combat Chaplain Ministries, 2011.

Burkes, Norris. *Hero's Highway: A Chaplain's Journey Toward Forgiveness Inside a Combat Hospital*. Self-published, 2015.

Chandler, Owen R. *A Bridge in Babylon: Stories of a Military Chaplain in Iraq*. Nashville, TN: Chalice Press, 2021.

Kittleson, Lance. *Meditations from Iraq: A Chaplain's Ministry in the Middle East 2003-2004*. Lima, OH: CSS Publishing, 2005.

Linzey, Paul. *Safest Place in Iraq: Experiencing God during War*. New York: Morgan James Publishing, 2020.

Snively, Cdr Sheri. *Heaven in the Midst of Hell: A Quaker Chaplain's View of the War in Iraq*. Jamul, CA: Raven Oaks Press, 2010.

Wismer III, Frank E. *War in the Garden of Eden: A Military Chaplain's Memoir from Baghdad*. New York: Seabury Books, 2008.

AFGHANISTAN

Ristau, Harold. *At Peace with War: A Chaplain's Meditations from Afghanistan*. Eugene, OR: Wipf and Stock, 2012.

Tyger, George. *War Zone Faith: An Army Chaplain's Reflections on Afghanistan*. Boston, MA: Skinner House Books, 2013.

GOVERNMENT DOCUMENTS

Book of Worship for United States Forces: A Collection of Hymns and Worship Resources for Military Personnel of the United States of America. Washington, DC: Armed Forces Chaplain's Board, 1974.

Brinsfield Jr., John W. *Encouraging Faith, Supporting Soldiers: The United States Army Chaplaincy, 1975–1995*, vol. VII. Washington, DC: Office of the Chief of Chaplains, Department of the Army, 1997.

Chaplains' Corps with a General Officer as Chief Hearings before the United States Senate Committee on Military Affairs, 76th Cong., 1st Sess. (24 March 1939).

Chaplain Service, US Coast Guard: Serving Those Who Serve. Washington, DC: Chaplain Corps, U.S. Navy, U.S. Coast Guard, 2000.

Coffey, LtCol R. Michael (CHC, USA). *Chaplain Ministry to the Millennial Generation*. Carlisle Barracks, PA: U.S. Army War College, 2006.

Committee on the Judiciary, Chaplains in Congress and in the Army and Navy, 33d Cong., 1st Sess. (1854).

Councell, LtCol Gary R. (CHC, USA). *Chaplain Roles in Humanitarian and Civic Assistance Operations.* Carlisle Barracks, PA: U.S. Army War College, 1994.

Greenslit, LtCol Lawrence P. (CHC, USA). *Religion and the Military: A Growing Ethical Dilemma.* Carlisle Barracks, PA: U.S. Army War College, 2006.

The Gunhus Years, 1999–2003: Courageous in Spirit, Compassionate in Service. Washington, DC: Office of the Chief of Chaplains, Department of the Army, 2003.

Gushwa, Robert L. *The Best and Worst of Times: The United States Army Chaplaincy, 1920–1945*, vol. IV. Washington, DC: Office of the Chief of Chaplains, Department of the Army, 1977.

Honeywell, Col Roy J. (CHC, USA). *Chaplains of the United States Army.* Washington, DC: Office of the Chief of Chaplains, Department of the Army, 1958.

Kibben, LCdr Margaret Grun (CHC, USN). *The Role and Mission of Chaplains in Humanitarian Assistance and Peace Operations (HA/POs).* Newport, RI: Joint Military Operations Department, Naval War College, 1996.

Norton, Herman A. *Struggling for Recognition: The United States Army Chaplaincy, 1791–1865*, vol. II. Washington, DC: Office of the Chief of Chaplains, Department of the Army, 1977.

Religious Support and Internal Advisement, ATP 1-05.04. Washington, DC: Department of the Army, 2017.

Stover, Earl F. *Up from Handymen: The United States Army Chaplaincy, 1865–1920*, vol. III. Washington, DC: Office of the Chief of Chaplains, Department of the Army, 1977.

"Terrorism: Radical Islamic Influence of Chaplaincy of the U.S. Military and Prisons." Hearing before the Subcommittee on Terrorism, Technology and Homeland Security of the Committee on the Judiciary, U.S. Senate, 108th Cong., 1st Sess. (14 October 2003).

Thompson, Parker C. *From Its European Antecedents to 1791: The United States Army Chaplaincy*, vol. I. Washington, DC: Office of the Chief of Chaplains, Department of the Army, 1978.

Venzke, Rodger R. *Confidence in Battle, Inspiration in Peace: The United States Army Chaplaincy, 1945–1975*, vol. V. Washington, DC: Office of the Chief of Chaplains, Department of the Army, 1977.

MANUALS, HANDBOOKS, AND INSTRUCTIONAL MATERIALS

Brown, W. Y. (CHC, UAS). *The Army Chaplain: His Office, Duties, and Responsibilities, and the Means of Aiding Him*. Philadelphia, PA: William S. & Alfred Martien, 1863.

The Commander's Handbook for Religious Ministry Support, MCRP 3.30D.4. Washington, DC: Headquarters Marine Corps, 2016.

Frazier, John B. (CHC, USN). *The Navy Chaplain's Manual*. Washington, DC: Secretary of the Navy, 1918.

Hammond, J. Pinkney (CHC, USA). *The Army Chaplain's Manual: Designed as a Help to Chaplains in the Discharge of Their Various Duties, Both Temporal and Spiritual*. Philadelphia, PA: J. B. Lippincott, 1863.

Kramer, Maj Philip A. (CHC, USA). *The Proximity Principle: Army Chaplains on the Fighting Line in Doctrine and History*. Fort Leavenworth, KS: U.S. Army Command and General Staff College, 2015.

Ministering to Jewish Personnel in the Absence of a Jewish Chaplain: A Manual for Jewish Lay Leaders. Washington, DC: Government Printing Office, 1970.

Nave, Orville J. (CHC, USA). *Nave's Handbook on the Army Chaplaincy*. Los Angeles, CA: published privately, 1917.

Nay, Maj Robert (CHC, USA). *The Operational, Social, and Religious*

Influences upon the Army Chaplain Field Manual, 1926–1952. Fort Leavenworth, KS: U.S. Army Command and General Staff College, 2008.

Religious Activities: Chaplain Training Strategy, Pamphlet 165-3. Washington, DC: Department of the Army, 1998.

Religious Ministry Team Handbook, MCRP 3-30D.3. Washington, DC: Headquarters Marine Corps, 2016.

Religious Support to Funerals and Memorial Events, ATP 1-05.02 Washington, DC: Department of the Army, 2018.

INDEX